MAKING IT HAPPEN

CARL HESTER
MAKING IT HAPPEN

THE AUTOBIOGRAPHY

First published in Great Britain in 2014 by Orion Books
An imprint of the Orion Publishing Group Ltd
Orion House, 5 Upper St Martin's Lane,
London, WC2H 9EA
An Hachette Livre Company

1 3 5 7 9 10 8 6 4 2

A CIP catalogue record for this book
is available from the British Library.

ISBN-13 978 1 409 14767 1

Typeset by Input Data Services Ltd,
Bridgwater, Somerset

Printed and bound by CPI Group (UK) Ltd,
Croydon, CR0 4YY

The Orion Publishing Group's policy is to use papers
that are natural, renewable and recyclable products and made
from wood grown in sustainable forests. The logging and
manufacturing processes are expected to conform to the
environmental regulations of the country of origin.

www.orionbooks.co.uk

'Some people want it to happen, some wish it would happen, and others make it happen.'

Michael Jordan

Contents

Acknowledgements

The idea of writing a book about what's happened in my life? It didn't seem worth a read, that is until Bernie and I sat down and started to talk about what had happened. Due to the number of people and horses that have come through my life, it seemed as if we might have some fun and interesting subjects. Of course, the fun part of this story is in how it developed – the norm would be to have born into a horsey family, become horsey, stay horsey, marry a horse, be a horse, have great big teeth and neigh. However, the fact that my parents were non-horsey, yet I was given the right direction by many people, that is hopefully an inspiration to those kids out there today who feel they can't afford to make it to the top professionally. I want to give them hope that they too can make it happen.

To my parents and my grandmother from Sark, thank you for giving me free rein to go and do what I wanted to do. To the Fortune Centre for actually recognising what I wanted to do and, of course, to Jannie and Christopher for helping me understand what a horseman should be – it is that, I feel, which has made me what I am today. To Dr Bechtolsheimer who gave me the break of a lifetime. Where would I have been without that I wonder? And to Kate and Stuart for giving me that base when I spread my wings.

Today, thank you to and thank God for Claudine who looks after all my bits and pieces, and Baz, Fiona and Alan who make this place work together with Katie and Amy. Thank you to Ben for continually printing out whatever Bernie and I came up with to review afterwards, and a huge thanks to all the people who have contributed to make the stories fit in place, especially Winnie, Dickie, Will and

Trickie, and to Jude, Dane, Claire, Mum and Jess for comments on sections of earlier drafts.

At Orion, having known Susan Lamb for many years has made this journey an easier, smoother passage. Alan Samson and Lucinda McNeile have been amazingly supportive throughout and fabulous for Bernie to work with. Thank you to Anne O'Brien for her sympathetic copy-edit – we're glad you liked the ending – and to our publicist Alex Hippisley-Cox.

Bernie and I have been friends for longer than we care to remember. Many of these stories have been shared together and the laughs we've had remembering them and realising everything that did happen has been a wonderful experience. I'm sure her husband Richard must have been delighted to have those free evenings once a week over many months while we've recounted these stories, and now he gets the dining table back. How lucky was I? As my career grew as a rider so did hers as a journalist. What better unison could we have wished for – my stories and her writing skills that have given me my 'voice' in print. I hope everyone enjoys the collaboration.

And finally, a big thank you to all the friends and horses who made these stories, and therefore this book, happen.

Foreword by Martin Clunes, President of the British Horse Society

When Carl asked me to write a foreword to his book I was very surprised – shocked, actually – as my kind of riding is plodding around the Dorset countryside on a Clydesdale and is as far away from the world of Olympic Class Dressage as you can get. What we do have in common, however, is an innate love and fascination for horses. Having found myself more and more immersed in the world of the horse in all its guises, I have come to realise that Carl is an inspiration not only to the top riders around the world but also to grass roots horse people at all levels. He's not just an immensely gifted rider, he also has a gift for communicating his skills and knowledge in a way that everyone can understand, inspiring us all. I have often watched my wife's and daughter's riding lessons and heard time and again, 'Imagine you are Carl Hester' – it's easier said than done!

There is something about Carl's journey from the back of a donkey on his home island of Sark to an Olympic Gold at Greenwich that will grab the attention of all horse lovers, regardless of their age or ability. The horse and its training is at the heart of everything Carl does. He understands the responsibility of finding the key to each horse to enable it to perform to its best, but also to flourish and be happy in itself. Carl loves his horses, he loves them enough to allow them to be horses. Olympic horses turned out to gallop, romp and buck in the fields to their hearts' content, not wrapped in cotton wool as precious and pampered pieces of sports equipment.

As Carl says, '*It often doesn't make sense where an all-consuming fascination with horses comes from, some people just have it.*' As you're about to read this book, I know you'll understand that feeling.

1

Greenwich Park

One week to go before the London Olympics were upon us and my nerves were totally frayed. Uthopia had given me a scare; he'd had bruising in a foot, which sometimes he can get with shoeing, and he decided to limp. We're about to go, everything's set and both the vet and the farrier tell me everything's going to be OK. But I'm terrified I'm not going to make it and I know how reliant we – the British team – are on these three horses: Uthopia, Valegro and Mistral Højris.

The day before leaving the television is full of Olympics, full of dramatic music, full of adverts and previews, full of when to watch the stars. Television's all over it and every time anything Olympic comes on I find myself bursting into tears. I don't know why. I don't know what's wrong with me. I'm just on edge about the whole thing.

Then I find out that my accreditation can't be delivered. We're all due to travel together on a bus up to the Olympics. The tack and equipment has been sent on ahead, the horses are ready to go and suddenly that vital piece of laminated photo ID without which you can't get anywhere no matter who you are or how important – blagging does not work at Olympic Games – is not in order and I have to pick it up in person. It was something to do with my passport needing the bespoke treatment, but thank heavens for Richard 'Dickie' Waygood, our chef d'equipe.

Dickie was absolutely brilliant. The idea was that we could all go in at the same time and Dickie had it all under control. He arrives, picks me up and off we set, separate from everyone else, crossing everything that this blasted accreditation would be ready. The whole thing was such a drama before I even got to Greenwich. The pressure of being a competitor, a trainer and an owner was catching up on me.

I have enjoyed my competing all my life, and yet here I was, looking forward to none of it, not one single bit. I was in an emotional place I had never been in before and it was especially difficult for me as I had never experienced before what I was experiencing then. There was nothing to draw on to help me out.

But the team support structure led by Will Connell, equestrian sport director at Team GBR and director of our World Class Performance programme, was geared up to what we as a team needed. It was about what the support team and the support structure could do to help so that we could be, as far as possible, our normal selves. There was a house where we could relax in the evenings, where we could sit outside and, in my case, have a drink and a smoke, so that did contribute to normalising the situation, which obviously helped me hugely. Anyway, with my accreditation sorted, we moved into the Novotel in Greenwich and the competition started.

The year before, at the Europeans, Charlotte [Dujardin] had been very buoyant. She'd set world records and this was her first Olympics with all the excitement that entails. I was lucky that she had the gloss of newness over the whole experience – far more shiny than a dull ache of pressure. I knew that as her trainer and mentor I could not show in any way what I was really feeling. There was I, at a major competition, visualising not the positive psychological imagery of everything going right but instead all the things that could go wrong. I don't do that, I never have done, but it is what I did in London and consequently I put myself under huge stress.

It was the first time the Olympic team competition was contested by three riders per team. Having been on teams of four since for ever this was a very different feeling. With only three in the team the pressure is colossal as there is no margin for error. Because of the fact that I was training Charlotte as well as riding myself I opted to ride first. I did that knowing it was not the ideal starting spot when you need the sort of scores that were expected of us. It might be a psychological feeling as a rider but you think 'Oh, I'm in the first group where everyone expects the weakest riders to be'. The classic strategy is to put the strongest combinations at the end, so if drawn first you are really presuming you are the weakest rider, the one to get out of the way first so the strongest come at the end. It's probably not the case that judges need to 'warm up' to giving higher scores but psychologically this is most riders' perception. And then Uti's foot was living in ice in case there was more bruising to come out, and that was in the back of my mind too. He did feel fine, we knew he was fine, but there was this nagging doubt. I was being very careful in training that he had no added pressure.

The competitor inside, however, comes back when you get on to ride. Thank heavens my inner competitor popped out of hiding and on the day of the test I was calm. I only had one problem and that was in the warm-up. Every time I did an extended canter Uti did a flying change before I got to the end of the diagonal. I have no idea why he did it, he had never done that before, and I ended up doing ten diagonals of extended canter and he did ten changes in the middle – and he damn well did it in the test as well! It was the one mistake he made, which of course will stick in my mind for ever. I don't know what I did in the warm-up or what caused him to do it or why he did it in the test. But, I had come from my last show, Fritzens in Austria, with a bad feeling. Uti had been inattentive. We'd won the grand prix on 77 per cent but in the grand prix special I didn't get the score I would normally expect so I was riding an Olympics off my last ride, a ride I really didn't want to be the one I had in my head.

Hartpury was supposed to be our final pre-Olympic show, but I had opted out. Charlotte and I knew that when it came to the individual competition with the draw run on FEI World Rankings she and I could be drawn very close together, too close. Charlotte and Valegro had the chance to go for individual gold, and knowing that she really needed me there to warm her up and guide her through the last test I opted out of Hartpury, so I hadn't had the luxury of a final warm-up.

Will Connell had been at a Performance Directors' meeting at Eton Dorney with the British Olympic Association and UK Sport discussing the potential pressures on athletes at London 2012. This was before the selection process but Will had presented the proposition that in dressage it could be that one gold medallist would also be in a position of training another gold medallist on the same team and how challenging that scenario could be. It was highly unusual, maybe even unique, and it did come to pass. We had to prove it was possible and I had to cope.

Being an owner as well – my third 'hat' – wasn't a problem. Roly Luard is my good luck charm in owning horses. She and I work together, we always have, and it works. I think we would each be worried about doing it without the other because we're good luck for each other as a team.

So we went into the Greenwich arena for that five minute forty-five second grand prix to come out with a 77.22 per cent score. When I came out of the arena a couple of people said to me 'you didn't go for it'. On no, I replied, I did go for it. Uti was soft, he felt good and that's as much as I could ask, considering how I felt. I just wanted that safe ride and – bar one mistake, the change in the extended canter – I got it. I was over the moon. It was a good start, it set the pace and most importantly we scored above the first German combination Dorothee Schneider and Diva Royal. We went into the lead.

On that first day you're thinking about being ahead of the other first riders – or 'third riders', if you take into account the self-imposed pecking order – and we achieved it. I came out on top of those third riders. That was my aim and I felt I had given the girls and us as a team that head start, for Laura [Bechtolsheimer] and Charlotte to go and do their bit. Laura is very much in her family unit, which gives her huge support. Things didn't quite go her way in the test; the highlights were there but she and Mistral Højris, known as 'Alf', made some mistakes and Laura was disappointed with her score. But Alf is a typical championship horse and gets better as the competition goes on, as he did in London.

We had a conversation on this medal subject one night. Laura, Charlotte and I had been out for dinner and we were talking about the medals. We said it didn't matter what we got, GB had never, ever had an Olympic medal in dressage before, so let's not put ourselves under that pressure that we have to win gold. If we win something won't it be amazing? That was two nights before the competition.

The Olympics had started on 28 July and the day before the dressage team competition started on 2 August the medals had started arriving for Team GB. Rowers Helen Glover and Heather Stanning had won the first British gold at Eton Dorney in the women's pairs, and become the first British female rowers to win an Olympic title, then Bradley Wiggins won the cycling time trial gold. We had another dinner the night before the competition, and we were sitting round absorbing the day's golds. 'OK,' I said, followed by an expletive, 'we now have to win a gold, we really have to or we won't be remembered. There are gold medals coming in here. We actually now do *need* a gold.' And we all thought we could do it.

We were a very close-knit group in that situation and it was a really, really good atmosphere. There were Laura's parents and her boyfriend (soon to be husband) Mark Tomlinson, Charlotte's stalwart mate Ian Cast, and Richard Davison, who was riding as an individual but very much part of the team, Dickie Waygood, then Charlotte, Laura and me.

You get to the Olympics and you're surrounded by your friends, your fellow competitors, team mates and you suddenly feel normal again. I didn't feel normal at home the week before the competition because I was on my own. That's what my problem was, but to get there and get into it with all those people who are either in it together with you or totally supportive, that's what helps you feel fine again.

Dressage is a competitive sport, but like all equestrian sports your main partner is your horse, and when you're in the ring, whether doing a grand prix test or jumping fences, it's down to you and the horse and you get in the zone. Once you're on two legs, you're in the same boat as every other competitor and everyone feels the same pressures, everyone wants to do their best. That's why when you're mixing with your mates again it's a 'normal' situation, however abnormal it is in reality. That is what competitive life is about. It was great going into the Olympics and being there. It was a show, that was all, and it was going to be fine.

Our hotel, the Novotel beside Greenwich Park station, was a short walk down the road and a right turn to the stables and the show ground. Every morning when we walked down to the stables there were people flowing out of the station coming to watch and it was one of the best feelings ever. Before we started the eventers were on, and the showjumpers were mixed in with us in the timetable, so Greenwich was full-on 'equestrian central' for the duration. There were bollards in place to widen the pavements and stop people walking in the road and the Gamesmakers with their 'big hands' and big smiles were cheerfully directing people to Greenwich Park. The whole place was throbbing with enthusiasm – it was bonkers! The walk from the hotel to the Greenwich Park entrance every day was a hoot because we got stopped left, right and centre for good wishes, for autographs, seeing people we knew. We got involved with everyone's enthusiasm, with everyone's feelings, and it was the best party atmosphere in the world. I don't think we'll experience the like of it again. It was tumultuous, incredible.

On the second day of the grand prix Charlotte had a great warm-up on Valegro, or Blueberry as we call him. She was her usual calm self, but I know when we walked down to that tunnel to the arena she could feel it. Hundreds of yards from the tunnel entrance my heart was pumping, I was walking but felt as if I was rocking, and that was only me, the tensions and excitement were palpable. I put my hand on Charlotte's knee and said, 'Don't forget, some people want it to happen, some wish it would happen, go and make it happen.' She trotted off down that chute and she went and did her thing. I couldn't have been prouder. I didn't cry, I just watched her as I do every day at home and it was a masterful performance.

On the following days those golds would come in thick and fast and people were starting to get very excited and expectant. The break between the grand prix and the grand prix special, the next round which would finally decide the team medals, had to be carefully managed as it would have been easy for the horses to go off the boil. We had to keep them happy, fit and relaxed. Then the night before the special the showjumpers – Nick Skelton, Peter Charles, Ben Maher and Scott Brash – brought home the first gold for GB in sixty years (before Nick Skelton was even born, but at least they had one!).

I felt confident that the special was Uthopia's best test so this was the part of the competition that I was most looking forward to. I wanted to recapture what I'd had the year before when I'd gone to the Europeans in Rotterdam not expecting anything, not having hit those 80 per cent scores, and I'd nailed them. I knew it was in there with Uti but I hadn't had it for a whole year. He'd got a little bit wiser, he knew the test and, let's face it, most horses that get to this level are intelligent but he's very intelligent and most of all he's a stallion so has his mind on other things at times. When they get there young, as Uti did – he was only ten when he first hit the high scores – it is because of that intelligence, so it follows that he was also intelligent enough to know the test. There is an old horsemen's adage: 'Tell a gelding, ask a mare, discuss it with a stallion.' I get that anticipation, and with a stallion that slight backward tendency, it's a constant, but with so much at stake there was not a lot of room for discussion. The fact was I just decided to sit down and ride hard. It's not my style of riding, but I was determined to get through with no mistakes. It was a bit knife-edge, but I hit that 80 per cent and as we rode out of the arena I looked at the scoreboard and thought, 'I've done it!' That was the test I set out to get, the score I set out to get, and I got them.

Alf and Laura had a few errors but she upped her score by 2 per cent and then Charlotte . . . well, Valegro was at the point where he was totally rideable; it doesn't seem to matter where you put him, he just gives it. Again he gave it.

The scores were added together. We could hear the roars from the crowd while we were out the back. We knew that the final Dutch rider, Adelinde Cornelissen, would have had to get an unbelievable score and, although it's not over until it's over, I think we all knew it was going to be a fairly impossible task for her.

To come in to that team prize-giving, to come through into the arena all together . . . We'd done it. That was all I could think. The horses had delivered, we'd delivered. I was just so excited for everyone watching. The majority in that crowd were British people who were witnessing something historic. We were feeling it and they were feeling it with us.

We all cried, laughed, and slapped each other. Everybody was relieved: the vets, the farrier, the physio. All our support team that World Class Performance put in place, the 'British Army' as I call them – they were tremendous. History had started, history had been made. That's all I could think: we did it. We won gold. And we did it in the right place.

I never thought it would happen in my life. When I started out in my competitive career I couldn't have known that in my lifetime the Olympics would ever be in London. When London was awarded the 2012 Games I wondered whether I'd be a part of it. I didn't know I'd have Uthopia and Valegro in my life, and I didn't know I'd have someone like Charlotte to complement the horses. But it did happen, it was a fait accompli. It was destiny.

You can't really explain what it feels like to be up on that podium – it's just a total rush to your body. The bronze medallists get up first, then silver and you're waiting and you're thinking, 'My God, they're going to go bananas!' Then they go bananas. It's a beautiful situation where you're looking to your left at the two team mates you've journeyed with, and looking either side at the Germans and Dutch a podium each down, and then out into the sea of waving Union Jacks. We went bananas too. We all felt – and it was certainly the thought in my head – that this journey had been worth it. It was a huge relief. The biggest thing of all was that it had worked, we had made it happen.

2

Island Life

Naughty Mummy got pregnant at school so was sent away to a nunnery to have me. In 1967, which might have been the swinging sixties but was only swinging for girls if they didn't get caught out, that wasn't anything out of the ordinary. It wasn't really a nunnery, I just think it sounds better so that's how I tell it; apparently it was a private house near Cambridge where she stayed and worked. Girls were sent away to this sort of halfway house before the bump got too big and the neighbours' talk got too loud. I was not put up for adoption, or at least it was halted when my grandmother decided I should be kept. I'm sure Mum and Nan have other versions of the history, but this is my story, so I'll tell what I know.

We lived on Byng Road in the London Borough of Barnet. I don't remember much about those London years apart from winning a goldfish and flushing it down the toilet. Oh, and the weird thing is I can remember looking out of an oxygen tent and seeing people peering at me through the plastic. But when I wanted a wee no one came so the inevitable happened. I had double pneumonia at the time. Then there is a hilarious picture of me in long socks, velvet trousers and a velvet waistcoat at the wedding of Mum's friend when she was a bridesmaid. I dread to think what Mum and the bride were wearing.

It was when I was four that my mother took me and moved to Sark, the fourth smallest Channel Island. The family used to go there for holidays and 'Chez Nous' was left to Mum and her two brothers by their godmother, the wonderfully named Winnie Tosh. Neither of her brothers wanted to up sticks and move to a tiny Channel Island, or at least not then, but Mum decided she did, probably because she wanted to gain her independence.

So we arrived on Sark. Mum was only twenty-one so it was a pretty big thing for her to do at that age, in those days. She got a job as a cleaner and chambermaid in a hotel and she used to take me to work with her so I expect the more Mummy cleaned the more I made a mess behind her. That hotel, Le Petit Champ, hasn't changed in all those years, at least not to me. My stepfather-to-be Jess Hester was a pot washer in another hotel, although he was a trained carpenter. My first memory of Jess is waking up in the morning and going into Mum's room and there she was with Jess for the first time. I was absolutely horrified that there was somebody in my mother's bed. Anyway, they got married.

Our 'house' was basically a wooden shack, a bit like one of those Caribbean-style houses with a tin roof. It had just one bedroom and a dining/living room, but it sat on the east coast of the island and so you could see France, even if the prevailing view was of a great big nuclear power station. Right next door to us lived the island's vet and because of dogs coming over from France the vet had built the first rabies quarantine kennels on Sark. I was strictly warned never to go over the hedge which separated the two properties, and I didn't, as the idea of getting bitten by a rabid dog and dying a horrible death was very scary for a little kid. But the vet also had donkeys, which I could see from our house as the garden sloped down towards their field, and he had goats too which I used to help him rear. Those were the earliest days of my life with animals and they're sweet memories. I assume, of course, that I was sweet too.

At the age of five I started school under the tutelage of Mrs Lefebvre (pronounced 'le fever' but lessons weren't conducted at a feverish pace, thank heavens). There were only two classrooms in the long, granite building: one for children under the age of eight and the other for ages eight to eleven. There was a senior school for after that, but in our little school the total number of pupils in my year was eleven.

The most fascinating thing for me about Mrs Lefebvre was that her husband was a carriage driver and so they had a couple of ponies. Sark was and still is a working island for horses. There are no cars, transport for locals and tourists is by horse-drawn carriage, and fields are ploughed by horses, so all the equines of the island are packhorses of the land. People didn't keep horses solely for riding, although a few families had ponies. Some of the children used to ride their ponies to school, then in the afternoon the ponies would be dropped off for them to ride home again. It's funny because it doesn't seem that long ago to me, but it probably sounds more like eighty years ago than forty.

I can't remember when it started, and there is no reason I can put a finger on as to why it did, but I was always fascinated by horses and ponies. I have, however, a very clear memory of my first encounter with a horse. Nan took me to a field and as I could see there was a horse in it I walked under the wire to go and say 'hello'. It picked me up by my hair! Obviously this made me cry and run out again. But Nan told me that the horse thought my hair was hay, which is why it tried to eat me. It often doesn't make sense where an all-consuming fascination with horses comes from, some people just have it. Needless to say, the 'hay-hair muncher' of Sark didn't put me off.

It's fair to say I was madly keen on pets. I was given Sweep, the guinea pig, for Christmas one year. Actually what I was given was a box with a load of curly wood shavings in it and I remember that awful sinking disappointment that there would be nothing else inside. But the joy of finally finding the guinea pig! Then there was Pharaoh the rabbit, which got savaged by a dog next door. Poor Pharaoh was wild, I hate to think my desire to tame him hastened his death but I suspect it might have.

Pigeons racing from France used to drop in on the Channel Islands and I was to become madly keen on pigeon racing. We (that is, me and friends from school) used to catch all these pigeons and while I wasn't allowed to keep them, I did keep one in the wardrobe once. I'm sure this confession won't make the French pigeon racers happy but it may answer a few questions for them. This one I kept for days in the wardrobe until Mum found it. I wasn't there when she did but can imagine there were one or two shrieks – and not of joy. I would feed the pigeon but couldn't think of anywhere for it to go during the day, hence the wardrobe. Mum released the pigeon, so when I came home I had the joyous job of cleaning all the shit out of the wardrobe.

Nan, as I've always called my grandmother, had also moved to Sark two years after Mum and me. She and Pop, my grandfather, bought a property called The Willows which they developed and ran as a bed and breakfast. It was lovely, bungalow style, all on one floor. Nan did the cooking while Pop did the serving. They produced home-grown vegetables and made it into the perfect B&B, which attracted lots of French visitors. This provided me with a big opportunity. Nan used to pay me – about tuppence, I think – to take some of the guests down to beaches they hadn't been to before and show them new places, or she'd get me in to play with the kids who were staying. It gave me a bit of cultural difference which I didn't get from being at school in a classroom of eleven kids and Mrs Lefebvre, who taught us for every subject, at every level, although the French teacher who taught the older group used to take us all for French lessons. Going to school on Sark was amazing though. Once we'd finished classes everyone used to pile down to the beaches. It was heaven. My friend Jamie and I always used to stop at the island stores to pick up a packet of chocolate biscuits, then it was straight down to the beach until six o'clock and teatime.

There was an increasing family gathering on Sark as Mum's brother David had also moved to the island. We used to see him after school on his rounds delivering fresh fish – his catch of the day. He wasn't a fisherman until he arrived on Sark. He'd been a rugby player, and a successful one at that. Since arriving on Sark as well as being a fisherman he ran a pub and had his turn at being the island's policeman. That's one thing about Sark: everybody gets a go at being the policeman. They are elected every two years and no doubt if I'd stayed there I'd have ended up doing it, which would have been my biggest dread. The job is mostly dealing with over-intoxicated people from the other islands on a jaunt to Sark for stag parties and that sort of thing. In the playground at school was an alleyway about three feet wide. Across from there is the Sark prison. It is famous for being the smallest prison in the world and consists of two very basic cells. A big green wooden door, with a grille of bars at the top, was the only thing that separated the inmates from us outside. Any prisoners could look out at us in the playground and we used to hurl stones and abuse at them like the ghastly little children we were. That's how close we were to the law.

The Dame of Sark, Sibyl Hathaway, was in her early nineties and by then unable to walk. When we were standing outside school in the morning waiting to go in, the Dame would come past in her electric buggy – she was the only person on the island allowed to have one in those days. As she made her way past it was rather like a royal progress, we all used to stand in a line and nod our heads to her.

When Jess and Mum married I became a Hester. Jess was gradually building our house up, first adding another bedroom. I didn't have any contact with my natural father, no birthday cards, not a word. Apparently when I was born he'd been told he could visit me after school, but obviously I didn't know whether he did. Maybe Mum and Jess felt it was a new life and 'for the best', but I never asked and wasn't interested. When I was eight Mum got pregnant again with my sister Polly. There was no hospital on Sark, just the doctor whose only means of transport was a bike. When someone was ill you would know by the speed the doctor was pedalling on his bike how bad their illness was. A few years after Polly arrived, having been safely delivered in hospital on Guernsey, my brother Jesse was on the way.

One really stormy, wet night at the end of August the ambulance, which was a carriage pulled by a tractor, arrived. The doors opened and we all piled in to go down to the harbour. It was a freezing night and there were rats running around everywhere on the harbour side. It was horrible. The ambulance boat, the *Flying Christine*, came to collect Mum. It only took twenty minutes to get to Guernsey, but between the two islands my brother was born. It was a breach birth, which must have been pretty damned uncomfortable for Mum. There are very few people now who are officially born 'Sarkee' – I only became Sarkee after living there for fifteen years – but Jesse could have been had people on Sark not thrown their arms up in horror, so Jesse's birth certificate states that he was born on the *Flying Christine* at the Albert Docks in Guernsey. Everyone thought he should be called Albert. Unsurprisingly, pregnant ladies are now expected to travel to Guernsey at least two weeks before their babies are due in case of any trouble.

At the age of eight I was still mad keen on the horses. During the summers I had this great nanny, Michelle (well, she wasn't a real nanny but she looked after me), who was the daughter of a proper old Sark guy and an Irish mother who was a proper old nagswoman, the latter in this sense being the term for a horsewoman, not a woman who nagged her husband. They had a farm with probably twelve or fifteen working horses and carriages, and a lot of dramas going on. Michelle was a wild child and very popular in more ways than one. There was a strapping Irishman, probably about six foot six inches tall, and a shorter, stocky chap. Both of them fancied Michelle and they'd fight over her. Michelle was a carriage driver, as were both lads. Anyway, one night a fight broke out and one of them took a shotgun to the other one. I think one of them got a minor wound to his leg. No one got killed, thank God, but both men had to leave the island.

In the summer when the carriages went out to take tourists round the island I used to hop from one carriage to the other; if one was getting too full I'd hop off at a stop and hop on another. My 'job' then was to do tours. The carriage drives lasted about three hours with six stops, including one for lunch. I would get paid at each of the stops to take the tourists down to see the beauty spots, or round the gardens of the Seigneurie, the home of the Dame of Sark. At places where the carriage couldn't go, we'd all get off and I'd escort the visitors round telling them the history of the island, such as what happened to Sark during the Second World War. The Channel Islands were the only British territory to be occupied during World War Two, but the only remaining evidence on Sark is the sail-less windmill which was used as a German lookout. We had to be jolly careful on the tours as it was never apparent which of the tourists were German . . . until it was too late.

It seems incredible to me now that aged seven or eight I could remember all the details. I hope I got everything right – although something tells me if I didn't my improvisation skills were already being developed – but the facts stuck when you were doing sometimes three tours a day. I've forgotten most of the history now. I met some great people, and some famous people like Pam Ayres and the violinist Nigel Kennedy, though I can't say I knew who they were then. Mostly it was all about being around the horses.

That obvious, almost instinctive fear that even people who are besotted by horses can have around them was never there in me. I used to go under their tummies and between their legs to get from one carriage to another – I never walked around them – and quite often at the stops I would crawl up the carriage shafts so I could sit on their backs. People used to love photographing this monkey-like kid who emerged from the danger zone underneath the horse and popped up to sit on his back.

Michelle's mother, Hannie Perrée, the nagswoman, would give me various jobs when I got back from the carriage tours at the end of the day. I'd either be tasked with doing her shopping – which meant I'd have to head straight back to the village – or to turn the horses out or bring the cows in for milking. I was a general gopher and I loved it, especially working on the farm, Le Fort, which is where the first settlement was made on Sark. I still hadn't actually ridden much, and then Hannie bought a donkey called Jacko.

Here was my first real chance to ride, so I used to use Jacko for the shopping runs. He was very happy to go to the shops as he soon learned he'd be rewarded with a carrot, but getting back was a different matter. Jacko would dig his heels in, deciding that waiting for a carrot was a better bet than carrying me and the shopping home. My solution was to get on, then flap the plastic shopping bag above his head. Only then would he go, and once he did he went jolly fast.

At the weekends we would take Jacko to the beach to do donkey rides. Anyone who's been to Sark will know that there isn't a beach you can easily get to. They're all quite hard to negotiate on an island 250 feet above sea level. All the sandy beaches on Sark have near-vertical paths going down to them, which made them very difficult to navigate, even for a hardy little donkey, so we used the pebble beaches instead. There wasn't a lot of riding to be done on the beach, but it was enough and the donkey rides were popular until Jess gave me a stern warning that I was going to be in trouble for making money without a licence. It was probably more about stopping me going to the beach every day, as at eight years old I was hardly going to be sent to prison for working illegally and making two pence a ride. All the same, we had to stop, although there were still ingenious ways of making money at the expense of dear old Jacko.

When at home, whatever time of day or night, if I heard a horse I would always run out to see who it was. Before 5.30 in the afternoon I'd know it would be a carriage, while after that any of the children who had a pony would be home from school so there was a good chance whatever I heard was going to be ridden. Vanessa, a girl from school who lived on the other side of the island, used to go past on her pony Spice, who must have been about thirty-five years old. I'd rush out and pull Vanessa off so I could have a go and ride down the road. Well, not quite, but I'd beg her for a quick trot and pay her back with a chocolate.

Another girl at school, Lizzie Dewe, whose family owned the La Moinerie hotel, had a pony called Jackie. She took me out one day after school and put me on him, telling me it was time for me to learn to canter. We went to a great big field and Lizzie got on her bike to ride alongside us. I didn't have a saddle – nobody did – but thankfully Jackie did have a bridle on. Lizzie pedalled flat out beside me as Jackie trotted faster and faster until my teeth were rattling in my head. Then suddenly he broke into canter and we were off, with Lizzie screaming at me to keep kicking.

I can still feel it now – it was the best feeling in the world and so comfy. That was my first experience of the wonderful feeling of canter and I wasn't going to let it stop. Nowadays we all understand that safety is important but wow, what freedom to be able to just get on and ride; no saddle, no hat, no back protector. The balance I acquired through that way of riding for many years has stood me in good stead. People do say that of bareback riding, and I am absolutely convinced of it.

Wherever I knew there was a pony on the island I would end up wheedling my way in there somehow. Little Sark is a wonderful part of the island with another famous award-winning hotel called La Sablonnerie, which is possibly the quaintest hotel in the world. Elizabeth Perrée, who was a cousin of Michelle's – a non-speaking cousin, there was always rivalry between the two although they're on good terms nowadays – lived right at the end of Little Sark. The cousins were as far as you could get from each other on the island, which was probably just as well what with all the fights. Elizabeth owned the most beautiful thing I had ever seen in my life which was a grey Arab stallion called L'Arret. Whenever I cycled past his field I would stop, sit on the bank and watch him, he just took my breath away. L'Arret was the one thing I wanted more than anything in the world but he was wild. When Elizabeth rode him I used to watch in awe – he would rear and scream. As the only stallion on the island he knew he was kingpin. Elizabeth finally let me ride L'Arret and he used to terrify the life out of me as whenever he saw a carriage horse coming he would scream his head off. He had several liaisons with some of those larger ladies who pulled the carriages, but fortunately didn't attempt such overtures while I was on board.

Any available time, weekends and holidays, I was up there having a go on these animals. When I was ten, Mum and Jess decided I had to sit the 11-plus exam, and that if I passed I would go to boarding school on Guernsey. The thought of it filled me with dread. I'm sure I wasn't the only one who passed the exam but I was the only one of my year who was going away to school, so that meant going on my own.

Elizabeth College was the only boarding school we went to look at. You could go to day school and board with a family, but the fact was it would have been too difficult to find a family to take me on for as long as I was going to be there, which was at least four or five years. That rather makes it sounds as if I had a choice, but I didn't, I was going anyway. I was really worried about going to Elizabeth College as it was known as an academic school, but my main worry was when would I be able to ride?

It was traumatic. The only thing that made it a bit better was that while I was very small at the age of eleven, out of between eighty and ninety boys there were three or four who were there at the age of seven. It was an international boarding school, so some parents travelled a lot and they'd left these lost little seven-year-olds who were tiny. It was the only saving grace that there were others smaller than me, but it was pretty horrendous all the same.

The college was founded in 1563 by Queen Elizabeth I. It is the most impressive building, gorgeous, and behind those turrets that run along the top of the main building are dormitories, or there were then. So my first boarding house was on the top floor of the college, which sits at the top of St Peter Port in Guernsey. I'd look out of the window in the morning straight over to Sark, nine miles away, wonder what everyone was doing and think if only if I could see a carriage horse in the distance – which of course I couldn't. That was the most frustrating thing about school, and the full boarding school terms meant we only had Easter, summer and Christmas holidays. Out of sight out of mind is one thing, but it's bloody well not when you live in a boarding house and can see home from your window! Mum and Dad – Jess – were over there and a wave didn't do any good at all.

There were eighteen of us in a dorm, a long room with nine beds on each side and lockers down the middle. We had to endure raids from the bastard prefects who used to come in and throw us out of bed and toss our clothes out of the window, the usual boarding school thing. In my year all the boys were very good friends, thankfully. I did hate it, but I wouldn't go back and change any of it. I don't think I would have been anything without it. It is said that boarding school is character forming, and it was.

I was so flipping shy when I went there, I had no idea how to speak to people. We had a lot of good housemasters and there was a full curriculum, but I wasn't much good at any of it. The most disappointing thing about this was that my mother's brother, David, among all his other skills, was actually a qualified maths teacher. He'd tried to take me under his wing and teach me maths because it was the one thing we didn't really do at school in Sark, but even so I failed year after year. I simply could not do maths and I think I took an absolute pleasure, after being forced to do it, in coming last every year in maths. Don't ask me why, but religious studies, which I also loathed, I somehow managed to pass.

Sport is prevalent among the islands; even now on Jersey and Guernsey all they can talk about is beating each other. We did a lot of running, and I enjoyed that. I was a sprint runner for the island over 100 metres. Looking back, I have no idea how I did it as it would take me twenty minutes to sprint out to the car now. I really enjoyed doing my Duke of Edinburgh award, despite being failed for getting back too early. You weren't supposed to return before noon and I failed three times for getting back at eleven thirty. We were supposed to clock it and I didn't.

Team sports were not for me. I was crap at football and always used to get put at the back, which I hated. I'd dive out of the way when the ball came towards me, thinking, 'Oh my God, they've broken through defence – run for it!!' That was my biggest dread and I could feel myself crumble when the goalkeeper screamed at me to go out there and kick it. How I hated football. I never played rugby, but did play a lot of hockey, and then there was swimming and sailing.

I am the worst sailor. I get incredibly seasick, so it was probably a good job I was a boarder because the way I felt on the sea it would have been very cruel to have had to face that every day. My friend Debbie, being a year older, had gone to school on Guernsey a year before me at Elizabeth College's counterpart for girls. Debbie was wicked. On the boat going there or back she'd unpick the stitches on the bottom of the sick bag before handing it to me. The contents, of course, dropped straight out. As I used to be sick three times on a crossing this was pretty bad. Ghastly, in fact. In the end, Mum took me to the doctor who said I would grow out of it, but I never did really, or at least not until some twenty years later. You learn where it works for you and I'm fine outside in the open air, but I still don't like being on boats.

I remember Debbie as a big girl – and bear in mind I was tiny at the time. She and her friend Belinda were the two big girls in their class and I think they must have reminded me of carriage horses; when we were at school on Sark, during breaks, I used to put a bit of string in Debbie's mouth and a bit of string in Belinda's and drive them round pretending they were horses. Belinda and Debbie would come in from the playground with big red lines either side of their mouths. Debbie eventually became a bespoke shoe designer; she was obviously pretty handy with stitches and once designed herself a short, tight dress to show off her 'Nigella' figure. We got on the boat in Sark, which meant negotiating about five steps down. When we got off in Guernsey the tide was much lower, meaning there were about thirty-five steps to go up. Encased in her hourglass number, Debbie found to her horror that she couldn't get her legs wide enough apart to manage the steps, so I had to go and get a pair of scissors and cut the dress up the side so she could get to the top. So I got my revenge for her making me puke through the bag!

Sark is so bleak in the winter. In spring it starts to come alive with bluebells in the woods and hedgerows and along the coastal paths, then some six hundred species of flowering plants all burst into life and colour as the Gulf Stream's currents warm around the islands. To paint a picture of Sark in summer with everything in bloom, the gardens are glorious and there are even palm trees. Sark in winter at its bleakest couldn't be more of a contrast. It's a plateau island of just over two square miles with the highest point 374 feet about sea level, so when the wind and rain come it's horrendous.

Going out for dinner in summer is great fun. You have to cycle everywhere, so basically if you're pissed the wind will blow it out of you. The winters are a different matter. You can liken it to the Arab women who wear head-to-toe black in the street then pop out at home dressed in head-to-toe Armani. On Sark in winter everyone goes out in their oilskins as there is no choice but to pedal, or to be very persuasive getting people to come to your place for dinner. Years later, when I worked in the evenings in the hotel bar, I used to have to dress for hell on the journeys there and back.

The island is totally seasonal; bustling in the summer, dead as a graveyard in the winter when the hotels close from mid-October to March. The islanders would turn into migrant workers, leaving their women and children behind and heading to the mainland to work – lots used to head to the Reading area to work on a Christmas tree plantation – with only a handful staying behind to work on the roads, repairing, re-gravelling and rolling (there's no tarmac) in preparation for the following spring.

My father Jess didn't have to do that. He'd upgraded his skills and was a fully-fledged carpenter and builder. People were starting to realise the importance of a house with a view, built of the natural Channel Islands granite which is a stunningly beautiful blue-grey or pink-grey, so he was starting to find his niche doing that. Mum had the three of us, and she worked with him in the building business doing the books as my father was really dyslexic.

I'd met Daniel on Sark when I was ten. Dan's family had a house on the island and a pretty interesting famous relative on his grandmother's side, the author Mervyn Peake. Derek Jacobi came to Sark to star in the TV mini-series of one of Peake's stories, *Mr Pye*. I remember them filming and it looking like a rather weird film. The main thing about Dan, though, was that in him I found someone who was as mad about riding as I was. Dan's family were also friends with Elizabeth Perrée, so when Dan tipped up at one of the gymkhanas we started chatting.

One thing that happened when I first met Dan is rather a claim to fame of mine. I was riding Patches, who belonged to Lizzie Dewe. As he wasn't very big, Patches used to pull a governess cart, which is a small two-wheeled cart. They have two seats, one fitted each side, so you climb in via a little door at the back and you have to sit sideways on when you drive it. They were designed to be suitable for ladies to drive, and the name comes from their use by governesses to transport their small pupils. Patches doubled up as a riding pony and I got to ride him at the annual horse show in the class for the best rider under sixteen. Dan was entered in the competition, turned out immaculately in his jodhpurs and jodhpur boots, and proved to be an immaculate little rider as he'd had proper lessons. Dan rode in the modern style – by that I mean the correct style – and had showjumped quite successfully in Guernsey. So there we were in this class and Dan was really my only rival. Dan trots in, wearing his hat and smart jacket, bouncing up and down very neatly on the correct diagonal as you're supposed to do in trot. To start with we all trotted round together, then we each had to do a little individual show in front of the judge. I seem to remember I had a saddle on Patches, but I certainly couldn't compete with Dan in the turnout stakes with my borrowed breeches and a huge pair of borrowed rubber riding boots. As I started my show, Patches had other ideas and napped it, shooting out of the arena. My natural response to this was to get him back in, which I did by flapping my reins on his neck and kicking him furiously with my boots flapping like waders and falling further down my legs. I got Patches back into the ring and was picked as the winner because the judges thought I was very brave. Dan was horrified, and I don't know how he has ever forgiven me. That was my first experience of feeling ultra competitive. Whatever the odds, I'd had to beat Dan, and I realised then that I really rather liked winning.

Dan and I would head on our ponies to L'Eperquerie Common at the north end of Sark, which sits on the headland facing Guernsey and the tiny private island of Jethou. It was one of our favourite places for riding as we'd construct showjumping courses out of the gorse bushes up there to canter round and jump. When we'd finished we'd gallop back up to the road. On one side there was a 250-foot drop down to the sea.

Our other favourite place was La Coupée. This natural isthmus – I'm not sure, but I think it's one of the longest in the world and certainly among the narrowest, being only about nine feet wide – connects Big Sark with Little Sark. We would ride two Welsh ponies named Penny and Bim Dougal. They were only twelve or thirteen hands high. Penny was the mother, Bim Dougal her son and they both belonged to Elizabeth Perrée. Dan and I would ride over to La Sablonnerie on our bikes, pick up the ponies, race over to Big Sark, go hell for leather round the island then ride all the way back. Bear in mind that these ponies weren't ridden for probably six months of the year, so they weren't shod and yet we used to pick them up and go like bats out of hell for the duration of the holidays.

All the carriage horses used to be terrified of Bim Dougal and would freak out when I rode towards them on this tiny pony. These days you're not allowed to ride a bike across La Coupée, but Dan and I literally used to gallop across, and race each other on this narrow strip with sheer drops for most of the way either side. It is eighty metres above sea level.

The annual Sark horse show was one of the highlights of the year. It still is, but when I lived there it was THE event of the year for me and I used to look forward to it with huge excitement. It's a proud thing for all the farmers to turn out their best horses and carriages, and much work goes in beforehand, bathing the horses, cleaning harnesses, et cetera. There are showing classes for all the different types of carriages and horses: harness horses, wagonettes, six-seaters, twelve-seaters, governess carts, heavy horses, middleweight, light-weight . . .

This fantastic spectacle culminates in the famous race derby, the one time in the year when the carriage horses were able to let rip and go. It wasn't that they were fast, but it was a straight line-up start then go, so that lot thundering towards you made for a pretty fearsome sight. I finally got a horse to ride from Hannie. All the other islanders would come over to Sark to watch and people would be pulled out of the crowd to stand at the corners and act as marker posts for us riders to go round. They were usually either tanked-up or unsuspecting tourists from England. The last time I rode in the race when I lived there I was leading on the first lap so hadn't seen what happened behind me. Coming round for the second lap all I saw was a wheelbarrow being pushed by two blokes and containing a girl with a bleeding nose – she'd fallen off at the start, been squashed, and they were transporting her from the field.

I wasn't bullied at school, although I did get dropped in the pool and once had my eyebrows shaved off, but on the whole us boarders stuck together. We islanders were allocated to one of the four boarding houses depending which of the islands we came from. There were eight of us out of some eighty boys in my year who were boarding, so when you have seventy-two boys who are going home after

school every day and eight whose parents had chosen to send us off
to school staying on, you can see why we stuck together. It was a very,
very good group and we were all completely different. Nobody else
liked horses, apart from me. One of the group was Paul Paint, who
was into powerboating and had his own powerboat even at the age
of fifteen. We all used to pile in and drop over to Herm, where Paul
would sip a couple of lagers thinking that was OK to do (the rest
of us would be on Pepsi Colas naturally!). Then there was George,
whose mother ran tea rooms; James and Pinky, who were going to be
lawyers; David Tucker, who wanted to go in the army; Tim, who was
deaf; and me. That was about it in our year in the boarding house.
The eighth member of the group was John Bell, whose father was a
maths teacher so John was around and about with us boarders.

Dan was at the grammar school, but his parents lived a ten-minute
bike ride from my boarding house so many evenings after lights out
I would climb through the window (we weren't on the top floor by
then) and bike down to Dan's. His bedroom was on the ground floor.
He'd let me in through the window, we'd sit there smoking for twenty
minutes, then I'd get on my bike and go all the way back to school
again. His parents were the ones who always picked me up from
the boat. Because I was sick I would be absolutely ravenous when
I landed in Guernsey, so Dan's mum would whisk me home and fill
me up with crisps and omelette. It was so good, they were such nice
people and became like family to me. Because Dan wasn't at Elizabeth College we always had a lot to talk about and a lot of fun, and
then there were the holidays, and riding.

Due to my birthday being in June I was actually in the year above
where I should have been – that is, I was a year younger than everyone else – and so I left school at fifteen. Probably, in hindsight, I'd
have been better off in the year below. You had to get four O-levels
to continue to sixth-form level, and I got three: English Language,
Biology and the dreaded Religious Studies, none of them useful for
what I wanted to do. When the results were released I remember the

look of pain on my father Jess's face, the absolute disappointment and the 'after all those years of sending you to this academic school' recriminations. But my feeling was that there had been no point in sending me there because I was going to work with horses. I'd argued that from the start and the response was 'you're going anyway' so this was really just vindication that I'd been right all along.

Being brought up by a stepfather – bearing in mind I didn't know and didn't want to know my real father – was fine, but there was that element of strain which is often present in a relationship with a 'step', especially when there are two other children involved who don't have any steps in the way of their relationship. I'm sure it's an uphill battle for many step-parents, but if as a stepchild you sense there is favouritism that can make you feel a bit isolated. I resented having to work in Jess's workshop several nights a week after junior school on Sark. My job was to bag up all the shavings from the saw mills. I hated it. There wasn't a guinea pig in sight and I was the bloody sweep, but he wanted me to do it. I'd say 'I'm going to ride' and he'd say 'No you're not'. That was my nightmare, to be told I couldn't go to the horses. If I'd been naughty or was late, and I mean a quarter past instead of six o'clock, then I couldn't go to the farm the next day. It was my absolute dread. I don't think it was unusual. Jess was a disciplinarian and I didn't bloody misbehave. Call it terror, respect or even both, I now think there should be more of it, but back then I couldn't wait to leave home. Despite being fifteen and a year younger than my peers, I saw myself as part of that group, and they were all thinking of jobs or A-levels.

My school reports read along the lines 'Carl is no trouble, he has a lovely disposition but does need to apply himself', and, to me, the classic: 'Carl goes along without a care in the world, certain he will obtain employment as a stable boy or jockey.'

My qualifications for the latter were that I was very small and liked going fast on ponies. Obviously I had no experience, but the careers master explored options for me and I sent an application to the Racing School at Newmarket. I didn't get accepted, but thanks to Mrs Gibson, one of the teachers on Sark, I had another option.

During my final year at Elizabeth College Mrs Gibson had rung to tell me about the Fortune Centre. The Centre's founders, the Honourable Mrs Baillie and Mrs Nelson, were coming over to stay at their holiday home on Sark and were planning to give a talk on their work helping physically and mentally handicapped young people through riding therapy. Mrs Gibson suggested that I speak to them, so I took a day out from school to come back to Sark. Then, during the Christmas holidays, I'd spent a week at the Centre in the New Forest where I'd been able to ride every day, learning to ride in a saddle, muck out, and basically do everything that I'd never done before, and do it properly. The ladies had told me that if I wanted to come over and take my BHSAI (British Horse Society Assistant Instructor certificate) I could. So once jockey school didn't work out, I had two choices: go to the Fortune Centre or return to Sark and live happily ever after working on the carriages and in a bar at night (which was probably what I would have ended up doing if Nan hadn't put her foot down). So, the Fortune Centre it was.

I was keen to go. I was so used to boarding school by then that the thought of being away wasn't scary. It was also around that time that Mum had said to me out of the blue 'Your father's on TV' and I'd tuned in to see him, the actor Anthony Smee. So, my move to the Fortune Centre and England was via London where I stopped to meet my natural father. Mum thought it was time I met him.

Guernsey was fog-bound and our plane couldn't take off, but Mum bumped into someone she knew who had a private plane and who was flying, and was prepared to take us to Heathrow. I'm a nervous flyer now and I blame it on that bumpy, foggy flight, but Mum and I somehow arrived safely in London.

Luckily my father was then married to Maria-Luisa. She was, and is, a gorgeous lady and made me feel very comfortable, but sitting there with someone I didn't know and my half-sister Vivien, who was then only two or three years old, waiting to meet my father was a strange feeling. I asked Maria-Luisa what I should call him: Dad? Tony? She said call him whatever you like, so I blurted out both suggested names at once, to which he responded, 'Call me Tony.'

I stayed two nights with them in London, which was absolutely horrific. Nothing to do with any of the people involved but because they lived on the Gunnersbury tube line. Coming from Sark I had only experienced dark nights with the only light from the stars. Gunnersbury at night was orange outside, and then every twenty minutes a flaming tube train would go past which would cause me to dive ten feet out of the bed. After two nights of this terror, I moved straight down to the New Forest and a fresh start.

3

A Kind of Fortune

Daily routine, what a shock to the system! I started off at the Fortune Centre living 'out' in a lovely village called Tiptoe in the New Forest National Park, where I had a room in a house owned by a lady named Mary. I'd have to walk across the road to the residential part of the Fortune Centre to take the bus to Bransgore and the main centre. We'd leave en masse every morning, thirty of us staff, students and residents, at 06.40, which was a bloody early start. The bus was always pretty lively, with the residents playing around in the back for the fifteen-minute trip.

It was strange, very strange, and yet compellingly interesting for me. A physical handicap is visible, obvious, but these disturbed young people had problems that were not obvious. You couldn't immediately see what, if anything, was wrong. These were kids who had suffered nervous breakdowns, kids who had been abused, kids who had some sort of learning difficulty. I also had to contend with the fact that, although I was only sixteen and a lot of the kids were my age or older, because I was a member of staff they would address me as Mr Hester. I'd never been called 'Mr Hester' in my life, so that was weird anyway, but by these people who looked exactly like me, who I didn't feel were any different to me? Bizarre is the only word for it.

If the hidden scars revealed themselves, there was nothing I could do. I was told that. I remember one girl who hadn't had an easy upbringing. The two of us were in the tack room one day and while I was busy focusing on the saddle soap, Her attention was on the cuts she was making in her wrists. She was having a particularly bad day, but, according to instructions, I had to ignore it. Obviously I had to report such incidents but I wasn't to get involved, as a trainee I was not equipped to do so. I didn't have the skills and expertise to deal with a vulnerable girl who was self-harming, my job was to get my BHSAI, but it took a while to overcome the natural instinct to intervene, ask them why they were doing that, or worse, just stare.

I was the only one who was there purely for the riding and horse management – the other staff-students were there to train as educational teachers – but I would join in on the physical therapy and some of the courses. I would also do evening duties and help out with looking after the residents, but I was primarily there to do my 'AI'. I was lucky that Mrs Baillie and Mrs Nelson had recognised the direction I wanted to take in life and had pretty much created a vacancy for me to fill.

Mrs Nelson, whose daughter Jennifer now runs the Fortune Centre, had been a chief instructor at Porlock Vale, which way before my time had been a famous mecca for training and riding and had produced some of the pioneers of eventing. Mrs Nelson had a particular interest in the art of dressage and on special occasions I would be trained by her. Then there was the famous 'flying nun', Sister Chiara, who used to come and take courses. I thought it was hilarious that I was taught by a nun – and yes, she used to wear her habit. I LOVED her lessons!

Sister Chiara – a British Horse Society Fellow, so right up there at the top of the teaching ranks – had a colourful background. Formerly Cherrie Hatton-Hall, she had been born into the Anglo-Irish aristocracy, presented at court and married to an army officer with whom she set up a riding school. Her most famous pupil was the young Princess Anne, now the Princess Royal. After the untimely death of her husband Nigel, Cherrie swapped her jodhpurs for the habit of a Franciscan nun. The Catholics venerate St Francis of Assisi as the patron saint of animals, so that was a good choice; although she had to take vows of poverty, chastity and obedience, she was allowed to use her talents and became a leading light in the worldwide development of Riding for the Disabled. I only found that out later, but I like the way her story connects – even to the Princess Royal being President of the RDA. I did find the whole thing very funny though, as a non-religious sixteen-year-old whose only exposure to God-following was at the Methodist church on Sark where I was a reluctant recruit to Mrs Deakes' choir.

I developed a fascination for dressage and getting horses 'on the bit'. Once I'd experienced the feeling of the easier, smoother ride that comes with the horse being 'on the bit' it became rather a quest. The Fortune Centre had a lot of good competition horses that had been donated or loaned on their retirement. One was the famous Mooncoin, who had been round Badminton with Olympic team gold medallist Angela Tucker in 1970 and 1971, and the following year with her husband Mike, now the BBC commentator. Well, to be able to ride a horse like that – awesome didn't cover it, not that it was a word we used back then. The Fortune Centre also held competitions, which I would watch with avid fascination. It was a world away from the riding I'd done up to then. I relished watching and most of all wanted to take part.

My lucky break was being allowed to ride a pony called Spot On. He was an Appaloosa, so he really was spotty, and we managed to get spotted on to all our Pony Club teams: eventing, dressage and showjumping. It turned out he was rather good at dressage. We were allowed practice times at the Fortune Centre when we could ride on our own without instruction. I used to go into the school with two other students and I would get myself in a corner and see-saw away on Spot On's mouth until he would finally drop his head. Bear in mind these weren't competition horses that were trained for the job – any more than I was – you had to do a bit of 'tweaking and eaking'.

Picture the indoor school at the Fortune Centre, with its row of offices upstairs with glass windows overlooking the school. Mrs Baillie and Mrs Nelson's office was up there and hanging down from the ceiling at X – the centre of the school – was a microphone. I remember getting in my corner one day, thinking I was out of sight underneath the windows, and furiously trying to get Spot On's head down. Then, suddenly, came this disembodied voice over the microphone: 'Carl, less use of the hands, please.' I appeared out of the corner, red-faced, and let Spot On poke his nose again for the remaining twenty minutes of the session.

They were good at the Fortune Centre to give me opportunities with the Pony Club. I'd never heard of it as there wasn't a branch on Sark. I was a working student as well, so I didn't have time to enjoy Pony Club as most kids do. Although I managed to go to the team trials and was successful at being picked for the teams, I didn't have a Pony Club life as such – rallies and camp and all that – only the teams.

I had some excellent teachers who were based at the Fortune Centre: Suzanne Kemp, who was a first-rate jumping trainer, and Debbie Freeman, who now lives in New Zealand. Debbie and Suzanne used to take it in turns to train me. Suzanne particularly I think used to enjoy it as she was very much into jumping herself and evented. Because they were 'competition' trainers rather than riding school teachers, Suzanne and Debbie made me realise that competing could help me to further my career, if that's what I wanted to do. There was a famous old judge called Mrs Guest who used to come to the Fortune Centre. We were only riding preliminary and novice standard (and I think she was a top listed judge), but I loved being judged by Mrs Guest. She was generous with her time and would always give me good advice afterwards.

I had developed a strong thirst for knowledge. Jane Holderness-Roddam, who is now President of the Fortune Centre, used to come and do two-day courses. She was famous as well, but no one went on about it; I was only conscious of it because it was my introduction to this big horse world of achievement. Jane had won Badminton,

Burghley and won team gold at the 1968 Olympics. The story goes – and it's true – that her first Badminton win at the age of twenty on Our Nobby was after she'd completed a night shift at Middlesex hospital where she was a nurse. Anyway, she's always been incredibly generous in helping riders and she doesn't stand on ceremony, despite being a lady-in-waiting to HRH the Princess Royal – although I'm sure I didn't call her Jane in those days! She was and still is eventing royalty, so I was in awe.

The person who made the biggest impression on me was Jackie Bickley. She was eventing then, but a few years later Jackie got onto the young riders' dressage team with her lovely grey The Rooster. I will never forget how it felt watching that big grey horse that walked, trotted and cantered so impressively. It was my first real impression of paces that stop you short and hold your gaze, and Jackie was a tall, elegant rider.

We were both eventing then, and I was so naïve. Fitness in the event horse was only just beginning to feature, both in the sport and in my mind. As you came out of the Fortune Centre you entered a New Forest enclosure, one of the timber-growing areas created in the fifteenth century, with a track all the way round which must have been four or five miles in total. One day I was told to give Spot On a 'ten-minute canter'. In complete innocence and having no idea I was supposed to warm up to this, I literally rode out the back onto the enclosure track and kicked him into canter – mostly flat-out gallop, actually – hoofing it all the way for ten minutes before coming back.

Despite me giving him a little walk at the end, Spot On arrived back at the yard with his sides heaving and his coat covered in a white lather. I was asked what on earth I was doing, so of course I responded that I'd given him a ten-minute canter. The reprimand was very sharp.

The workload was huge and the hours long. For my final year I moved from Tiptoe to Bransgore and the main Fortune Centre, which comprised some twenty-eight stables. The night checks used to take me over an hour, starting at 8.30 in the evening, often on my own. At that time we had to skip out the stables (remove the droppings), top up water buckets and give all the horses more hay. It was quite lonely living at the Fortune Centre, and doing evening stables on my own even more so. I was paid £10 a week for the first year and for the second I think I got £20. That was fine, I didn't think about money then. The BHSAI exam then was in two parts: the Horsemaster's and the teaching certificate. For my teaching exam I was driven to Catherston Stud, the original Black Knoll Farm where Jennie (née Bullen) had moved when she married Anthony Loriston-Clarke. I realised Jennie was Jane Holderness-Roddam's sister with the growing awareness that dressage in those days was rather dynastic, although of course without the shoulder-pads. For the riding bit of the exam I was driven to Huntley School of Equitation, four miles from where I live now. My examiner was Carole Broad FBHS, who founded the school with owner Torrill Freeman. Then I had to do the Pony Club 'H' test, which was all stable management, apart from having to ride one horse and lead another. Sounds simple enough, but you had to do it in a double bridle. I'd never ridden in one before, so it was rather an 'Oh my God' moment, trying to sort out which reins were the important ones and not dropping the washing lines. I took that exam at Deirdre Scrimgeour's – another name that was to become familiar, signed at the bottom of future dressage score sheets.

Jolly Dolly had been evented by Suzanne Kemp and was already an intermediate-level event horse. It was a very generous offer, made by the Hon. Mrs Baillie who owned her and Suzanne, that I should take her on to do junior eventing. They had decided that Dolly shouldn't go on to advanced level with Suzanne as she had one leg which had shown a bit of weakness.

In those days, Windsor was the final trial for the junior eventing team. To me it wasn't merely big, it was flipping mahoosive. Especially given that my partnership with Dolly hadn't got off to the most auspicious start.

Our first event together was at Peper Harrow; I had ridden on the Pony Club teams and I had competed at the Pony Club Championships, which I'd got round though I only managed a low placing, but this would be my warm-up to the junior trial. Even back then, dressage was my thing. Dolly and I got a score of just 14 penalties and led the dressage with a lead of about 15 penalties. In the mid-eighties there were no intro or pre-novice classes – you went straight in at novice. Dolly was a great showjumper, she had a massive jump and jumped a clear round. Then it was time for cross-country.

Dolly had not done an event for about eighteen months and was absolutely bloody wild. When the start gun went off she flew out of the starting box leaving me literally about to come out the back door. Down the hill, over the first, over the second, then we turned a sharp right to come back up the hill and all I can remember was that she was running away with me and that I couldn't see a thing. We got to the third fence – a big parallel – and she took off early, taking a couple of strides out. Dolly paddled the fence, turned over and fell in a heap on top of me. There was I, lying on the floor as Mrs Baillie and Mrs Nelson came running over, not to see how I was but in true British fashion urging me to get up, get up, get back on and off you go. I got up. They had caught Dolly and I had to get on and do the rest of the course. It was my first experience of loss of nerve. I was winded and windy. I think I galloped (Dolly hadn't slowed down) all the way round to the bottom of every fence – not the ideal approach, and a kind of protection mechanism that kicks in when you don't want to kick on and jump the wretched things. I gave Dolly a terrible ride but we did manage to complete.

By the time we got to Tweseldown, having had a bit of practice across country and having got Dolly's and my confidence back, we finished second. The team selector then was one of those famous 'Major someone-or-others' – they all seemed to be majors – and we were all to gather round at the prize-giving. Beforehand, Mrs Baillie had taken me to one side and told me I would be selected for

Windsor but, bearing in mind that we had to think of Dolly's leg and the speed at which she went, it would be 'chic to say no'. We were all given a letter at the prize-giving which we then had to go away and open as it revealed whether or not you were selected. How they organised that I really don't know, as I couldn't imagine the Major sitting there bashing out letters on a typewriter, but I was selected, which was nice, and we graciously declined the offer.

It was decided that Dolly and I would concentrate on dressage. We went to our first competition – I don't recall where it was apart from that it was on grass – but it was a Young Rider Trial, which we won, so we qualified for the Young Rider Championships at Goodwood. The tests were at medium level and we'd had to learn a bit of half pass, my first lateral movement where the horse moves forward and sideways at the same time. Suzanne taught me, as Dolly had been her horse, and with her help Dolly and I learned half pass together and simple changes – not the flying sort yet, but the canter-to-walk then strike off back to canter on the other leading leg variety.

In the meantime I was still riding in pony classes. There weren't any pony eventing classes at that time but there were dressage classes. Mrs Baillie had bred a New Forest pony called Stafford Malteser. He came from a long line of chocolates: Stafford Chocolate Box was his mother, and there was Stafford Aero, Stafford Curly Wurly, Stafford Mars Bar (well, not literally but near enough). I called him Mouldy. We entered the trial for the Pony European team and came about eighth, so missed out there. After years of being below average height I had started to grow – and when that happened I grew like Topsy. When I arrived at the Fortune Centre I stood around five foot six, then suddenly within about a year I grew to nearly six foot. Mouldy only stood around 13.2 hands so I was very big on him. Oh, the absolute joy when I returned to Sark and walked into the kitchen. The sheer shock and glee as everyone exclaimed, 'Oh my God, your voice has broken!' It was only about two years after everyone else's.

When I tipped up at Goodwood for the Young Rider Championship

I knew no one. Having been isolated at the Fortune Centre and done only the one qualifier turned out to be an advantage in some ways, as I knew nothing about Goodwood's celebrated status as a dressage venue – or even as one of England's premier stately homes, for that matter – so I took it all in my stride and went in the arena to do my test. The Dutch international judge Els Mouw was judging, although I had no idea who she was at the time, and suddenly I became the 1985 Young Rider Champion. It was one heck of a shock. I was just embarrassed. I didn't want to go up and get my prize as I felt this overwhelming embarrassment about being there. No one knew me and I didn't know anybody. Jane Kidd wrote in *Horse and Hound* along the lines 'this boy from Sark appeared and is now young rider champion', which was about the size of it I suppose, while Anthony Crossley, who was the biggest dressage critic, commented that I seemed to have some talent but needed to do something about my hands.

Looking at the photograph of me winning still makes me cringe. I'm wearing a pair of rubber riding boots, my legs are stuck forward and my hands are slightly turned over the wrong way. Dolly's head is behind the vertical, but then the picture was taken in a medium trot and I'd hardly ever done that before. It was the trend to put a strap round the top of the rubber 'Stylo' boots to a) hold them up and b) make them look like proper leather-top boots; because mine had the strap, I thought I was the height of fashion.

I wasn't afraid of the media as I didn't know what it meant to talk to them – to me they just seemed to be a couple of people milling about. Everybody would read *Horse and Hound*, but all I knew from my limited experience of being 'in' dressage was that the two you had to watch out for were Anthony Crossley and Pegotty Henriques, as they could make or break you in those days.

Having done the championship the next aim was to try and get Jolly Dolly ready for the following year's team selection, but before that I went forward for Talent Spotting. The scheme had recently started at the suggestion of Arnold Morgan, husband of former international rider and top judge Domini Morgan, and was designed to provide an opportunity for young people, even those without access to trained horses, as competitions were few and far between back then. I went along to Cholderton in Wiltshire for a trial day and was selected from that to go to the final at Talland, the well-known Gloucestershire equestrian centre (although I'm far from sure it was well known to me then!).

It was a special day, but incredibly nerve-wracking. We all turned up at Talland, horse-less, to be assessed and have conversations with our assessors. Mollie Sivewright, Talland's founder, assessed our riding and I got to ride her Talland The Snow King, a great big grey and a proper dressage horse, the likes of which I had never sat on before. John Bowen won, Paul Hayler was second and I finished third, and we're all still going today in our own capacities. In her report afterwards Mollie (or Mrs Sivewright, as we undoubtedly called her) said that I had feel but was an extremely crooked rider on a straight line. That's the only comment I came away with from the day. However, my prize was a voucher for £25 which was to be spent with a trainer.

Jennie Loriston-Clarke generously said that she would give me two lessons for that money. So I set out on a hack – and if anyone knows this hack from Bransgore across to Brockenhurst it was about fifteen miles across commons, over main roads and under tunnels to where she lived. I would turn up, have an hour's lesson, then hack back, so Dolly did five hours apiece for each of her two lessons with Jennie. That, by the way, was nothing to Jennie, who'd hacked Desert Storm to compete in the stadium in Aachen down the main road and over traffic lights.

Dolly didn't know flying changes, she didn't need to for medium level, so I needed Jennie's help to teach her, especially as I didn't know flying changes either. Jennie was brilliant, and she has frequently been reminded by me of that £25 for coming third and her offer. She has been 'The Baroness of Brockenhurst' to me ever since.

The follow on from Talent Spotting, and the best bit in many ways, was taking up the second part of the prize the following year of a two-day course with Domini Morgan at Goodwood. I had got the ride on another horse at the Fortune Centre, a chestnut thorough-bred named Easter Ruby. I'd done the first event of the season on him and won, so it was Easter Ruby who came with me to Goodwood.

Above the supremely elegant mid-eighteenth-century stable court-yard close to Goodwood House is a maze of dormitories where we riders stayed. Of those I can remember today there was Paul Hayler (who was far too goody two-shoes to do anything naughty), Rhett Bird and Jackie Bickley who had so impressed me on her grey, The Rooster. I palled up with a girl named Sarah. Our first night in the dorms was like being back at school. That night after lights out Sarah called for me. Her boyfriend had driven up through the dark and was waiting outside the stables in his Porsche. Sarah, her boyfriend and me got in and went off to the pub for a night out – which we managed to get away with.

Early next morning on the first day of the course I came up with the bright idea of taking Easter Ruby up to the gallops at Goodwood. Rhett Bird came too. For me, eventing was still the great passion, don't forget, and the gallops was a good idea, but off in the woods was a very large trakhener (a log over a ditch fence) which I decided we were going to jump. Easter Ruby, however, did not want to jump said fence. After several failed attempts and a walloping from my jump whip, Easter Ruby decided he'd had enough of me and took off at a hundred miles an hour. I couldn't stop him and we ended up tangled in some barbed wire alongside the racecourse. In my youthful naïvety I kept attempting this bloody jump but Easter Ruby wasn't having any of it so eventually I gave up and went back to the stables. By that stage he had cuts all over his legs from the wire. It was a nightmare. Rhett had come back to the stables with me and when I got off I saw the extent of the damage – superficial though it was there was no way of disguising it. With a sense of foreboding I got ready for my lesson with Domini, bleating at Rhett, 'I'm in so much trouble.' Domini was a force of nature to be reckoned with even at the best of times. Some quick thinking was required as I appeared on this horse grazed up to the eyeballs, ready for Domini's interrogation. Asked what on earth I had been doing, I said we had gone up the gallops, a bird scarer had gone off and spooked Easter Ruby and we'd ended up in the hedge. I got away with it. That was my first Goodwood stay-over and every stay at Goodwood has a story to it. That one, the getting away with it bit, ending up being the first of many Goodwood laughs.

I was eighteen by this time and getting itchy feet. I wanted to have some fun. Knowing that all my friends at home were out having a ball – Sark in summer was the best place in the world with barbecues, swimming, horses, the beach – I decided I'd had enough of life at the Fortune Centre. Much as I loved the riding, the hours, routine and isolation were getting to me. I wanted to do my own thing and have my own life, which I didn't have there. And the more they tried to chain me down, the more I resisted.

Crunch time came when I was called up to the office, having been naughty on more than one occasion. Walking into the office that day was horrendous, like walking into a board meeting or something. It gives me the shivers even now. There were about eight people sitting round the table and I was asked to sit down. One of the ladies, I can't recall which having been too paralysed with fear to take it all in, said, 'I would like to ask everyone around this table to tell Carl what they think of him.'

There were a lot of red faces, presumably they were embarrassed, but one by one, in sequence round the table, these people that I had worked with, that I had thought were my friends, took it in turn to tell me that I didn't work hard enough, I spent too much time going out, I was too cheeky, I was this, I was that. It reduced me to tears.

At the end I was told to go away and think about my future. I had until the following morning to produce a letter which would be placed in a designated drawer in Mrs Baillie's office, saying whether I would stay or go. So I went back to my room in the bungalow behind the stables and I thought.

It wasn't about being mortified by the comments, which I suppose had been the intention, it was the feeling of being totally let down. The way it was done was so atrocious. Then suddenly a weight was lifted from my shoulders and I thought, 'This is my time, I want to leave, I want to go back to Sark. I have had enough, I don't want this career, this life, it's not as important as my fun and I haven't had enough of that.' So I wrote my letter – all it said was 'I would like to leave' – and put it in the drawer.

The following morning I was called up to the office. That was hardly surprising, under the circumstances, but the tune had changed. Now it was, 'You can't leave, you've got too much to think about, too many things to do.' So before I knew it the decision was reversed and I was staying. It took about a week and it felt almost as if they'd had to make me stay, and decide to stay, so that they could fire me. I wasn't going to be allowed to just leave. Sure enough, after that week they told me to go. I don't think I did anything specific during that week, it was simply that they wanted to take it into their own hands to tell me I had to leave. But it was still a huge relief.

I phoned my friend Alison Markland. She had left the Fortune Centre the previous year and lived nearby at New Milton. I asked her if she could please come and get me. It didn't take any pleading, she came that night and picked me up with all my stuff – I'd been there for two years and had a school trunk and school case's worth of stuff – and away we drove, me and Alison, and we went wild! The relief was overwhelming: it's over, I'm finished, I'm done, I'm FREE!!

I couldn't wait to get home. The Fortune Centre had been like a boarding school in many ways that my actual boarding school wasn't. I didn't have any muckers, for a start. The residents and students were there and locked in to be there, while all I had to rely on were the other members of staff, who apart from a few exceptions were a lot older than me. I was in a place doing something that it wasn't set up for, although they'd made special allowances for me. I do raise money these days for the Fortune Centre, now that I'm not signed up to what at times felt like penal servitude.

In those days money was not important to me, which was a great thing really. I could live on what I got, but I was a young guy in a place that was out of town, down a mile-long drive, and I needed to break out. Having been painfully shy when I arrived at the Fortune Centre, I was finally beginning to get social, to find my feet, and naïvely I suppose I thought I could grow up and they'd accept it. I was wrong.

I couldn't drive and I'd shared the bungalow behind the stables with a couple, Jane and Richard, now both Moseleys. I was best man at their wedding, which was hilarious because when I did the customary speech the sound didn't record on the video so I had to go and do it again in a studio afterwards. Without reactions or the background noise of general wedding-guest hubbub, it sounded completely ridiculous. They were lovely to me and a lovely couple, but it was just us and twenty-eight horses! Leaving was the right decision for an eighteen-year-old who needed to grow up.

The drama finally came to an end when Alison put me on the plane to go home. I had rescued these two kittens at the Fortune Centre. They were feral. I'd had the kittens in my bedroom and was hand-feeding them. One died in my bed and the other one I ended up taking back to Sark with me. Alison put me on the plane back to Guernsey and on arrival I got pulled over by Customs. My hair was dyed black then (I was to be a keen experimenter with hair colour for the next few years), I had an earring in one ear and I was wearing combat trousers. The Customs officers obviously took one look at me and thought, 'Aye aye, we've got a right one here. Let's pull him over.' They opened my case in front of everybody, and there they were: two syringes on top of my things. They all stared at me with that kind of sideways look and asked what I'd been up to. I replied that I was raising a kitten, at which they all burst out laughing and proceeded to literally clean out my case. I had nothing on me to interest them naturally, but I missed my boat back to Sark and had to spend the night on Guernsey having been looked over like some major drug dealer.

The kitten had travelled on the boat and we had to pick it up. I finally got it back to Sark, and having persuaded my mum and Jess that we had to have a cat, got the basket into the kitchen, opened it, and the bloody thing flew up onto one of the kitchen units where it stayed for the next twelve hours refusing to come down. When the kitten did come down it made a run for it and we never saw it again. It disappeared into the wilds of Sark, whereas I was just intending to go wild on Sark.

4

A Sark Idyll

I'd get up between eight and nine in the morning to go over to the hotel, get the horses in from the field and harness them up. We had to be at the top of the harbour hill at La Collinette, which is basically the taxi rank for horses and carriages, by ten thirty. Sark was getting a thousand visitors a day so there was plenty of business to be had. It was good to be driving again and I was 'official' having taken my driving test, for which you had to do a two-week probation period with an experienced driver then the test with two constables sat in the back of your carriage. I'd already taken my skilled junior driving certificate and had been on the inter-island team for competitions so it was good to be driving my own carriage – I was too tall to do the monkey climbs any more.

You could hire the whole carriage out for £18 or pay £3 per person – the carriages could take six people. With a tour of the island taking about two and a half hours the maximum number of tours you could do a day was three and that was enough to be able to keep up the sparkling entertainment which ensured more tips. So usually I'd be finished by four thirty or five o'clock, turn the horse out, clean the harness then get home an hour later. It was a quick turnaround, though, as I would have to be at the La Moinerie Hotel at seven o'clock to work in the bar. I'd finish work between ten thirty and eleven. It was a long day, but it was also a great day.

I was making eighty pounds a week, half of that from the bar work, so with tips on top was taking home between £150 and £200 a week.

It was a hell of a lot of money for me then. I didn't miss riding as I was leading a gypsy kind of life, not hedonistic but certainly idyllic, even though I was working six days a week. Sunday was a day of rest; under feudal law no carriages or tractors could go out, and there were no boats to the island so it really was the day of rest.

There are two churches on Sark, the Anglican St Peter's and the Methodist chapel which has been there since the eighteenth century. During schooldays not only did Mrs Deakes, the minister's wife, recruit me to the choir via singing the heads off everyone on the island like Kiri Te Kanawa in full flow, but she had, bless her (and I'm not sure that's appropriate but never mind) taught me baby stuff on piano and guitar. I did learn, only this summer there were other things to do.

Sundays were days for the beach and cream teas. We wouldn't touch the horses on Sundays; they had a day off too. Sark fulfilled everything you imagined you would want to do as a teenager. Not only was I getting my horse fix, I was also, at last, getting my social fix. At that point at the Fortune Centre where I knew I had to leave, all my friends had been telling me what they would be doing on Sark and how good it was going to be. Like a siren's call to come back to the rock it was a huge draw. And they were right.

There were ten, maybe twelve of us, all carriage drivers who were close friends and we'd do everything together. When we finished work at the bar we'd all go back to mine or someone else's digs. Nobody had a house, but I'd rented a cottage from Nan for £15 per week including an evening meal. Nan and Pop had converted an old stone shed into a one-up, one-down and I didn't want to live at home any more so Nan said I could rent that for the summer. Basically I think she did it so she could keep an eye on me.

Justine was one of my first girlfriends. A pretty, and if I remember rightly church-going girl, she had come over to Sark to work as a nanny and we started going out. On Sark everybody knew everyone else. Even the seasonal workers there for the summer soon got know everyone. It was like having our own paparazzi network: there wasn't much you could get up to without being spotted.

Nan was dead against sex before marriage, so when Justine stayed over at mine the best way, we decided, was to do it undercover. Justine and I went over to Guernsey one day and bought a wig in one of those novelty shops. In case Nan ever clapped eyes on Justine in the mornings when she had stayed over I'd put the wig on her before she would run out of the door. I don't know what we were thinking, apart from the fact that this was a long blonde wig whereas Justine had dark hair. We clearly hadn't thought the whole thing through but we got away with it.

I liked girls and I had a lot of girlfriends. I still do, but in a different way. Back at that age, in that situation I didn't think 'I'm this', 'I'm that' or even 'What am I?' On Sark there were no role models; it didn't occur to me that I was gay because I wasn't aware of anyone that was. So the question 'Am I gay?' never came into it.

It was a brilliant summer and it came to an end, as always, when the last hotels got ready to shut down on 1 October. I'd seen that time and again over the years, but this year was different because when the seasonal workers left for the winter it meant my gang of friends would be gone. The island would become desolate as usual, but even more desolate for me. I knew about isolation by then and even on my wild island it was not a prospect I wanted to face. So, at the end of that summer when Nan asked what I was going to do, I told her I thought I'd go and work on the roads like everyone else. Oh no, she said, you're going back to England.

In typical Nan fashion, a copy of *Horse and Hound* was produced (which thankfully had made its way to the Channel Islands by then). Nan put it down firmly on the table as she issued her instruction: 'There's the job section. Get looking!'

There was only one vacancy that appealed to me. Well, two: there was an advertisement for a job at dealer Cheryl Milner's, but it looked a very big job. I did apply and was asked for interview but I didn't go. The one that really appealed simply said *Rider/Groom. Live in as family* and the telephone number. A little job, which was what I wanted.

That summer on Sark was the start of growing up but it would be thanks to that little job that I would shed the last remnants of being a kid, not that I realised it at the time. A few months in, I told my new employer (rather than asking) that I'd be taking a week off for Christmas and going back to Sark. 'So you're leaving me to do eight horses?' she responded. My answer, a typical teenager's, was 'Yeah'. But it turned out that asking for that week and being allowed to have it was best thing that could have happened to me. I spent the entire time thinking about the horses and wanting to get back, wondering what on earth I was doing sitting around on a rainy old island when all my friends had gone. I knew then I would never want to return to live there permanently. The summer before that realisation hit had been the perfect summer, but in the months that followed I'd undergo a sea-change, and there was no going back.

5

An Eccentric Children's Home

After winning the Young Rider title on Jolly Dolly I had been invited to ride on the first national dressage convention. It was taken by Hans Erik Pederson. I wouldn't fully recognise what a 'national convention' was all about until I had to take one in 2012. The most memorable thing about that first experience was being approached at the end by a rather eccentric-looking elderly lady. She said to me, 'You have a God-given talent. We need to find the right place for you to go.' Her name was Vivian Eason and she kept in touch, writing when I went back to Sark.

I had rung the number in that tiny *Horse and Hound* advertisement. When I said I had won the Young Rider Championships, the dark brown voice on the other end of the phone replied that she thought I was overqualified for her job. No, I insisted, I really want to come and see you. It was agreed, so I got a flight over to England and my friend Sue from the Fortune Centre picked me up and drove me to Gloucestershire for my interview. In the meantime I had written to Mrs Eason to tell her I had applied for a job with Jannie Taylor at Bourton-on-the-Hill and to ask whether she knew Jannie, and whether it was anywhere near her, as Mrs Eason's address was Bourton Far Hill Farm. She replied that she knew Jannie Taylor very well.

We drove up the A44 from Moreton-in-Marsh into Bourton-on-the-Hill then turned left into the one-car-width's worth of drive. Halfway down the drive there was a gate with all kinds of strings attached – of the baler twine, not the entryphone and security type.

You had to pull a string and the gate would open. This automatic gate system was completed by a brick tied to the end of the string, which would pull the gate back into place once you'd gone through.

It was certainly small; every bit of space available in what was essentially the cottage garden had been put to use. There were five stables on the left-hand side, which I later learned had been converted from garages, while the stable on the right was a converted garden shed. Behind that stable and past the chicken run there was a dirt patch measuring about twelve by fifteen metres which had originally been a walled garden.

Jannie wanted to see me ride; not to see what I could do on a trained horse, but to help with breaking in a young horse. We lunged him first on the dirt patch then I got on. Well, I hadn't been on more than ten seconds before this thing bucked me clean off. I landed on my back and lay there, totally winded and unable to breathe while all Jannie did was shriek with laughter. I finally managed to kneel, gasping for breath, at which point Jannie stopped laughing long enough to tell me to get back on. That was my interview.

We went into the kitchen to talk. I never asked how much money I was to get, but it turned out to be £15 a week as I would be living in. I remember asking whether I would get a day off, to which Jannie replied, 'If you want one, you have one,' which I took to basically mean 'no'. It didn't matter to me, I wanted this job. Nowadays it's considered part of the interview process to ask about salary and conditions, but things were different back then. As an employer it always sets alarm bells ringing when an interviewee's first questions are how much will they get paid and when are their days off. When I started out it was almost a sin to ask if I would get a day off, and that was how it worked all the time I was there.

As soon as I mentioned to Jannie that I knew Mrs Eason she burst out laughing. She had rung Mrs Eason (she used to train with her sometimes) and told her I was coming for an interview. Jannie related amid peals of laughter Mrs Eason's response: 'Don't you dare employ him! Riding all those babies and eventers – his seat will be ruined!' I went there anyway.

Jannie thought the best way to appease Mrs Eason would be to take me for lessons with her. She was in her eighties by then, but you could tell that she must have been a beautiful woman in her time. She used to wear bright blue mascara.

Mrs Eason was the epitome of 'classical' in her approach, very 'Podhajsky' as I would put it much later, after having been subjected to the old boy's words of wisdom over the years. I didn't know what 'classical' meant at that stage, but I was about to find out. Mrs Eason opened my eyes. The telling of it sounded a bit hilarious to me: how one must carry one's hands as if one were carrying a tea tray, and when you were on the horse you had to pretend you were a teapot – all that sort of rubbish. Not that she said those exact words, but it all sounded like mumbo jumbo to me. Seriously, Mrs Eason would go on for hours as we sat beside the Aga in her kitchen, telling me how one's legs must do this and one's hands that, and so on. The crucial part was that it made me realise there was much more to dressage then I'd ever thought possible. I was learning, and not just about riding.

Jannie and Norman Van der Vater, known as 'Van', were great friends. They were thick as thieves, in fact. Very famous in his day, Van was a three-time Olympic eventer who rode for Ireland, mostly on horses that had come out of Jannie's yard. They called each other 'Sissie', short for sisters, and those sisters were definitely doing it for themselves. They used to play the most terrible pranks on everybody and encouraged me to do the same.

Jannie had grown up in Majorca. She spoke fluent Spanish and still had connections on the island. She announced one day that there was a boy coming from Majorca to work for six weeks, and as he was due in a fortnight she was going to teach me a greeting for when he arrived as this was the polite thing to do to make him feel welcome. I knew nothing of the language at all so I practised this line for two weeks with Jannie working on my inflection and pronunciation.

The day came and we heard a car arrive. Jannie pushed me out of the door urging, 'Say it, say it.' So as the boy, his mother and his father walked over from their car, I greeted them with my carefully rehearsed phrase: '*Hola, mi nombre es cabroncito y tú, hijo de puta. ¿cómo te llamas?*'

How I didn't get smacked round the face by the mother I really don't know but from the three of them there was stony silence while I stood with a huge smile on my face having remembered this line – I'd worked so hard on it and I can still remember it to this day, which is totally bizarre. A moment later there were shrieks and peals of joy from behind me and I turned to see Jannie collapsed on the floor in fits, thinking it was the best thing she'd ever done, training me to say, 'Hi, my name is little goat and you, son of a whore, what's your name?' Of course what she didn't bank on was that his parents would bring him. She thought he'd arrive in a taxi. Not that it mattered one bit to Jannie.

Another time Van rang to say that he was bringing his friend Shirley Thorpe – known as 'the Duchess' as she had this regal aura about her – to dinner. Shirley was allergic to garlic so as soon as Jannie had finished making the mashed potatoes she got a load of cloves of garlic, chopped them up and mixed them in. Shirley, bless her, took one mouthful and knew exactly what Jannie had done. But discovery took nothing away from the look of pure glee on Jannie's face.

The one person who remained completely unmoved by Jannie's pranks was Christopher, her husband. Saturday afternoons in the Taylor household were devoted to watching the racing on television. Whatever else was happening, it was vital that the horses and all chores had to be finished by one. From one thirty onwards we'd all have to wind our necks in while Jannie and Christopher sat glued to the racing.

One Saturday, we were sitting in front of the TV with our plates of food, Jannie was having her usual lunchtime red wine and tonic

(*left*) Waiting for tourists on Sark Harbour – I think I'm tied up! (Author's collection)

(*right*) Jesse, me, Polly – early years on Sark (Author's collection)

(*left*) How I first learned to ride: on Jacko, Sark 1976 (Author's collection)

(*right*) My first rosette was won on Patches (Author's collection)

My first pout (first row, directly behind teacher in white and girl in white)

(Author's collection)

Jumping Mitch during the summer I returned to Sark – his talent was obvious

(Author's collection)

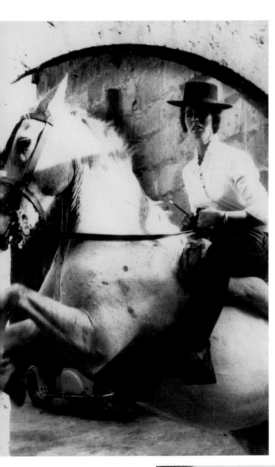

This picture says it all. Jannie, an all-round horsewoman (early days in Spain)
(Author's collection)

This Jannie and Christopher purchase turned into a successful show horse (Author's collection)

Posing with 'Posy'
(Author's collection)

Debbie Carré and I
reunite: modelling
for her boot and
clothing collection
(Author's collection)

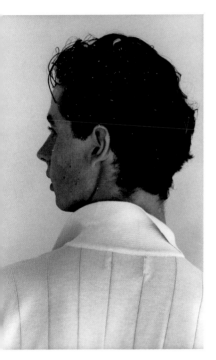

Modelling for *GQ* in 1991

(Alan Beukers/GQ © The Condé Nast Publications Ltd)

On Heather's dear Merlin, 'Merl-the-Pearl', Goodwood 1989 (Author's collection)

Early days at Dr B's with Waffentanz and Wesley (Author's collection)

With my first teacher, Rubelit von Unkenruf, and my team debut at
Stockholm in 1990 (Author's collection)

Mrs Slocombe, Miss Brahms and Captain Peacock take on Egypt (Author's collection)

Giorgione, who took me to my first Olympics (Author's collection)

Night out during the
Barcelona Olympics
with Bent Jensen and
Charlotte Bredahl
(1992)
(Author's collection)

Back to eventi
On Aberlord
Milton Keynes, 1ϲ
(Author's collect

water, and I started talking while there was a race going on in the background. Jannie picked up a sausage and threw it at me, telling me to 'shut up'. I picked up a potato and chucked it at her. Well, that sparked what rapidly turned into a full-blown food fight. Christopher just sat there – he didn't look left, he didn't look right – while all this food went backwards and forwards across the room, spattering the walls.

The horses' mode of transport, Daffodil, was a very small two-horse wagon which looked exactly like a converted ice-cream van. Unsurprisingly Daffodil was painted yellow. Once, on our way to a competition at Hartpury, the man on the gate, who was directing the traffic, stopped Jannie as she pulled into the competitors' entrance and pointed her off in the other direction. When she asked why, he replied, 'All deliveries that way.'

Event rider Sophie Martindale and Jannie were old friends. At the end of one event, Jannie got into the driver's seat and turned the ignition. There was an almighty explosion. Sophie had shoved a potato up Daffodil's exhaust. Jannie stopped the lorry and got out, hands on hips, head held high as she swept her gaze around the lorry park. All she said was, 'Where's Sophie?' Sophie had run for it and gone to hide in a Portaloo, thinking Jannie couldn't get her. Jannie marched back to the lorry, took out a lunge line and attached one end to Sophie's Portaloo sanctuary and the other to the back of Daffodil. Firing up Daffodil, Jannie calmly accelerated, leaving the lunge line to do its work pulling the Portaloo over with Sophie – literally the trophy – still inside. While Sophie screamed and wailed, incarcerated in the upended loo, Jannie told me to get in the lorry and we set off home with Jannie laughing her head off.

Then there was Sam, whom I nicknamed Tabitha Twitchit. He was a Bearded Collie and certainly twitchy. We all knew he would bite, and I used to have to move him around the house with a broom. The technique, if I wanted to go into a room and Sam was in the way, was that I'd poke him with it. Sam would then savage the broom, leaving me free to enter the room. He lived to a ripe old age. Then there was Mut-Mut the cat, who had no teeth and yellow eyes and lived with 'Muther', Jannie's mother. I had to look after 'Muther'.

The house was L-shaped, with Jannie and Christopher occupying the section facing the drive and Muther in the section that ran parallel to the drive. She was over ninety when I arrived at Jannie and Christopher's. Her name was Beatrice Minella (Manila to me) MacDonald-Brown and she had been side-saddle cross-country champion three times, I think. There were wonderful pictures on the wall of her in her habit and veil, careening across the country and flying over fences that would strike fear into the bravest Badminton winner.

I had the room below her bedroom. Every night Mrs MacDonald-Brown would have two poached eggs, a salad and a baked potato – it was the same for all the years I was there. Jannie would make this supper, put it out on a tray and at seven thirty I would have to take it up to Muther, who would be lying in bed. Thankfully by the time I looked after her she was stone deaf as her two King Charles spaniels – the vicious Pedro and his mate Muffin – would begin barking, yapping and shrieking the minute I started up the stairs. I would come through the door, put the tray down on her bed, engage in a few pleasantries – we had to be very respectful of her as she was a terrifying lady – and she'd tell me exactly what I had to do with the horses, the way I should be riding and generally issuing instructions. It was naughty of me, but as soon as I was safely at the bottom of the stairs I got great enjoyment from whispering, 'Pedro, Pedro . . .' (it was a stage whisper, but she couldn't hear anyway). I'd stand listening as he went berserk on Mrs MacDonald-Brown's bed, followed by the sounds of shrieking and walloping. Once I'd got that out of the way I could go to bed. When I got Pedro on his own it was a different story; without his mistress's backup he was terrified of me and would never utter a peep.

Mrs MacDonald-Brown was still driving at the age of

ninety-something. She would reverse her Mini out of the drive onto the main A44 and proceed down the hill to do her shopping in Moreton-in-Marsh with complete disregard for any other drivers, or anyone for that matter. If she wanted to go to the butcher's she would park outside, leaving the car door open and the engine running, go in and make her purchases. When she came out there'd be a queue of people behind her beeping and hooting. She'd get into her car, give them a wave, and go on to the next shop, which might be only a few yards down the road. She never walked anywhere – she couldn't as she had a hunched back, so it was difficult even with a stick – but she thought she owned the Cotswolds.

One day as she pulled up in the yard and got out of her Mini, Sam (Tabitha Twitchit, that is) slipped through the open door and hopped in the back. What followed was like something out of the *Benny Hill Show*. First she got her stick and tried to pull Sam out so she could retrieve her shopping, which was still in the back. Then she stuck her hand in and, well, Sam grabbed her and pulled her into the back. All we could see was Beatrice Minella MacDonald-Brown bouncing about in the rear seat as Sam tried to savage her. Finally Sam popped out and I got Jannie. We had to take poor Muther to hospital as she'd been bitten. It was terrible, of course, but in a ridiculously funny way.

Another time eventer Erica Watson was walking past the lorry and failed to see Sam's lead, which was hidden by the long grass. She was duly tripped over as Sam, growling, took up the slack, leaving her suspended with one leg in the air. You wouldn't be able to keep a dog like that nowadays, or at least you couldn't let him out in public without a muzzle, but Sam adored Jannie and would do anything for her. She could pick him up, turn him over and tickle him. In fact she used to lay him on his back and 'hoover' the floor with him – he'd stiffen his legs and she would push and pull him up and down the carpet while he emitted little squawks of delight at being brushed up and down. He never went for me because I'd always go in broom-first, but none of us would go near him. Only Jannie could deal with him.

Sam came from Heather Miles, a neighbour who lived in a beautiful Cotswold farmhouse with her husband the Canon. Heather had got him from the dog pound, found she couldn't cope with him and so gave him to Jannie. That was Jannie all over: the home of last resort. Any horse that couldn't be ridden, or that had been deemed unrideable, she would buy. Then she and Christopher would truss them up in baling twine – their system of training-aid attachments; these days you can buy something very similar made of leather with a hefty price tag and a posh name, but string was good enough for Jannie and Christopher – and get them going.

They acquired one racehorse that was so unrideable it had seriously hurt people. The first day 'Toffee', as we called Christopher, rode it at Posy's school – which was round the corner and up the lane. This horse went through the fence with Toffee still aboard, turned upside down and rolled down the bank on top of him. Toffee calmly got up at the bottom of the bank and sat on the horse as it lay there. He kept it on the ground for what seemed like ages, then he got up, the horse got up, and from then on the horse was absolutely fine with him.

Christopher worked as a horse physiotherapist so spent a lot of time out visiting his equine patients. Meanwhile Jannie and I had our routine. I would muck out seven horses, then at 8.30 I'd come in for my breakfast, which Jannie would have ready. At 8.45 we would go out and tack up two horses each, then the pair of us would ride one while leading the other, heading up the main road to the top of the hill where we'd turn right and arrive at our training ground, the old quarry.

Many of the horses we had were unbroken, just broken, or newly arrived from Ascot sales. Ascot was Jannie and Christopher's first port of call to buy all these difficult horses, but others came from locals who would ring Jannie if they had something they couldn't handle. We'd ride these crazy things up the road as lorries thundered past. In hindsight it was pretty hairy, and I wouldn't dream of doing anything like that now, but then we thought nothing of it.

The quarry that we used for training was a playground for horses and was known to us as the 'Faerie Glen'. In the middle was an area with a sand surface, more like a sandpit than an arena, and Christopher had built a variety of obstacles around it: a bank you could jump down, barrels we could bounce over, a corner with an elephant trap (rails sloping over a ditch), and the whole central area was littered with bedheads, barrels, poles. Horses got trained for eventing, for anything they might meet on a course, in that quarry.

It was easy to box up (that is, put a couple of horses on board Daffodil for a little outing) and go somewhere to introduce them to water. The beauty of the Cotswolds is that there are so many slipways and fords you can use to introduce horses to water, and we would go to various points, most on the River Evenlode, to do just that.

We would often turn up at an event with a horse that had never been near a showjumping or cross-country course. We'd arrive at a novice event – which was the first level in those days as intro and pre-novice had not yet been introduced – and the fences were bloody big. I think the height maximum was 3' 7", which is the fourth level up these days! But the horses were so well trained. Christopher, who had point-to-pointed and trained racehorses in the past, did all the hacking, riding them round the countryside and jumping the hunt fences. Jannie and I would do all the schooling, and the technical side of teaching them to be controlled to jump fences at related distances and bounces. Jannie's joy in all of this, and in fact her motto, was, 'Whatever we paid for it in hundreds we have to sell it for in thousands.' So a cast-off racehorse secured at Ascot sales for £500 would sell for £5,000, or a punt taken on a tricky so-called unrideable horse at £1,000 would result in a sale for £10,000. That was big money in those days. She sold Todd to Princess Anne, and rode Smasher herself to win the Riding Horse title at the Horse of the Year Show.

Looking back, it was incredible the knowledge of those two people and the passion that they had. It was a unique situation, farcical at times on the surface, so the choice was to soak it up and learn, or decide it wasn't for you because of the rough and tough of it all (Jannie's jokes as well as the unrideable horses). Personally, I loved it. English I may be by birth, but this was an alien country to me, having left the mainland so young. Aside from my early childhood and my time at the Fortune Centre, where I'd been pretty cut off anyway, all my life had been spent in the Channel Islands. It's something you only understand if you've experienced moving away from the very safe place where you were brought up. But Bourton-on-the-Hill was amazing. And it was a real eye-opener to see what Jannie and Christopher had. They gave me my first experience of riding a horse that wasn't a natural mover but could be trained to move with looseness and swing.

The pranks were relentless, they never let up. Dear 'Posy', whose school we used, was concerned about one of her horses which appeared to have lost weight. 'How do I feed it up?' she asked Jannie. 'Boiled barley' was the emphatic reply. Posy's confused expression was like a red rag to a bull so far as Jannie was concerned. She went on, with a completely straight face, to tell Posy to take a bag of barley down to the butcher's in Moreton-in-Marsh and ask them to boil it for her. So Posy queued up with all the Cotswold ladies ordering their racks of lamb and dinner-party specials and on getting to the front of the line she handed her bag of barley to the butcher and said, 'Boil this for me, if you would.' Well, that was one of the best ones. You can imagine the faces, and Jannie roared with laughter for weeks on end.

I lived at Muther's house for the first year I was at Bourton-on-the-Hill, then moved over into Jannie and Christopher's house. They had advertised for a carer for Muther. The advert went something along the lines: *Character Cotswold accommodation in return for looking after elderly lady, also of character.*

You think you're mature, having flown the nest and gone to live in another country, but I was very immature and so was Jannie. Although they were three times older than me, Jannie and Christopher were my great friends, huge fun to be with, and they became my second family. Jannie didn't have kids of her own but she saw me through my immature years injecting some of her own unique take on life. She was the one who guided me to my first dressage job at Dr Bechtolsheimer's, and through to my first Olympics. I know she saw this transformation – well, they both did – and were very proud. But there were a lot of adventures before that.

Archie was a fabulous horse. He won one of the first futurity competitions for young event horses at Stoneleigh, and I won three events on the trot on him. Jannie phoned up the six-time Badminton winner and general eventing legend Lucinda Green, who came to watch me ride him at an event in Wiltshire – Dauntsey, I think. We got an amazing dressage score, something like thirteen penalties, and Archie jumped a fantastic clear showjumping. He was really pinging that day and as we went cross-country I got a bit clever three fences from home. It was a hedge, nothing trappy, and I set Archie up to jump it on an angle and save some time. He thought otherwise and ran straight down the hedge. I thought Jannie was going to kill me. She was fuming, as I would have won by a mile without the penalties for a refusal. Lucinda came up to me at the lorry at the end and said, 'He's a fabulous horse, a fabulous mover and a fabulous jumper, but the way you angled that hedge a horse with a killer instinct would have jumped it. He's too much of a gentleman for me.' It made me feel a whole lot better, and I learned a lesson about what a top-class event rider looks for in a top-class horse: you need a horse that will attack the fences. Archie wasn't going to win Badminton, but Sophie Martindale then took him on and did a few advanced classes and eventually Archie was sold to Dutch eventer Hans Brugman, so he had a good career.

There were three siblings, two full brothers and a full sister, of Polish breeding that Jannie had found on a farm near Evesham. They were all still with their mother, they had never even been weaned. Jannie picked them up one by one. There was Easterman, whom we nicknamed Petal, and who was sold to US Olympic rider Peter Green;

then there was Clue, who went on to place at Bramham Three-Day event with Tamsin Owen – he was a bit quirky and didn't move as well as Petal, but had a big, bold jump. And then the final sibling, the chestnut mare Velvet. Jannie went to collect her on a Friday and took her straight up to Stoneleigh the following day where legendary American horse trainer Monty Roberts was doing a demonstration. Velvet, aged seven and never having been touched, was there for Monty to break in, watched by a crowd. Needless to say she went on to an eventing career too.

I hadn't given up on dressage, or at least Jannie hadn't let me give up on it. She took me to meet Kate Masek, who was the only dressage person she knew of in the area, and suggested us two be friends and go out together. I hadn't met Kate's parents but I knew Kate worked at Coln Kitchens. We decided to go to the cinema in Cheltenham and Kate said she would have to drop in and type a letter at work on the way. I went in with her. There was this huge fat man sat at the end of an executive table with a cigar in his hand – a kind of Alan Sugar type, only much more scary – who glanced through Kate's letter, gave it back and growled 'not good enough'. I was looking at my watch thinking we've only got fifteen minutes to get to the film while Kate was tapping away, doing the letter all over again. We finally managed to get into the car and I exclaimed, 'Oh my God, I couldn't work for a fat f***er like that!' At which point Kate turned and said, 'That's my dad.' A good start to our friendship!

Kate was kind enough to lend me Billy Can, her Welsh cob cross thoroughbred. Then Patricia Anderson, a lovely lady who was a friend of Posy's, said that I could have her horse Craigievar to ride. So suddenly I had two horses to do the dressage Young Rider trials on. I didn't make the team on either, but Billy ended up second at the Young Rider Championship to Nicky Barrett and Slightly Trendy.

Nicky and I had met a couple times, then she and her grandmother Lady Craddock, who owned Slightly Trendy, had an almighty falling out. As a result, Nicky and her fiancé Richard (they were married shortly afterwards in 1988) left the scene and I got a call from Lady Craddock asking whether I would like the ride on Trendy. I went to see her and try him, and the first thing Lady Craddock said to me on my arrival was that I should 'get that earring out of my ear'. It was a command, not a request.

I would drive down to Hampshire to ride Trendy twice a week, which meant an overnight stay. I wasn't allowed to stay in the house as I was deemed too dirty, so I camped overnight in the stable flat to ride the next day. I was permitted to eat with her in the kitchen, but it was one of those situations where something inevitably went wrong. I'd knock my glass over or food would drop out of my mouth, and I'd get that disapproving look from Lady Craddock across the table.

Lady Craddock used to get a German trainer named Herr Kueser – I'm not sure how to spell his name but as I recall it sounded like accuser without the 'a' – over to teach me, but Lady C was never far away. I remember one day stopping Trendy and complaining that he was so heavy in my hand. 'Well, you just have to use your legs,' said Lady Craddock, adding with a level of exasperation: 'Come here and get off.' She hitched her skirt up, climbed on board Trendy, booted him three times in the ribs, gave him a pull and handed him over saying, 'There, he's much lighter now. Get back on!'

She was feisty. When we'd go to shows she'd drive the horsebox all the way in the middle lane. She would never use the inside lane. Drivers in the cars going past would wave their fists at her or stick two fingers up and she would wave back as if they were being friendly. She had a horrid little miniature Schnauzer called Wonky. He hated me because he was so protective of her and used to bark like fury at me; Wonky was another one I would persecute if I got him on his own.

We were getting ready to go to a show one day, a Young Rider Trial at Sarah Whitmore's yard near Edenbridge, and Lady Craddock reversed the lorry up to the doors of the indoor barn where the stables were, leaving a crack just wide enough for her to sneak through so she could supervise me as I put the bandages and boots on. I was kneeling down, carefully bandaging Trendy's legs because she was such an old stickler. She was talking to me – or rather telling me how to bandage properly – and I looked up and thought, 'That's funny I could swear there was a lorry there a moment ago.' Lady Craddock was still talking. The next moment there was a terrible crash, so we dropped everything and rushed out. Well, Lady Craddock had neglected to put the handbrake on and the lorry had rolled down and hit the wall at the bottom of the drive – luckily side on, not front on. We both ran down there, and who was sat in the driving seat but Wonky, looking absolutely terrified. Lady Craddock opened the door of the cab and exclaimed, 'Wonky, you naughty boy, you let the handbrake off!' It was one of those airbrakes, so no way could that miniature devil Wonky have let the handbrake off.

Anyway, with the side of the lorry caved in we got hold of all the masking tape we could lay our hands on, taped up this huge hole – luckily in the living area not the horse area of the lorry – and drove off to Edenbridge. We got there in one piece, despite Lady Craddock's terrible driving, and I did my test on Trendy after lots of shouting from Lady C in the warm-up. We got on the team, though I'd never been to an international. In those days you went straight to the European championships having done national shows.

Having been picked for the team – along with Jackie Bickley on The Rooster, Lizzie Loriston-Clarke on Horsted Bright Spark and Laura Shewen on Quarryman – I went home to Jannie's. I was to have four days riding the eventers before heading off to Lanaken, Belgium, and the championships. I tacked up Megan, a chestnut mare Jannie had acquired, another work in progress, and took her out to do some fitness work. We were cantering along a slope, side on, when a pheasant flew up. Megan spooked and fell over on top of me – and that was the end of the team dream.

My ankle was broken in several places. I was carted off to A&E at Banbury, where they put my leg in a cast. A few days later I was resting up at Jannie's and got a phone call from an old Sark friend, Stephen Henry, who was by then working at the John Radcliffe in Oxford as an orthopaedic surgeon. He told me he'd like to see my leg because, as a sportsperson – if I was going to be a professional rider – it was important to check how the ankle had been set. At the John Radcliffe they decided my ankle had been set wrong: my foot should have been at right angles when it had actually been set with my toes pointing downwards. They took the cast off, put a strap around the ball of my foot then tried to get me to pull. I wasn't that much of a masochist, so two nurses were enlisted to stand either side of me and pull. God it was painful! Then they set it in a fibreglass cast, which was quite new then, and for which I am eternally grateful. It was a bit grim at the time though.

I spent the next few weeks looking for things to do to keep busy. I'd met Bernie at a party before the accident. She was a stylist and worked in London or on location, coming up at weekends or on days off to ride her event horse, which she kept with our mutual friend Simon Lawrance. I didn't know what a stylist did, but it all sounded rather glamorous and when I heard she'd worked on the ads for Silk Cut as well as, like me, puffing furiously on them, I rang and invited her to come over and have coffee at Jannie's. She left around ten o'clock that night and we haven't stopped yacking since. We bombed about the Cotswolds in her Mini 'Cricket', me with my cast up on the dashboard, visiting people and probably getting in the way until my ankle finally mended.

Jannie's all-time favourite horse was Wickett. He was a lovely chestnut thoroughbred by the stallion BP and stood 16.2 hands high. He was the only one she never sold, which shows how much she loved him as she'd sold horses all her life. Heather Miles found Wickett, and as he cost £1,500 Jannie should, according to her philosophy, have sold him for ten times that, but he was the one she wanted to keep until he died. He had his own special stable, the converted shed in the garden, rather than living in one of the garages.

Wickett was a lovely ride, but he had low-slung fetlocks at the back so Jannie decided he shouldn't event. I did some combined training competitions with him – that is dressage and showjumping.

We were at one show, in Warwickshire, I think. Bernie and I, having done our dressage tests, were sitting on our horses by the showjumping as we wanted to get in and get done so we could get home. It was a hot day. The class going on was over a tiny course and after it had finished we waited for the fences to go up to 3' 6" but nothing happened. So we sat there, puffing on our Silk Cuts, legs hooked over the knee rolls on our saddles. 'Don't you two think you should be warming up?' enquired Jannie. 'We have and the fences aren't big as the ground's hard,' we responded. Well, at that point my name was called to be ready to go first – and an arena party descended on the ring, hoiking all the fences up to full height at a rate of knots. Bernie left me there as she wheeled Massey off to the practice fence sharpish, while I fumbled to get my feet in the stirrups. Wickett stopped at the first fence. Jannie was absolutely fuming as he'd been jumping jolly well. And Bernie jumped clear, which made it worse. But all was redeemed when I won the final on Wickett. Although he had a lovely jump, with his fetlocks the way they were Jannie decided he was at risk of breaking down if he continued to jump and she wouldn't have let that happen. So he was kept as her dressage horse and Jannie competed him up to medium level.

Heather Miles had a horse called Merlin, whom she absolutely adored. I christened him 'Merl the Pearl' privately. Heather was getting on a bit and Jannie had suggested that she might like me to ride Merlin for her. It was to be the start of some lovely adventures, but the first time I went to ride him it was a warm day and I turned up at Heather's in my shorts and half chaps. Heather rang Jannie up later to say how absolutely disgraceful it was that I'd been wearing a pair of hot pants to ride her beloved Merlin. It was at Heather's that I had my first break, literally. She made me go up a step ladder – I can't remember what I was supposed to fetch, but I didn't get it because when I reached the top of the ladder it folded under me. I fell off backwards, bounced off Heather, landed on the rockery and broke my shoulder. But Heather was a brick in more ways than one and lent me the money to buy my first horse.

I'd already caught some of Jannie and Christopher's wheeling and dealing ability when I brought Mitch over from Sark to sell on behalf of Rossford de Carteret. I sold him to the local showing producer, David Tatlow, and he went on to do brilliantly as a pony showjumper.

Jannie had told me about a friend of hers who, she said, was one of the most beautiful dressage riders she had ever seen. Celia Limbrick was a farmer's wife. She had a gorgeous grey dressage mare that she had put in foal to Odysseus, a graded Hanoverian stallion and Grade A showjumper. The result was Limbrick. I still to this day can't remember what he was really called, but Celia had sent him to Jannie to be sold. I fell in love with him. It was love at first sight because he was the first horse I'd come across that could do a natural medium trot, and that's what I fell for. In fact he was a spooky, hot, tight little toad, but I loved him for that trot.

I told Jannie I wanted to buy him and Heather stepped up to the plate. I think we paid £2,000 for him, which was quite a lot of money then. I novice evented him. He was tight to ride, he had a huge jump, but when he was in the ring he used to get so tense he'd always roll a pole or do something to get faults on the cross-country. Because we couldn't remember his name, Jannie asked what was I going to call him and of course I couldn't call him Limbrick so it obviously had to be 'Limprick'. Fortunately for him, his competition name was less giggle-worthy: Limmy's Comet.

That's how I met Vanessa Ashbourne. Vanessa had been on the Young Riders event team and when I finally advertised Limprick she bought him. He was brilliant, he ended up going round Badminton. He was crazy brave and I was watching on television when Rodney Powell took him round. He got to the water and he galloped through the lake at Badminton as if there was no fence there. Lucinda Green, commentating for the BBC, said she had never seen a horse so bold through that lake. But that boldness was his downfall, because he'd run himself into the ground before he got to the double of hedges. It was a very wet Badminton that year and he jumped the first hedge then spread-eagled when he landed. He turned over and just lay on the ground. It was horrendous watching it on television; obviously Limprick was a big part of my life even though I'd sold him. It is far more stressful spectating than riding. Limprick was on the ground for what seemed like ages, then he got up, and he and Rodney wandered back to the stables. In spite of that, they went on to win Blenheim that year, 1992, after which Vanessa sold him to Germany and he was never heard of again. He was a terrific horse, but he came onto the scene in the days of roads and tracks and that was the era of thoroughbred stars, whereas for today's eventing courses without the endurance factor he might well have been a superstar. He certainly would have been a contender.

Jannie could nip up on any horse in a pair of floral trousers and green court shoes, and frequently did, although the shoes might have varied – her red 'stillies' were favourites – and she was fond of cords. Her philosophy was that if you could get a horse to take the contact with the rider's hands – any horse – that horse would start to move through its body and swing in its paces. She was so right, but that's not the sort of thing that's understandable when you're young, when you think all you want is the horse 'off the bit'. My idea of lightness back then was to have nothing – no weight – in my reins. Jannie was always trying to teach me and get the message through; we'd trot horses over poles all the time and round the woods in circles, round the nettles, through the nettles, through water, getting horses to use themselves. Although it was all done in the greenest, rough-around-the-edges way possible then, today's dressage riders aim for exactly the same thing – except they do it in a 60m × 20m arena.

Every Christmas (I'd long since got over the idea of taking a holiday at Christmas) Jannie, Christopher and I used to go out for a ride. Jannie's philosophy was that no one would be out and about on Christmas morning, so we'd head up to Batsford Park, where we were not allowed to ride, and help ourselves to the cross-country course. There was a well-known wall at Batsford in a long avenue of trees. Jumping with 'competition blood' up is one thing, but jumping in cold blood is quite another. We would gallop up the avenue of trees to the wall, alongside which there was a tractor trailer. You used to have to bounce onto the trailer then over the wall. It was an Open Intermediate fence, I think. I was riding Limprick and Jannie and Christopher were standing their horses either side of this fearsome fence with Jannie daring me to do the 'Batsford wall'. Galloping down the avenue Limprick just took off with me as we headed to the wall. As we landed in the park on the other side, Jannie was screaming at me to get out of there as fast as I could before someone saw us. It was the most exhilarating Christmas I can remember.

6

A Bit of Wing Spreading

Jannie encouraged me to take on three stables just up the road at the Barrington-Wells', halfway between East Cottage and Posy's school, so I could start to make my own living. Going out at the rate I was at the time necessitated rather more funds than I had available, and opportunities to teach lessons were starting to come in. Jude, a friend from the Fortune Centre, had moved in to Jannie and Christopher's as groom/rider, so I had a bit of a break in the stable duties. Not much, but some, and I was learning to dish it out too, as Jannie discovered when I dunked her in the water trough one day amid shrieks and turned the hose on her. At the same time, though, Jannie was turning me loose.

Slightly Trendy was supposed to go to Nicky. Lady Craddock, however, didn't want anyone else to have him, least of all Nicky, who had brought him up. Lady Craddock had Trendy put down, which was horrendous for Nicky, and something for which she was never to forgive her grandmother. It seemed an utterly senseless waste.

Craigievar had gone back to Patricia and Kate had started riding Billy again, but a new dressage ride turned up through Dane Rawlins. Dane put me in touch with Terry Greenwood, who owned Virtu, knowing I needed something to ride. Virtu had been a bit of a dazzler of a young horse for Chloe Chapman, then Dane had trained him to unfinished grand prix level; Terry had bought him but had not done anything with him. Virtu had been out of work and turned away for a long time. He was hugely fat; in fact, he was a porker to the extent that when looked at from behind he had a ridge down his spine with blubber either side. Bump rump or what! I kept Virtu at the Barrington-Wells' and attempted to get him fit by bumbling him up the banks behind Posy's school, but while he was with me if there was such a thing as boot camp for fat horses he should've been on it.

There ought to be a blue plaque at Tesco in Stow-on-the-Wold. Back in the day on that land there was an indoor school and a few stables which I'd occasionally encroach on to board an extra horse, thanks to Ann who owned the premises. She lived there with a company of parrots, which may be the reason I have one now. I don't know, but it was a quirky place in those days.

There would be unaffiliated competitions at the Stow indoor school, showjumping and dressage, and when Danny Pevsner came to teach there Mrs Eason insisted Jannie and I should go and observe. This was the first clinic I'd been to watch, apart from when I was at the Fortune Centre, and we joined about twenty people in the gallery.

Rachael Trice-Rolph, who was local and married to point-to-point rider Jonny, came into the school on her horse. She must have ridden round for twenty minutes and Pevsner didn't say a single word. I whispered to someone 'How much are lessons?' The reply was that a lesson cost forty or fifty pounds – a HUGE amount in those days. I was waiting for these pearls of wisdom and obviously so was Rachael, who finally halted her horse and asked him, 'What do you want me to do?' After a long silence he replied, 'If you don't know what to do after all these years of me teaching you, you might as well get out of the school.' Poor Rachael burst into tears and rode out of the school. I was gobsmacked. Although I've heard people say he is brilliant at times, the lesson I learned was that I wouldn't want to teach like that and hoped I never would.

It didn't take long before I was seriously freelancing; riding absolutely everywhere, spending most of my time in the car and having more accidents than getting to places. I had passed my test by then but my vehicle choices weren't always informed and my driving skills, lacking a background of even being driven due to the lack of cars on Sark, owed less to the Highway Code than the need to get from A to B. I got mowed down by a school bus one time, went into the back of someone at a roundabout when I didn't think I was insured, then got a blow-out on the Fosseway and went straight into the Stowell Park wall. I had three accidents within about six weeks and thought I wasn't destined to drive a car. I'm sure cars thought that too.

One of my first and most loyal pupils was Betty Nicholas on her dear horse Ivan. At least she was nearby. Betty was kind enough to invite me to dinner; sensing it was a bit serious, I took Bernie as my escort as she knew Betty too and more importantly knew her way around a dinner party. I had a fear of what I thought of as 'fogey parties' and not knowing what to do. My fears were not groundless. At one point in conversation with an eminent Cotswold lady I suddenly noticed to my horror she had fallen asleep.

After dinner all the ladies stood up and as I went to rise from my chair Betty placed a hand and whispered, 'No, you sit down.' The ladies withdrew and the boys got left round the table telling stories about the old days, passing the port and smoking cigars. Such was my launch into Cotswold life. Betty was a dear, she came to my twenty-second birthday party and brought me a bottle of vodka, but she dropped it on the way in.

I was riding Merlin at Heather's and she offered to lend me the money to buy a lorry (or we went halves, I can't recall quite how it worked). So Dilys was purchased: a converted former Ryder truck which had to be named in the tradition of Daffodil's family as she was yellow. We had her fitted out with a living area including a pull-down bunk bed – a platform suspended on chains – and I thought she was marvellous. Her Ford Cargo engine went like the clappers.

At the time Jannie encouraged me to branch out I finally got myself out of her hair and rented a cottage in Oddington with Annabel, who worked for Posy.

I met Becky when she worked in the garage in Stow – it was the nearest shop to Kate Masek's – and when she started doing some part-time work for Kate we found we all had a laugh and got on, and we thought it would be a good idea to share a house together, so we moved into a cottage on Pig and Whistle Hill at Icomb, just outside Stow. I dare say we weren't ideal tenants, and in fact over the next couple of years I'd go through as many houses as cars, trying to find cheaper rents, I suppose.

On one occasion Becky said she was going to do Sunday lunch for me and Annabel, and I arrived back, starving, to find fire engines outside the house. Becky had put the roast in the Rayburn, gone out and forgotten about it, and it set the kitchen on fire.

I also acquired a puppy from 'Crabbers', a barrister who was mad about horses. Rupert was a Jack Russell who grew up to be a strong type with tricolour markings and a healthy sense of adventure. Later I had to train him not to chase horses and so he learned that when I picked up the reins to work he had to leave the arena. At the end of the session, when I dropped the reins, he would run round like a little bolt of lightning barking his head off with joy. He loved coming to events and invariably would be first dog into the water. He also loved being with horses, as did Crabbers, who used to help out on the yard like some sort of superannuated weekend helper in return for a ride at Jannie's. I guess it was his weekend change from a wig and gown.

Crabbers lived in Blockley with his wife Lizzie, a travel agent. One evening they had invited Jannie, Christopher and me for dinner and we arranged to meet in The Crown and then take the short walk back to the house for dinner. We were late leaving, so Jannie said, 'Let's go straight to the house.' We walked in and no one was home. Lizzie had lovingly prepared all the food and there were all the vegetables in pots ranged on top of the cooker ready for when we got back from the pub. Before leading us up to The Crown, where Crabbers and Lizzie were obviously waiting for us, Jannie put a squirt of Fairy Liquid into each of the pots. When we all returned from the pub, Lizzie lit up the stove and before long it looked like a flipping witches' coven as every pot was bubbling over. Lizzie was not happy. We went back to the pub to eat. Needless to say the short walk was to the accompaniment of Jannie's hoots of laughter, and mine too. Christopher rarely, if ever, rose to any of the considerable amount of bait that was strewn across his path.

The fact that Jannie and I were thick as thieves and she was in her fifties just shows how immature she was, but for Jannie it was all sport. 'Sporty' was her favourite word, used to describe anything from an indescribably unrideable horse to the process of wrecking other people's dinner parties (or her own). Nothing was ever naughty, only sporty.

Thanks to my eccentric upbringing in that atmosphere, I enjoyed hunting but the field etiquette wasn't high on my agenda. On one occasion I was riding a horse for Lady Aird, a big grey called Timber Wolf that we thought would benefit from a bit of hunting. I wish I could remember who I was with, but can only be sure it wasn't Simon Lawrance as he was far too correct (he was later to become a Master of the Heythrop). Anyway, we decided that as nothing much was happening it would be a good idea to go and get some jumping practice as there were a few inviting logs around. At least it seemed a good idea until we got bawled out by one of the masters, Liz Wills, and sent home.

Hunting was excellent for embryonic event horses and great fun on a run, but I can't say I ever entered into the spirit of it as sitting around having a chat – known as 'coffee housing' in hunting speak – was considered off in hunting circles but far too up my street.

Merlin and Virtu had qualified for the National Championships at Goodwood and I was doing it on a shoestring. Bernie volunteered (or was 'voluntold'?) to come with me as groom and we set off in Dilys with Virtu and Merlin aboard. We stayed over with Dane Rawlins on the way. He'd offered me some free help and I leapt at the chance to give both horses a tune-up, which we did, and it was good to ride with other dressage riders, including Jackie Bickley, who by then was a firm friend. What I hadn't reckoned on was Dane, who'd been so bloody supportive, expecting a hod-carrier's support in return. Pointing to a pile of bricks, he said: 'We're building a barn, mate, get stuck in.' Bernie retreated to Dilys to read *Vogue*.

We had a problem. 'Merl the Pearl' was recovering from ringworm. Actually there are no worms involved; it is a contagious fungal skin infection. He'd been treated with whatever the topical application of the day was and he had to wear a rug to cover the residual bald spots in case anyone thought that he had the plague. We drove down from Dane's to the stables, not on the grand estate, which at least I knew given my 'previous', but way round the Chichester ring road to the race-course stables. It was a bit of a scary drive and all I was thinking about was getting there. We made it, but on opening the ramp we found dear Merl scrunched up cuddling Virtu in the back as the divider between their spaces had come loose. I was mortified. They, however, were thankfully fine, although Merl was a trifle warm in his rug. We didn't trouble the leaders but I'm pretty sure we came away with rosettes, and Goodwood was always a wonderful party.

I enjoyed a few months of competing at prix st georges level on Virtu until something happened that would change the course of my life. Oh, and Tony, my father, turned up to watch, so he finally got to see what I did.

I met Marc on his fortieth birthday at The Feathers in Woodstock. I'd been invited by mutual friends. Marc, I was to learn, had stables at his home in Nether Westcote, but this meeting was nothing to do with horses. Blond with a stunning smile which illuminated his pale blue eyes, I was smitten. I knew by then I was gay; I suppose I had always known deep down, once I knew what 'gay' was, but the difference was I had grown old enough to feel something, old enough to have a real relationship, and old enough to actually understand what it was like to share your life with someone – and I was to love it.

It was complicated and pretty secret for a while. Marc was living with Felicity, and although we laugh about it now – that's me, Marc and Felicity – there was an awful lot of torment and trouble at the time as Felicity and Marc had been talking about getting married. It was a difficult period and crucial to all of our lives, but it was a signal to me that this was going to be a really significant relationship otherwise it would either never have developed or would have stayed secret, which would have been worse all round. Felicity and I are now great mates and I joke that I did her a huge favour as she went on to become Lady Blyth.

Marc was to become a big stabilising influence in my life and that was something I'd missed out on, like a lot of things you don't know you miss until they're there. I was off and doing my own thing, that was my life, but you can do that when you know there's someone who is always there for you. That's what our relationship was about.

The fact was I'd never before spent time with anyone who'd lived life in the way Marc had. He'd been a model, a designer, and then he learned to ride, took his BHSAI and set up his riding school, which he did in his own style, in his own way. He was also a dab hand at those life skills I was so lacking – such as how to get insurance and how to buy a car. Through Marc I met people outside the horse world, interesting people. He had a lot of intellectual friends, but mainly they were a diverse crowd and I've always enjoyed older people's company. To me Marc had lived life to the full, and it was just great, as it is for everyone lucky enough to experience it, to be with someone who was looking out for you.

Annabel and I had been living together, and Annabel had been thinking we were going to get married; in fact she'd already booked the registry office at Moreton-in-Marsh, which had been a bit beyond my control. The one person who had been to the registry office at Moreton was Bernie, and I wish I'd known as I'd have stopped her – but that's her story and maybe she'll write it one day as she wrote her way out of the disaster that followed.

But everything was about to change anyway, and Marc was totally supportive. He wasn't going anywhere and this was a chance I had to take.

7

On to the International Stage

One phone call changed everything. Even if it had ended up with one of the other candidates (I think I was one of three) getting the job, life was different straight from that moment because it brought into focus a possibility which had only been a hazy dream before.

Dressage then was all about Germany: German horses, German riders, German trainers, German tack, German breeches and probably even German pants if anyone had thought that wearing them would have helped get higher scores. They'd kept hold of every gold medal since dressage competition began, they were the best and everything everyone else aspired to be but couldn't (unless they were German, of course).

Heinz Schweistries had swept the board at the previous year's national championships riding Dr Bechtolsheimer's horses. They were based in Gloucestershire and it was as if Germany had taken up residence in England with the result that everyone else's efforts were in the shadows and no one could have failed to notice.

The phone call was an invitation to interview for Schweistries' job. He was heading back home to Germany and Mrs Gold, one of the top dressage judges of the day and a former team rider who had trained in Germany for many years while her husband was stationed there with the army, recommended me. Dear 'Mrs Bold', as I called her, or 'Paddington' on account of the red duffel coat she sported, looking as if all she needed was a Marmalade sandwich, I will always be grateful that you spotted me for the right reasons not just because of my then frequent changes in hair colour, which alarmed a number of senior judges when I doffed my hat in salute.

Not normally known for becoming flustered, that was one of the rare occasions when I can safely admit that I got to know the state of flusterdom. Having accepted the invitation to interview, next problem was getting there. Not that it was that far away, just the other side of Cirencester, but I was car-free at the time. I borrowed the famous 'Cricket minuet' and set off in confidence which rapidly drained as I drew up to what appeared to be a smarter version of a normal white farm gate until I looked a little further up the curved drive. Plan B had to be swung into action.

The Cricket minuet was beloved by me and her owner Bernie, but the black Mini had her 'sunroof' taped down with duct tape and her bonnet held together with wire so I'm afraid she got dumped at the end of the drive. I decided a walk might give a better impression.

I rode Dramatico, Dr B's schoolmaster, and Glanzpunkt. My experience of one-time changes, now one of my favourite movements of the grand prix test, was limited to trying them on Virtu bundling up the hill and it was a bit mortifying to have to ask Dr Bechtolsheimer how they should be done, but he talked me through it and those were my first proper 'ones'. Swinging from side to side is a cardinal sin in the flying changes, but I like to think that Dramatico and those changes swung it for me that day.

I had to wait a week before I heard I'd got the job, which was one of the most agonising waits of my life and certainly THE most at that point, but in October 1989 I moved into a gorgeous flat and started work. When Dr B asked me how much money I would like I was in total shock at the idea of wages, having been on a maximum of £30 a week since I began working with horses. I thought for a minute he was expecting me to pay him! I wasn't allowed to take any horses, which was to prove fortunate for Emile Faurie as Dane Rawlins, through Bernie, helped him secure the ride on Virtu. So it was just me and Rupert the Jack Russell who moved in to begin life at the Bechtolsheimers'.

I no longer had to muck out stables first thing in the morning. My day began with riding under Dr B's eagle eye until lunchtime, then a two-hour break which I used to the full inviting friends over most days. In the afternoon there were horses to be hacked out and various jobs relating to keeping the place itself groomed and manicured, such as harrowing the arena surfaces, plus giving the occasional staff lesson and minding the horse walker (more on that later). The horses were given six-star care by the team of girl-grooms with head girl Tracie in charge. I had never been part of a yard regime where the summer sheets and bandages were IRONED! Actually, I'd never been part of a yard where said items matched. I had to smarten up as well and before long I got my first pair of proper dressage boots from the well-known maker Schnieder in Bond Street. The catalyst was a picture of me on Rubelit in my old hunting boots in *Horse and Hound*, so you could say it was media pressure. It was only later I was to discover the joy of zips; these boots took me hours and a hell of a lot of pain to remove. Anyone else who has ballet dancers' arches ever tried getting your feet into concrete cylinders?

Having always lived previously as part of a family or latterly with housemates, I was slow to acclimatise to the regime of living on my own. My eating habits were up and down, and I had days of burning the candle at both ends – I was supposed to be in bed by ten every night but often this involved going out ten minutes later. Then there were the fated German lessons which Tracie and I were supposed to work at. Needless to say I didn't work at them and to this day the only German phrase I know is '*alles klar Tchuss*', which is jolly handy. 'OK, fine, bye for now' can see you through numerous kinds of situations. Dr Bechtolsheimer also gave me a copy of the 'dressage bible' that Mrs Eason had quoted from so often, *The Complete Training of Horse and Rider* by Alois Podhajsky, the famed trainer and director of the Spanish Riding School who secured the safety of the School's white horses from the Germans in World War Two. Unfortunately, although they made a film about the Lipizzaners, there wasn't one of this particular book; though I swapped the bookmark around a bit I'll admit now that it was more for effect rather than reflecting the amount of knowledge gleaned from its pages. The daily lessons were lapped up, however, and the afternoon hacks were my chance to reflect on the morning's school work.

When the Bechtolsheimers were away, Rupert's favourite trick was to jump up from the wall onto the front of my saddle when I was hacking Rubelit out for his afternoon constitutional. Part of it involved hacking back along the main A417 and one afternoon while doing just that I was passed by Sheila Wilcox, the legendary eventing pioneer who had helped the Bechtolsheimers set up in the UK, driving in her car. I knew straight away what was going to happen and sure enough within a matter of hours came the phone call – I'd been shopped by Sheila. Mrs B was not amused, to say the least.

After lunch much of my time was spent in the 'heated phone box' which housed the controls for the horse walker. The equine athletes had to be watched while taking their afternoon constitutionals but I have to admit for me it was a bit of a chance to have a snooze in the 'Tardis'. When the horse walker was first installed we all took a turn trying it out in the actual walking bit, but when I got to play with the controls the speed mysteriously rose a few notches for Mrs B's turn – a sight not to be forgotten!

Trixie, Mrs B's niece, had arrived to stay at about the same time as I started. She proved to be something of a sister act but the difference was that, as family, she was able to get away with everything. I used to set her over-ambitious jumping distances and she fell off her pony too many times until the point where she refused to have lessons with me. When we were reunited years later at Mrs B's sixtieth birthday party, Trixie told me she felt she'd paved the way to provide Laura with a smoother path to adulthood. She certainly must have the full complement of tips on how to bring up children as she was such a

wild child herself. Laura was only four when I arrived at the Bechtolsheimers' and not having much experience with small children I
was probably of the school of thought that they should be neither
seen nor heard. On one occasion when Laura failed to observe that, I
shut her in the feed room as a punishment – then promptly forgot I'd
left her there. When the door was finally opened she scarpered like a
scalded cat up to the house. I can vouch for the fact that there was no
long-term psychological damage, but Laura remembered it and got a
bit fed-up with it being mentioned during the Olympics. Needless to
say Mrs B was again not amused.

The selection trials for the 1990 World Equestrian Games were
held in March that year. On the way there we had the radio on. Simon
Bates' *Our Tune* was a must on Radio One every morning and featured a listener's personal story together with a significant song. Most
of them were sad; lost love, that sort of thing. Well, it was only a short
way into that day's story that I was overcome by a sick feeling of dread
and before long I was hanging out of the lorry about to kill myself.

Although they said on the show that all the names were made up,
this girl's story related how she had fallen in love with a guy, a rider
from Sark in the Channel Islands, that they were going to get married, and then he'd left her for a man. I was absolutely devastated that
everyone would know the story. I remember getting out of the lorry
thinking does everyone know it's me? Well it was highly unlikely
that Trish Gardiner, Diana Mason, Domini Morgan, Joan Gold and
other judges and selectors – being of a certain age and a certain ilk
– would be listening to *Our Tune*, but that was my perception of the
show's importance at the time. Annabel had turned up at the Bechtolsheimers' a few weeks after I'd started there and slapped me round
the face, but I'm happy to report that she went on to marry a rugby
player and have two lovely children. It was not however the greatest
start to my first selection trial. Then during the competition Richard
Barrett nudged me furiously saying, 'Oh my God, there's Mr Ridley
from *Coronation Street*.' 'Where, where?' I responded excitedly, then

we spotted him. 'No it's not, that's my father,' I said to Richard, not realising at that point they were one and the same.

I'd been told that to be sure of a team place you had to come in the first four, but the controversial dressage journalist, the late Pegotty Henriques, made it clear to me that it was not the placing but whom you beat that was important. I was the youngest rider up for selection – by quite a long way – and since former model Anni MacDonald-Hall had been selected the year before, injecting a bit of glamour into the sport, there was a lot of interest. It was the time of an obvious 'changing of the guard' and I was entering the ranks of Jennie Loriston-Clarke, Diana Mason, Trish Gardiner, Bar Hammond and Chris and Jane Bartle (although Chris had retired from dressage competition by then and returned to eventing), who all had many years of life and experience on me.

At the selection trials Rubelit and I were fifth, but beating well-known combinations, so were selected for Schoten, a popular outdoor show in Belgium which was run by the frankly rather scary Mariette Withages, a leading international judge and later Chairman of the FEI Dressage Committee. Like Diana Mason, she could wield a handbag with as much aplomb as Margaret Thatcher. Set in a park near Antwerp beside a fairy-tale castle, the arena was next to a zoo. While it was one of those shows that made me realise that English shows had about as much atmosphere as a public library, riding a test to the accompaniment of roaring animals was a new experience.

It also gave me the novel experience of staying in a hotel during a show. In the hotel lift I met Miranda, now the Duchess of Beaufort, beautifully turned out in full tails and top hat. The thought crossed my mind that I'd got it totally wrong and we were supposed to dress like that all the time.

There was a lovely dinner all the riders were invited to. Again this was pretty glitzy in my limited experience, as was having to wear a suit and tie. Bernie and I sat with Jennie and Anthony Loriston-Clarke and two lovely Swedish lady riders we got to know well over the coming year. The conversation turned to dressage horse breeding and Anthony grabbed the opportunity to proudly present the virtues of the Catherston stallions, including their use for artificial insemination. As the main course arrived he remarked in a loud voice, 'Dutch Gold is very good frozen,' which sent the rest of us into fits of silent giggles and would have put us off the chicken completely had we not been so hungry after all the champagne.

It was my first international show and it was a great laugh as well as being the introduction to some real characters. Christine Doan, who rode her lovely Dondolo for Australia, was immediately nicknamed Rapunzel due to her long blonde plait. We met beside the warm-up when she offered us apples and asked the name of our chef d'equipe. 'Diana Marie-Therese Francine Dubois Mason,' I responded. It came out of nowhere and Diana has been 'Diana Marie-Therese' to me ever since.

I finished about halfway down the list with Rube. On our return we contested the then key national show at Barnsley near home and won the Grand Prix. We beat Jennie and co. and it was my first grand prix win. The fact that we all warmed up on grass (the lawn or field variety, not the other one) rather than on a specialised surface would bring some of today's competitors out in a rash.

Within a few months Rubelit and I had done enough to be selected for the team, so in July 1990 we were off to the first edition of the World Equestrian Games, held on the renovated site of the 1912 Stockholm Olympics. It wasn't only dressage but showjumping, eventing and all the equestrian sports, so apart from the excitement of being on the team there was massive excitement in the horse world generally. It was the first time the British team horses had flown to a competition outside an Olympics, but they had a lousy flight due to two planes breaking down and subsequent delays. We riders, however, arrived in style and stayed in a super hotel.

The whole performance of a big show was a complete revelation, from getting the accreditation (without which you can't get anywhere, let alone into the stables), to being allocated times to ride in the arenas. Of course it was inevitable that I wouldn't be able to keep my nose clean for the entire time, and I got caught out walking back to the hotel smoking a cigarette. I heard a loud beep and promptly turned and stuck two fingers up, only to realise too late that it was Dr and Mrs B in the car. Then I seriously boobed by giving Rubelit a sugar cube, which led to him being dope-tested. I received the biggest bollocking from Domini Morgan, who told me I could have got the whole team eliminated.

The serious business of my first international championship resulted in sixteenth place individually for me and Rube, and a start in the individual grand prix special, only the second time I'd ridden that test. We were fifth as a team, which was pretty good, but I have to confess my enduring memory is of going to the show party, with Anni MacDonald-Hall looking terrifically glamorous in a black leather strapless top, and her husband Caspar – and Caspar leaving me to pay the taxi. Oh, and of being photographed sitting on the rocks paddling my feet in the water, which reminded me of being home on Sark. That photo was used for years.

Back at the Bechtolsheimers' I did buck the system by keeping the second horse I'd bought, Tomato, just down the road. I'd got to know Andrew Barrons, who lived in the next village and whose father had trained Seagram to win the Grand National, and his mother had Tomato to stay until I sold him to become a brilliant hunter in the North Cotswolds. Polish-bred, the huge chestnut was aptly named. I'd found him in Worcestershire in a stable which he hadn't been out of for so long and hadn't been mucked out for so long that it looked as if a lift had been caught between floors. It took ages to dig poor Tomato out. He wasn't going to be an eventer, but his new owner regularly rang me up to sing the big horse's praises as the best hunter he'd ever had. He became a renowned star of the North Cotswolds, but tragically he got a thorn in his fetlock while hunting one day and had to be put down when infection resulted.

One enduring memory was of my first taste of modelling. My Sark friend Debbie Carré had produced a collection of leather boots and clothing based on equestrian designs, and me, Posy and Nicky were the models. It was fun hamming it up in front of the camera, adopting moody-looking poses, although I was astonished at the trowel-loads of make-up applied to all of us – I've still got the photos up at home. I wasn't exactly a dab hand, but I was invited to model for *GQ* magazine's January 1991 edition along with rugby player Jeremy Guscott, javelin champion Steve Backley and boxer Tony Collins, which was huge fun. I have joked ever since that if I'm feeling remotely apprehensive or keyed up about an occasion, I just think 'make way for the supermodel'. It works for friends too, but of course only when in my company.

At the 1991 European Championships in Donaueschingen, Germany won team gold with Isabell Werth and Gigolo taking the individual honours. With the introduction of the freestyle to the championship format these championships were something of a landmark, but not when it came to British performances. Dutch Gold was fourth in freestyle though many thought he and Jennie Loriston-Clarke should have had the medal in front of the Russian, Nina Menkova, whose music was famous for eliciting comments on the fate of cats. Anky van Grunsven made her team debut with Bonfire and the Dutch team got bronze. We were last as a team. There was a very glum picture in *Horse and Hound* of the team lined up at the bottom of the pile. What a whirlwind though! In less than eighteen months I'd gone from not knowing anyone on the international scene to competing with and against some of the major names of the equestrian world and the stars-to-be who would dominate the sport for decades, not least Isabell and Anky.

I was busy with young horses as well. When I arrived at the Bs' I brought with me the love of being taught that I'd always had – and no ideas of my own. I soaked up everything and enjoyed every minute of those lessons with Dr B and with Harry Boldt (or rather, Herr

Boldt) who periodically came over from Germany to assess our progress and who sat in the corner of the school casting a wise eye over us and every now and then uttering the phrase '*Ja, gut*'. Having seen Anky and Isabell ride, I was fascinated by their training methods. In the summer holidays while the Bechtolsheimers were away I decided to practise the 'deep and round' method on the small tour horse Waffentanz. He was a lovely character but very large and rather slow. I had nicknamed him 'Elephantanz'. He was the opposite of the right type for this sort of training and I was told in no uncertain terms that this was NOT the way to do dressage.

With dear Rubelit getting on in years, the decision was made to retire him. By the end of the season there was a whole new batch to concentrate on. As a grand prix hope the Bechtolsheimers bought Robert Dover's grand prix horse Walzertakt after flying me to the US to try him. We stayed in the Plaza in New York. My first horror was not being able to find my room, and then at breakfast I was hauled to one side and told that 'Sir' needed a jacket. I still had no idea of those sorts of rules and regulations. Walzertakt was nicknamed 'Walter' by the Bechtolsheimers and 'heart attack' by me, as he always seemed to be either on the verge of giving me one or having one himself. This was one of my first experiences with a really hot and sensitive horse. He'd try and scrape me off against walls when we were out hacking, which was not very nice, but he was the most beautiful and talented horse. His temperament was not, however, at all easy to channel and one of the first things I had to master was the art of removing and replacing my hat in salute while still on the move. He was thought of as a front runner for the Olympics but was actually lame when we got him home and remained so intermittently, despite all Dr B's efforts to get him right. Dr B had bought Giorgione from another legend, German trainer Herbert Rehbein, who, among other things, was famous for being able to ride a line of one-tempi changes while smoking a cigar. 'Gino' was intended to be Dr B's ride, but he generously reassigned the chestnut stallion to me, which was to lay the ground for our biggest adventure yet.

One of the real perks of the job, and there were many for me, was to get a month off every year in October. It was fabulous, and my holidays were always good. I went to Israel, Egypt and the USA. It was the first time in my life I had ever been able to afford to do anything for a holiday, let alone travel like that.

I went to Israel with Jannie and Julia, a Cotswold friend who worked for event rider Owen Moore. I came up with a different story every time someone asked me how long I'd known Julia, knowing that if the person then asked Julia and got a different answer they would think she was lying. We had a family room as it was the cheapest. When Julia and I stayed up in the bar one night we went upstairs to find ourselves locked out, with a fast asleep Jannie either not hearing or more likely refusing to hear our urgent knocks on the door. We slept outside on the sun loungers.

Egypt was with Simon Lawrance and Owen Moore (nicknamed Miss Brahms and Mrs Slocombe). Simon changed the goalposts every night with his stories of what we did for a living. I'm good at telling stories anyway, but these got more and more embellished. While we coped with being dancers I found passing myself off as a lawyer rather a challenge intellectually, although aided and abetted by Simon I got through the evening. One night Simon had a gippy tummy and disappeared for about half an hour. Having identified the right 'engaged' door I tipped a cup of water over it, quietly left and returned to the restaurant. Five minutes later Simon arrived, bedraggled. He said nothing, then with a cheeky grin picked up a cup of tea and poured it over my head. I too said nothing and quietly removed myself to my room.

Then it was 1992, Olympic year, and the team question was to get under way with the selection trials at Stoneleigh. But before that Gino and I were selected to go to the huge indoor show in Holland at S'Hertogenbosch (I could hardly pronounce it, so ever since have called it 'Sloggenbosch' but will call it Den Bosch for now) which was a baptism of fire for Gino as it was only his first grand prix season and third grand prix ever. Despite two major championships and a few international shows, this was something else for me too. The show venue is a vast complex which is normally the regional market, and it attracts huge crowds. The restaurants and shopping are amazing too.

The first thing was to get Gino settled in, and Mrs B swung into action to secure him a double stable at the end of a row of the temporary wooden indoor stables (it took a while as the 'special treatment, please, he's a stallion' argument didn't wash at a show which was awash with stallions, but she won in the end). The place was buzzing and I can imagine the horses don't get much sleep with all the coming and going as classes go on until late at night. The warm-up arena was like Victoria station in rush hour. This was my first experience of Dutch audiences and it was quite a shock to hear how much noise they made in appreciation after each ride; people walking around clutching trays of *frites* and sausage were the norm as horses entered and left the arena. Gino loved it, the electric atmosphere working to his (and my!) advantage and giving him extra expression in the piaffe passage. Fourth in his third grand prix was brilliant and qualified us for Gino's first grand prix special. Going first after the break, whether it was intentional or not, the band heralded us with a pretty dramatic drum roll which put Gino's eyes on stalks and his feet on hot coals but we managed to keep the tension at a manageable level to place sixth. There have been a few since but the rosettes, I remember, were gorgeous. Anky van Grunsven was second in both classes on Olympic Bonfire. The excitement about the pair who'd go on to dominate the sport for so many years was just growing then.

We'd travelled via Hook of Holland so headed off in convoy to get the overnight boat, along with Richard Davison who had got half his Olympic qualification on Master JCB – it was 60 per cent in those days! Having eventually boarded the boat after Richard had sorted out his horse's papers (he'd arrived via a different route and you had to have stamps into and out of each country back then – happily one of the showjumping grooms managed to sort it) we headed up to the restaurant and bar. It was a buffet and the crossing was getting rough. Trying to walk in a straight line to pile our plates full of seafood required careful aim to arrive at the right place and gradually the numbers at the table dwindled. Finally we went off to find our pretty spartan cabins, grab a few hours' sleep before breakfast. Munching through a full English breakfast we ignored the calls for people to return to their cars only to eventually go down and find the decks deserted apart from two horse lorries.

After Jannie's Daffodil and my ex-Ryder truck Dilys the HGV lorry at Dr B's came with the luxury of a driver. That was until Dr B decided it was time for me to take my HGV test. I thought it was possibly the biggest mistake of his life as driving was definitely not one of my strong points. I was terrified manoeuvring that lorry over roundabouts and turns, let alone getting on and off ferries, and it didn't start well.

The beginning of the ordeal was being sent to Gloucester for a week's HGV course. Since I didn't – and still don't – sport any tattoos, and my jeans and baseball cap weren't exactly the height of 'trucker' fashion I probably looked more Milky Bar Kid than Yorkie Bar.

End of week and my first fail. I can't remember the reason; it was something trivial like running over a pram or an old lady on a zebra crossing, but it allowed me to go home gleefully feeling certain there was no chance I'd be sent back for more. Wrong.

There were two instructors and I had a different one the following week. It was a swift fail, this time reversing over the cones, and I was rather unhappy that I had to take the rest of the test. I was convinced that at this point Dr B would surely realise this whole sorry exercise was a non-starter, but Dr B didn't believe in giving up. You can imagine my utter horror at being sent back the following week.

Instead of setting off with my heart in my mouth I was filled with a feeling of inevitable doom. Sure enough, there he was: the original examiner. Don't ask me how it happened but at the end of the test – which I was resigned to having to go through all over again, judging by past experience – he went and informed me I had passed. He then asked whether he had seen me before. Naturally I smiled and said yes, but I'd seen his friend in between! Dr B was so delighted he came up with the disastrous idea of me driving the lorry to Wiesbaden.

We set off to the south-west of Germany, it looked a bloody long way on paper, with me at the wheel, Bernie in the passenger seat in charge of the map and Tracie in the living area – I think we'd had a bit of a falling out – but she was in charge of coffee and keeper of the biscuit tin so things were of necessity smoothed over in record time. We arrived at Dover and parked up in order to take the horses' papers for clearance at Customs, which entailed queuing up for a free window behind a long line of truckers. This process was slightly more complicated as we had one horse on board to be returned to Germany, the Bs having decided not to proceed with the purchase. Negotiating on and off the ferry in one piece was a major relief and it was off to our first port of call at sparrow's fart o'clock in the morning at Aachen border crossing where we had to wait for the vet check and the German horsebox. The girls took their wash bags and had a quick freshen up in the ladies' room – I don't recall the habitual fat-boy breakfast being on the cards for some reason, either the cafeteria wasn't open yet or we didn't fancy *bockwurst*, but in any case there was no grub.

When the German transport arrived there was a bit of confusion over something missing. It certainly wasn't the horse, and it had a head-collar on, but the mystery was solved when Tracie descended down the ramp bearing a full, long, flowing chestnut tail which was not attached to said horse. Doubtless this was not the reason for the poor creature's return, but as the image swam through my mind of a tail coming undone mid-test rather like a supermodel's wig falling off mid-catwalk, I bid the chestnut goodbye with some relief.

Onwards to Wiesbaden, which meant hitting the full German rush hour on the autobahn. It was up to Bernie to keep nudging me awake as the lack of sleep kicked in. One of the most God-awful road trips of my life. When we got to Wiesbaden all our eyelids were drooping and while we couldn't wait to arrive at the blasted show, there were no helpful signs indicating where the entrance was, at least to this blur-brained crew to whom the *nur für turnier* signs read as 'not for the competition'. Bernie woke up first to the yellow brick road-like realisation that what they actually said was ONLY for competition, which on my part necessitated turning the truck back onto the road we'd just turned off. As I was carrying out this manoeuvre I had the misfortune to engineer the meeting of wing mirrors between the horsebox and a vehicle driven by the German equivalent of a white van man, which caused the *Weisses Lieferwagensmann* (or whatever they're called and no, it doesn't have the same ring, does it?) to leap out and start swearing and cursing in German. Funnily enough, we did understand this part quite well. Being higher up and with a girl at the nearest window to him meant the obvious thing to do was to drive off with a wave, which I did.

Arriving at the show entailed parking in a residential side street to unload everything – horse, equipment, hay, etc. – then wheelbarrow the latter articles to the stables. Wiesbaden show takes place in a beautiful park in front of the historic seventeenth-century Schloss Biebrich, a baroque pink-and-white confection that was the residence of the Duchy of Nassau (which I always associate with Barbados, but never mind), so I suppose it was to be expected that we couldn't park outside the front door. Nevertheless this whole exercise entailed a lot of to-ing and fro-ing, which I was anxious to get done as I wanted to ride Gino before the Bs arrived.

Gino always caused me problems in the zig-zag, a grand prix movement that involves half passes from one side to the other, with a flying change, clean change of direction and specific number of canter strides either side of the centre line. If anything, it's easier now as at least one 'zig' has been taken out, but in the Gino days it was the full deal, and setting off from A on course to end up at C seemed more like undertaking a downhill slalom as he leaned on the bit and took me skiing. Dr B liked Gino to be ridden in a nice, thick snaffle bit. It's the 'kindest' sort of bit for the horse, but not necessarily for a rider trying to control a horse with a stallion neck. So it was the perfect opportunity to pop my version of a suitable bit in Gino's mouth in preparation for the forthcoming competition. Ironically, it's called a Dr Bristol, so known to me as a 'Dr B', and very well Gino went too giving me a confidence boost ahead of the grand prix that we wouldn't zig-zag straight through the judge's hut at C and on into the Biebrich castle drawing room. Back at the stables it was a quick unhook to detach the bit from Gino's bridle as Tracie heralded the approach of the Bechtolsheimers. The well-mouthed 'Dr B', the evidence, went straight into Bernie's Mulberry handbag. Home and dry, I thought, but how wrong I was.

There was a police car waiting at the horsebox; even with my limited German it was pretty easy to work out the meaning of *Polizei*. Less obvious was what they wanted. Richard Davison, who has the knack of being useful in times of communication difficulties as well as being in the right place at the right time, managed to elicit from them that I was the one they were after as the driver of the horsebox. The blasted white van man had reported me!

Apparently they'd been waiting for me for two hours and were pretty cheesed off about it, so when Richard tried out his best Perry Mason impression they told him if I didn't go with them they'd arrest me, and if 'Perry' didn't stop making excuses they'd arrest him too. We were carted off in a police van, complete with bars on the windows. Oh, and I had parked outside the Schloss gates.

I thought after giving our details we would be delivered back to the show ground, much to the relief of the rest of the British contingent – and of course me, thinking how lucky I was to get away with a few stern looks. Richard, however, reminded me it was a bit more involved than that. In the event, I gave my statement but then we had to wait an hour or two until they could get a judge on the phone. To-tally bored by then – after all, this was a huge fuss for a wrong turn at traffic lights – I just let Richard get on with it.

A huge fuss for a wrong turn at traffic lights? I was disabused of that notion when Richard, who'd been on the phone with the judge and the police, charged over to me hissing, 'Stop picking your nails – what's this about the bodily harm and the damage to the van?' Well, I'd forgotten about kissing wing mirrors, but bodily harm was a bit far-fetched! We'd needed to get out of the way of the traffic behind us blowing their horns and the guy was irate and we couldn't under-stand his German so there had seemed little point in hanging around any longer. I told this to Richard, and left him to explain it all to Judge Judy or whoever it was on the end of the phone. Richard managed to get the fine down from 1,000 DM to 800 DM, which I could pay with a credit card – but my wallet was back at the show. So poor Perry Mason ended up bailing me out, literally, as apparently this was like a bail bond to be held until the case was heard. It was a lot of money in those days and Richard had to ask Dr B to pay him back before leav-ing the show so he could be sure he had enough for diesel on the way home. I was probably hiding by then. It was many months later, after an increasing number of incomprehensible letters with an increasing amount of red ink had accumulated, that I thought I'd better ask Dr B what they were all about. The short answer was that the fine was huge!

The actual competition went really well, with Gino and me seventh in the grand prix and fifth in the special against some of the German team riders, and Olympic fever was setting in as the Americans an-nounced their team after the grand prix. It was also where I first met Robert Dover.

Robert has been part of the dressage world for decades. Nutty, in-telligent, successful, terribly political and one of the most interesting people in the sport, Robert was to become a great friend, mentor and someone I can even now ask any question about dressage and he'll always have an answer. Back then it looked as if he was conducting a 'Robert séance' outside the warm-up arena. All the US riders were standing around in a circle holding hands as Robert intoned, 'Melindurrrr, I wan' it awl and I wan' it now.' Poor Melinda looked absolutely terrified, her eyes nearly popped out of her head, and off she went and did a disastrous test! Robert would ride her horse Lectron in Barcelona while Melinda herself would be named reserve on him for the 1994 World Games.

At the final selection trials on a windy day at Addington, which Gino and I won, the team order changed again. Carol Parsons was selected and Jennie Loriston-Clarke was off the team amid much controversy. It was the beginning of a new team order and suddenly we were matched with contemporaries. Anni MacDonald-Hall had tragically lost both her two grand prix horses, The Optimist and then Floriano, in a very short space of time so was no longer in contention. Looking back post-London Olympics and removing the gold-tinged spectacles for a minute, one of the things that strikes me about those key events twenty years ago is the press presence. Alan Smith of the *Daily Telegraph* led a press pack of ladies who were always there with their notebooks on these occasions representing the 'dailies'. Jenny MacArthur of *The Times* is the only one of that original cohort who was still tapping away at her keyboard in Greenwich!

Around this time I got my first taste of television when I was asked onto the *Jim'll Fix It* programme. I was surprise guest of honour at a birthday party for a girl who loved dressage. I had to drive up to Shropshire in that tinted-windowed Rolls Jimmy Savile always turned up in while outside the house cameras and lights were set up. When we knocked on the door my biggest fear was that the girl wouldn't recognise me. Anyway she did and afterwards I presented her with her badge in the studio. The show was watched by millions. Who would have imagined the scandals that would later emerge. To have been on the show is an odd feeling.

A fun part of the Olympic build-up was the moonlight laser ball organised by Anni, David Hunt and Russell Christie. It was a glitzy black-tie affair. The team performed a quadrille in the laser-lit outdoor school with everyone watching in their finery clutching glasses of champagne. In reality, 'lit' was not quite accurate and the quadrille was more like four of us fumbling around in the dark to a live band. Whether spectators could see anything other than shadowy shapes I have no idea, but we were bloody lucky no one bumped into anyone else.

The Bechtolsheimers' Olympic parties were out of this world, and it brought real meaning to being selected on the team, having it celebrated in such a fabulous way. The team send-off party was hosted at home, where a beautifully decorated marquee featured tastes from around the world concocted by famed chef Anton Mosimann. I was glad I only had to walk down the path to my flat after that.

Getting accreditation had seemed a huge thing two years before but nothing prepares you for the Olympic bureaucracy of security checks on every entrance and having your pass scrutinised every five minutes. It's not something that comes naturally to me, but thank heavens I didn't lose that photo ID. Having arrived in Barcelona at the Olympic village, our chef d'equipe Barry Marshall (nicknamed Muttley because of his laugh), Emile and I went to find the team apartment we were to be sharing with the showjumpers (Laura and Carol, of course, were in the girls' quarters). It looked pretty spacious and we were first in, so we bagged our beds and went to the stables. We returned to find our bags outside, the showjumpers moved in, and us crammed into the smallest room. The next day as we all piled onto the bus to go to the stables, Tim Grubb made it clear that the 'young ones go in the back'. The showjumpers ruled back then.

It was before the days of mobile phones and I'd been yapping for a long time in one of the phone boxes at the Olympic village when there was a furious rapping on the door. I looked out to see Steffi

Graf, telling me to get a move on and get out. It wasn't the first time I'd encountered a bossy German.

The opening ceremony was eye-wateringly uncomfortable, not because of the hours of waiting around to walk in as a team, but something far worse: I had a boil on my bottom and it burst. Enough said.

The highest temperatures that century in Barcelona were recorded on the first day of the team contest. When I saw all the Union Jacks waving and heard the cheer from the British supporters I grinned from ear to ear. Wolfgang Niggli, lead judge and Chairman of the FEI Dressage Committee, wrote in the *L'Année Hippique* annual that Gino and I did a 'not very brilliant test which nevertheless earned a place in the final', but he placed me much lower than the other judges so maybe he was a bit piqued that I made the final. Admittedly, Gino's passage was never his forte but his walk was better and he'd given the judges something to look at with his extended trot. I had an awkward moment when one of the pink umbrellas collapsed just as Gino was piaffing in front of it. Gino was hot – his eyes were on stalks the whole way through – and so was I. Never before or since have I sweated so much in a tailcoat, and you could have wrung my shirt out, but at least I'd made my second final on my first Olympic and second world team appearance.

Being first to go in a competition is always tricky. People are still settling into their seats and the atmosphere's unsettling; it's a hard job for an experienced horse, but for a first-year grand prix horse at an Olympic Games it was going to be a big task. I was conscious as we entered the buzzing stadium that the prize we were most likely to get (had it been available) was the one for the fastest round. It was great for the piaffe and I was relieved to get into canter as at least the hotness could be converted to expression, but the walk was way too on edge to be anything other than a jog and the salutes at beginning and end were made in record time.

When Carol Parsons, the final member of the team, went in she would have had to achieve some ridiculous score for us to claim bronze and it wasn't going to happen. I was watching on one of the monitors, and as Carol rode her test with Vashkar's neck getting shorter and shorter the camera panned to Princess Anne's face contorted in a sort of grimace. I remember thinking, 'Oh, I don't think we've won a medal.' When Carol came out she wasn't at all happy about her score, which she felt deserved more for Vashkar's, as she put it, 'effing good pirouettes' – which is what I called her after that, or 'FGP' for short.

I've always been an admirer of Isabell Werth and Gigolo, who didn't halt either and had a few mistakes but certainly enough to claim silver for the reigning European champions. Rembrandt was on a knife edge but he and Nicole Uphoff were totally concentrated. It was one of the most mesmerising tests I have ever seen, a goose-bump inducer, and they won the gold for Germany. In fact, Germany won all the medals, but Holland's Anky van Grunsven and Bonfire, who came fourth, were set to change that in the future.

Off to the Juan Carlos Hotel where the Bechtolsheimers hosted lunch for all the riders, owners and team support. That was the first time I'd ever had to show ID to get past armed guards just to be admitted to a hotel. The IOC big cheeses and royalty were staying there.

The Olympic experience had seemed pretty daunting until we got there. In reality the atmosphere at the Barcelona polo club turned out to be more like that of a friendly CDI (international dressage show). The pool at the Juan Carlos was a favourite haunt, and I'll never forget the day when Laura's husband Simon Fry managed to pull Desi Dillingham, then leading light of the British Dressage Supporters Club, into that pool – it looked as if a large pink marquee had landed in the water. We'd also hung out a fair bit with the US team, especially Robert Dover – who walked round with his boyfriend Robert Ross and their two Jack Russells looking very movie star-like – and the lovely Charlotte Bredahl. Equestrian events were, until London, a bit removed from the main Olympic fervour, but at least we were technically in Barcelona, albeit at the end of the underground line. The main thing for me was that I'd done it, and in the process I'd become the youngest rider to represent GB on an Olympic dressage team. I only wished they'd provided showers for horse and rider on leaving the arena; as I told Australia's *The Horse* magazine, it was the closest to cooking I've ever come in my life!

It had been an unforgettable year, but I didn't settle back into the routine when we got home. I had always enjoyed teaching and also knew that realistically I could not make a living just being a rider, I had to start laying down something for the future. I went to Dr B and talked to him about the possibility of doing some more teaching in the afternoons, but the answer was 'no'. Dr B, perhaps sensing that I was thinking ahead, also wanted me to commit to stay for two more years. It took a week of soul-searching and a fair few late-night phone calls with friends and finally with Dr B, but at the end of it I agreed to stay on.

Before the year drew to a close there was still the National Championships to come. Goodwood was always a special place to ride and with Shell Gas as national sponsors the nationals at that time had a real wow factor. Gino and I had won the intermediaire national title the year before, he had done nothing but get better in every outing since and with his best test ever we clinched the National Grand Prix title. It was my first and it was amazing. I had desperately wanted it and had put myself under more pressure than at the Olympics. I went all out to get it and Gino was with me to bring it home by nearly forty marks. I had the ride of my life, one of those where you have a dream feeling throughout the test. It was great for the Bechtolsheimers too, as it was the one title that had eluded them. Afterwards I was ready for a holiday, but pleased I'd decided to stay. After all, where would I ever find another horse like Gino and a team like the Bs?

The New Year started well and I'd been thrilled to accept the Spillers

Dressage Rider of the Year award having been voted winner by the readers of *Horse and Rider* and *Pony* magazines – despite having to make a speech, something I still dread. Then I won the grand prix on Gino at the Addington selection trials, together with the small tour classes on Limmat, which Dr B had bought the previous autumn. The international show at Goodwood was fabulous as always, especially coming in third and fifth with Gino. There was a certain amount of pressure, which I'd added to by declaring that a medal was the next aim both for me and for Dr B. But at the same time, the more I had watched, the more I had seen of horses, horses' riders, different ways of training, the more I wanted to try out my own thoughts and ideas. I felt under pressure to do things the Bechtolsheimer way, which was fair enough, the horses were theirs, but the question was how long could I keep accepting the spoon-feeding? The answer was not much longer.

I'd been helping Vanessa Ashbourne with Limmy's Comet, the first horse I'd produced with Jannie's help. Seeing as this, in reality, meant trips on my days off to stay at Vanessa's for socialising, I didn't think it was that big a deal. It was when Dr B rang home one afternoon asking to speak to me and I wasn't there.

I had hacked Gino, as I had been told to while Dr B was away, just up the road and back. A few hours later, Caroline, the head girl after Tracie had left, came to me and said Gino had a big leg. I went to have a look and, sure enough, Gino had some heat in one leg. I informed Mrs B, who called out the vet. It all felt a bit cloak and dagger; the vet didn't tell us anything, but he and Mrs B spoke together, after which she came to me and asked what had I done with Gino. I told her exactly what I had done, that I had hacked Gino up and down the road as her husband had instructed, but I got the feeling it was presumed I must have done more. The atmosphere became extremely tense, there was a bit of a showdown. Granted I'd been caught out a few times and Mrs B and I didn't have the easiest of relationships, but this time I knew I'd done exactly what I'd said I had done. With my feeling my version of events was not believed I knew there and then there would be consequences. Something was going to happen.

At about eight that evening I heard Dr B coming up the drive. The following morning I went to the yard at seven o'clock as normal. There was always a list on the wall each morning of the horses to be ridden, by whom and in what order. That morning my name was not on the list. Dr B was down to ride them all. He arrived at 7.45 to ride his first horse. I sat and watched him ride, which is what I would normally do with the one horse he would ride every day. Then he got off the horse and said I'd like you to come up and see me at the house in fifteen minutes. It was almost a relief as I knew what was coming and I had got to the end of a great time.

Up at Dr B's office he said to me, Carl, I heard what happened yesterday, you must realise you cannot speak to my wife like that. I said I had told the truth and I would not be called a liar. He said OK, but you do realise we can't go on any more, and as with everyone that leaves here you will have to be out in twenty-four hours. I replied that I was really sorry, I'd so enjoyed being there, that he and I had got on very well and we've never had a cross word, and again, that I was sorry, but I had told the truth. I want you to do one thing for me, asked Dr B, I want you to apologise to my wife. 'OK, I'll do it for you,' I replied, Mrs B came in and I said, 'I apologise for shouting at you, but I was not lying.' Mrs B was obviously angry. There were words to the effect that I wasn't a horse-person, nor a sports-person. At that point I didn't retaliate, I simply said, 'Thank you very much, we'll see.' And I left the office, packed my house up and drove away.

It was a perfect time to leave as I then had four days at Badminton and eventing was still a great love. It was a relief, as we'd had that break six months earlier when I'd said I needed to do something else other than just be at the Bs'. I wanted to start teaching and they wouldn't have that. All the same, I'd grown up there, I'd had the best time of my life there. I think the only sad part about leaving was the fact that I did go to the Europeans three months later and watched the British team take their first medal ever. Dr and Mrs B also came out to Lipica to watch and it was very uncomfortable. But I let any animosity go over my head, and suffice to say now we are all great friends again and I appreciate everything they did for me. Without them I wouldn't be where I am. When we get together we only talk about the good times. And it was good until the day I left. With a few exceptions, like my run-ins with Mrs B, I never had a bad time.

I arrived at Badminton to find the place was abuzz, and Badminton being on the large side that meant a heck of a lot of buzzing. Jane Kidd, with an official hat on, came up to me and said a press release had been faxed through to the Dressage office about my leaving. I was told in no uncertain terms by several well-known figures, including a particularly larger-than-life dressage supporter, that I was a 'stupid boy' for having thrown away such an opportunity. These were people who had high ambitions for British dressage and in their eyes I'd let the side down. I was given strict instructions not to talk to the press, while people who didn't understand the sport and certainly didn't understand me were all too ready to voice their negative opinions. I wondered later how much of that reaction was due to the fact that they'd become accustomed to the Bechtolsheimers' generous hospitality, which would now be off the menu.

The dressage worthies didn't get their way. Bernie got me into the press tent where I was surrounded by dailies before I'd had time to turn round. I will be for ever grateful to those journalists – Alan Smith of the *Daily Telegraph*, Jenny MacArthur of *The Times*, Genevieve Murphy of the *Independent* especially – for treating me like a sportsman and not a 'naughty little boy', and for being so interested in my future plans and positive that this was a beginning not an end. Jenny MacArthur made me promise that I wouldn't disappear, as what on earth would she write about in dressage!

As hard as it was to pack my bags and leave those horses I had grown to love behind, and as daunting as it was to think about starting over from scratch, I didn't see it as a case of going back to square one but of going forward. I just wasn't quite sure of the direction yet.

8

Back to Square One – But Not for Long

I went to live with Marc in Nether Westcote at Far Furlong Farm, which would eventually become the home of Henriette Andersen and Ulrik Molgaard, my good dressage friends. Jannie was elated that I'd come back and absolutely determined that I should get going with the eventing again. She had just the horse, she told me.

Aberlord, known as Alfie, was a five-year-old little grey gelding. He was another of Jannie's Ascot sales purchases. So right away I started heading straight up to Bourton-on-the-Hill every morning to ride again with Jannie.

I will never forget my first event on Alfie, at Milton Keynes. Jim Fox, a four-time Olympian and team gold medallist in Modern Pentathlon at the 1976 Montreal Olympics, was there, giving me a 'well done' as I came out of the showjumping; he was like an old dad to me, always full of encouragement. One of the developments since I'd been away was the use of video, and this was the first time I'd been videoed across country (I'm so relieved VHS technology has been overtaken). I went round shitting bricks and missing at every fence. I remember the commentator saying that 'Aberlord had the advantage of having Olympic rider Carl in the saddle' and thinking, 'Oh no, he doesn't, Carl has the advantage of having Aberlord underneath him, taking him round as fast as he can despite Carl hanging on for grim death!' After three years at Dr B's I was not letting go of those reins. We managed to come second, but I could not bring myself to let go and gallop. That's when it dawned on me that this was an avenue

I was not going to follow, despite Jannie's exhortations. In the end, Jannie agreed with me. I was more than happy to produce the novices for her and do the odd event, but it was not the path I was going to choose.

I realised that I wanted to have my own yard. I met up with Kate and we decided we would try and run her yard in Stow-on-the-Wold as a business. Literally within about two weeks of leaving the Bechtolsheimers, Kate and I had got our heads round sorting the yard together. She was busy working, so it was quite easy for me to rent the yard, have horses there and take care of Kate's as well. In those days we didn't have an indoor school, just the outdoor arena right on Stow Hill where horses had to quickly become accustomed to airbrakes applied by passing lorry drivers.

Donnersong, 'Otto' for short, had been bred by Kate. He was by the great German stallion Donnerhall out of a Pik Trumf mare, Pastiche, that Kate had bought quite cheaply in Norfolk. We broke Otto in as a three-year-old ourselves. He had me on the floor. Otto would be a horror until he was eight years old; he always had a cold back. He had a terrific canter but if he was excited he'd buck like hell. He was to become famous for it in prize-givings. Otto was destined to be the first grand prix horse I would train from scratch.

Requests for lessons began coming in and because of my successes people started to ask if I would teach clinics. While I'd done my bit of freelancing, becoming a trainer – if I could have called myself a trainer then – or an 'imparter of knowledge' at least, was quite daunting. But I started to do clinics and Gleneagles in Scotland became one of my monthly ventures. I was back out there, having to make a living, and I got cracking. I'd be up at Jannie's most mornings then on to the yard, then off teaching or away doing clinics.

In 1994 Gleneagles provided me with my first experience of doing a lecture demonstration. I took Lucinda Marchessini's Marocco, who was only five at the time but went on to grand prix. Emile Faurie came, bringing a more advanced horse as I didn't have one, and

Legrini, who was seven. Scottish eventer Fiona Stuart rode her advanced event horse Young Lochinvar. Even today demonstrations are something that I dread doing, but that day at Gleneagles launched my lecture demo career with an audience of over seven hundred. I've got used to it now that I've done a lot of them, and I enjoy showing our horses to people, but back then I had a severe case of tummy ache for hours before.

Life became very busy running between yards and I was starting to pick up new rides. I had to ride everything that came in to the yard as that was the only way to make the business work, and some of those horses were good to get stuck into. And of course I had to get used to the idea that they wouldn't all be around for the duration. Boucheron, known as Bertie, was sent to me by Nicky Barrett and co-owner Toni Parkes. Bertie was a little hottie and it was about turning his tendency to explode into controllable impulsion, but he won everything and was a nice little horse to get me started making my name again.

Horse and Rider magazine had suggested a competition, 'Search for a Star'. It was supposed to be a prize of a couple of lessons for someone and a bit of fun all round. Bernie was doing the words and had sorted out a short-list of entries out of the hundreds sent in. We sat down and looked through all the letters and photographs; we had ponies, cobs, Arabs, thoroughbreds. There were some lovely-looking dressage horses but the whole point of the competition was to try and pick from a picture the person that we thought deserved the help and wouldn't normally have access to it.

Among all those pictures one stood out. There standing on a hill was an enormous bay horse, almost a carriage-driving type, with a tiny lady sitting on top. At the same time we said to each other, 'It has to be her!' We wondered how someone that small could ride a horse that big. And so, a few weeks later, when they arrived for their lesson, we met Marcia Kelsey and Democrat. Little did I know at the time, but I had met my next international grand prix horse.

Suddenly the yard was full, the dressage horses had started coming in and I had to start making decisions on what sort of horses we were going to have and what the priorities would be. I was to have a really nice time during those years, in charge of my own career again and therefore my own destiny, and I started doing all the things I wanted to do.

There was plenty of fun too. I'd lived three minutes from The Fox in Oddington before going to the Bechtolsheimers and The Kings Head at Bledington was another 'local'. They're such an integral part of the Cotswolds scene now and were to us then. I'd enjoy three or four nights a week out with friends, usually at one of these two venues. At the time, The King's Head was run by Mike and his wife Annette, who was absolutely charming to boys but practically ignored any females in the party, which was hilarious as the girls would scope the bar to avoid placing an order with her. The present owners Archie and Nicola Orr-Ewing are equally friendly to all guests.

I'd started teaching eventers too. Mark and Carolyn Todd had moved to Adlestrop. We became friends then I started helping Mark and riding some of the horses. They ran what seemed to me a huge operation; you think you work hard as a dressage rider, but eventers must be the hardest-working people in the equestrian business, or at least among the hardest when you count racing people. They were also great fun socially. We started the Monday Club on the basis that nobody did anything interesting on Mondays so we would each host a dinner and invite someone new. It comprised me, Mark and Carolyn, Bernie (who was living up the road from the Todds), Lucinda Marchessini and Rosie Northampton. Being the leading Cotswolds socialite, Rosie held court, although there are many priceless tales of those evenings. One Monday, having arrived to pick Bernie up en route to Rosie's, I managed to steer the bright yellow sporty-something I was so proud of into a ditch, at which point Rupert the Jack Russell shot up Bernie's suede skirt. There was much shriek-ing. Trying to get a mobile signal on that back road was less than successful, so we thought 'hurray' when a black Range Rover pulled up behind us. However, the man coolly smoking a cigarette as he got out of the car merely wished us well and drove off – bastard!

Eventually we were rescued by a farmer returning home. We set off to Rosie's, horribly late, and on bursting in and complaining bitterly about being left by the side of the road by someone with a suitable vehicle to help, quickly reverted to 'Good evening, how do you do' on seeing the blasted man stood there.

On another occasion Rosie invited us with the instruction that a special guest would be present. Bernie, being au fait with these things, schooled me into the correct form: 'Good evening your Royal Highness' first, 'Sir' thereafter. We bowled up, on time thankfully, and I strode into the drawing room where Prince Michael of Kent was standing by the fire, proffered a hand and spouted, 'Hello, I'm Carl.' Oh well, it stood me in good stead when I met the Queen many years later. Actually it was a great evening.

One day this guy appeared at the yard, he just walked in when I was teaching and said to me, 'I want a lesson.' I told him fine, I could fit him in in about three weeks. He replied: 'I don't want someone who can fit me in three weeks, I want to come tomorrow. I AM coming tomorrow. What time can I be here?' The time was the only negotiable bit and the following day Vaughn Jefferis turned up with Bounce.

Vaughn had been a showjumper and had switched to eventing a few years before. He'd ridden as an individual for New Zealand at the World Games in 1990 on Enterprise, his first event horse which he sold to Christian Landolt, then Bounce had come along.

Many people have been involved in my life, watching me grow and develop, and now I got a chance to experience what it was like, being in at the start of an incredible journey for this pair.

Vaughn could not ride dressage. He'd had a serious car accident and, as he said, he had a left hand that had a mind of its own, he couldn't sit to the trot and if flying changes had been introduced at that stage it would have been like world war three – he simply couldn't do that sort of thing. So Bounce made the trip up to my yard two to three days per week. I rode Bounce and I also put Vaughn on some of my horses so he could get the feel. Vaughn said that the best thing that could ever happen was to 'plonk him on'. Basically the horse had to be trained so that Vaughn would be able to simply get on and steer him round, and that's what we did. Bounce was an amazing mover by the time we'd got him to loosen his back. He began to swing and his lovely canter was matched by a big expressive trot which replaced the neat row of stitches he'd previously produced.

How was it that someone who was the most natural jumping rider, who looked like a dream across country, couldn't sit in a dressage test? The plan was to get Vaughn sitting, and we did. He was so dedicated and he worked hard; he'd run in bin liners to lose weight and he put in hours of training outside the arena, then he'd do all his work in the arena without stirrups to improve his seat. He did everything he possibly could. But Vaughn loved nothing better than being out of the saddle, galloping from fence to fence and it was one of the best sights I've ever seen. Vaughn and Bounce going cross-country were absolutely stunning.

At the World Equestrian Games in The Hague I was standing at the entrance to the showjumping arena having followed Vaughn and Bounce into the arena. A few minutes, a few fences, and I think a few more riders before we knew, but when we did and Vaughn was World Champion we were all in tears of joy. He wasn't in the lead after the dressage, but Vaughn and Bounce did a lovely test that put them in touch so they could work their jumping magic. I was so proud.

Being part of the New Zealand camp gave me an introduction to post-event partying on an entirely new level. The British team – Mary Thomson (later King), Karen Dixon, Tina Gifford (later Cook) and Charlotte Bathe – had won team gold, with Karen taking individual bronze. Having called in to congratulate them at the supporters' tent I repaired to the 'Down Under Club' next door with Bernie. Having blitzed Badminton – Mark won on a catch ride, Horton Point, and was also fifth on Just an Ace, Blyth Tait was second on Delta, and Vaughn and Bounce were third – the New Zealand team had been expecting medals. Only Vaughn had come out shining, but the Down Under Club was rocking while the Brits next door were still on the dry sherry.

It was there that I was first subjected to the Haka. Vaughn had done his speech thanking everyone and then I nearly died as he made me stand on a table while he told stories about me. For anyone who is not used to being put on a pedestal let alone a bloody table, to have a group of guys then come up to you doing the Haka . . . well, it's one of my best memories. We partied until three or four in the morning then had a mad rush to get to the airport, only to find our plane was delayed until the afternoon. That was my first major training success, the 1994 Eventing World Champions.

Back at home Boucheron, who'd won the medium winter championship earlier that year, bagged me the advanced medium national title. I managed to get the medium title too, on Royal Academy, who'd been sent to me by his owner Caroline Stubbs while she was pregnant, and had rather surprisingly relegated the unbeaten 'Bertie' Boucheron to second. So at my first national championships after fifteen months on my own I'd not only bagged two titles but second place in both classes as well, as Brabham was runner up in the advanced medium.

Brabham had been sent to me by List One judge John Mead. He was a challenging horse that I had to work hard with to develop his trust. He would be coming back next year after a winter's rest, but Bertie had been sold – Nicky having done a very good deal of which I was not a major beneficiary – and Royal Academy was on the market.

The following year, 1995, was to be the year of the chestnuts. Gershwin came to me not having competed for eighteen months and was as exciting a ride as he was a prospect, being extremely talented but volatile with it. I was also riding for Lady Bamford and competing Garbo at small tour level; Nicky had another designer number for me to bring on, the stallion Versace; and there was a special chestnut that came after a terrible event.

Christopher turned up at the yard one day in late March. I was teaching. He parked his car and walked across to me. 'I've got some awful news for you,' he said. 'Jannie was killed this morning.'

I didn't cry, I just looked at him. Christopher said he was going home. I told him I'd be up to see him later. Because Jannie had been killed in an accident – a young horse had fallen on her up at the Faerie Glen – there had to be an inquest. Over the next ten days, two weeks, however long it took, I never once cried, I never let anything get to me. Every evening I'd go and sit with Christopher for an hour. Another one of Jannie's favourite words was 'stunning'. And here we were, stunned in a different way. It hadn't sunk in.

The funeral was arranged and I remember saying to Marc that I wanted to go on my own, that I'd see him at the church. I wanted to go to the house and as I turned into the drive there was Christopher with Jannie's best friend Janet, the district nurse. Some other people were coming and we were going to walk up to St Lawrence, the ancient church at the top of the hill that we used to ride past every day.

Janet unfortunately did what I know she thought was the right thing. She came up and put her arms around me saying, 'I'm so sorry.' That was it. I went into the house, so embarrassed that I was crying. I stumbled upstairs and lay on Jannie and Christopher's bed where I sobbed, and sobbed, and sobbed. Christopher came up and, being Christopher, in that gentle, gentleman's voice of his, said: 'Are you all right? Come along, we've got to go to the funeral.' That was Christopher: so strong, as ever. His words will always stay with me: 'I'm glad it was her and not me so she doesn't have to go through what I'm going through.'

I knew for Christopher I had to, so I pulled myself together and we walked up to the church, and I made myself sit there until it was over. I couldn't get out of there fast enough. I just ran down that hill and I was the first one back. I went into my old bedroom and wailed some more. But we had a wake to get through, I had to help Christopher, hand round drinks, talk to people. So I came downstairs and off we went, for Jannie.

A month almost to the day of Jannie's death I took Wickett to the Badminton Dressage Championships which Miranda organised at the Badminton indoor arena. Jannie had left Wickett, her special chestnut, to me. We won.

I'd been to the selection trials with Gershwin and realised someone was likely to be in the way that year. Vicki Thompson beat us on her reigning national small tour champion, Elaine Smith's Enfant, another chestnut. Enfant, known as 'Impy', and Gershwin made a good pair as we would find out a few months later.

Gershwin was owned by Jennifer Oldham, an American, and her husband Philip. If there was ever a horse that knew how to twist his owner round his little hoof, it was Gershwin. In June we were selected to go to Copenhagen CDI. It was a fun trip; Peter Storr was riding too and Bernie came along as a reporter. Peter was an old friend from young rider days. Always immaculately turned out, when we were in ripped jeans to go clubbing Peter would accompany his pressed version with a pair of Gucci loafers. Dear Peter was then and is now subjected to ruthless ribbing from me. When the Channel Tunnel opened I completely scared him off it by telling him you could see sharks as you travelled through!

The thing with Gershwin was to get him thinking forward and it was still at the stage where getting his mind on me rather than his surroundings would require a bit of firmness. With Jennifer present that was not going to be possible as she thought her darling Gershwin was scared. She'd employ various alternative remedies, many of which seemed completely barmy to me, while Gershwin in her presence looked at me like the most spoilt of spoilt brats, as if to say, 'You can't tell me off when Mummy's here.'

The time came to get on and I was ready. But when I got to the stables, to my utter horror, Gershwin was standing there in his massage rug, his tail in a plait while Jennifer fussed over him. He wasn't even tacked up. Naturally, I was fuming but couldn't say anything. Copenhagen is a long way to go to lose a class through insufficient warm-up!

It felt good to be back in a tailcoat and I had plenty of chances to wear it that year. The European Championships were to be at Mondorf-les-Bains in Luxembourg. Probably as a toast to the introduction of the freestyle as the final test for the individual medals in preparation for its historic inclusion in the Olympics, Mondorf had added a new competition, a pas de deux to music at small tour level. Vicki and I were off to Mondorf with Impy and Gershwin.

It was a beautiful show. We were all in a hotel in Luxembourg City and as we did quite often to save expenses, Bernie and I shared a room. It was an ultra-modern new hotel and one of the features was the power shower. The problem was it had transparent doors and wasn't in the bathroom but in the middle of the bed/sitting room. It was a race to get in and out of there before the other had a chance to ring the nearest friends and invite them up for drinks.

Vicki – I've always called her Queenie – is still one of the most elegant lady riders and was trained by Franz Rochowansky. 'Rocky' was in his eighties then. During the Second World War he had been instrumental in hiding some of the treasures of the Spanish Riding School from the Nazis. He had many fascinating stories to tell and much training wisdom to impart, once you could decipher his incomprehensible accent.

Our pas de deux went beautifully. It was all choreographed to a single piece of orchestral music, 'Santorini' by the Greek composer Yanni (Sven Rothenberger later pinched it), which had a lovely dream-like quality and it flowed. We won by miles. In the prizegiving, as the crowd went wild Impy stood bolt upright and seemed to hang there for ages before promptly sitting down on his bottom. Queenie didn't move. I remember thinking thank God they hadn't yet given her flowers!

It was at the height of the duel between Isabell Werth and Gigolo and Anky van Grunsven on Bonfire. Isabell won. The British team did not have a good show, despite hopes raised with their third place at Aachen, but they'd lost front runner Jane Bredin when Cupido got injured.

'Queenie' and I were asked all over the place to perform our pas de deux but we never got it to the same matchless, seamless state as we did that day in Mondorf. We reprised it at the nationals but resumed our rivalry for the actual championships. Gershwin and I took the prix st georges, Queenie and Impy the intermediaire I. Well, I had to do the gentlemanly thing.

The sadness of that time was that my relationship with Marc had come to an end. I wasn't ready for the garden, neither designing it nor sitting in it, and I wanted to be with the horses, not because of some workaholic tendency but because that was where I wanted to be. It wasn't where Marc wanted me to be. We're great friends now but obviously there was a lot of hurt at the time. I moved into a rented cottage at Daylesford.

I went to the Atlanta Olympics as trainer to the New Zealand event team (or most of them, as Andrew Nicholson did his own thing as usual and Fiona Craig helped Blyth Tait). It was a big team too, as for the first time there were to be separate team and individual competitions run over different courses, which was a bit weird. It was an eye-opener to be on the other side of an Olympics as a trainer. We were all together in a shared house, and the Kiwis as ever had a brilliant support team and loads of team spirit. They needed it, because things didn't go smoothly, but in the end the team got the bronze medal despite Andrew's stop, Vicky Latta's fall from Broadcast News, and Vaughn's struggle to get a heat-depleted, very tired and unbouncing Bounce home. Blyth's individual gold on Ready Teddy was hugely popular and Sally Clark's close run for silver on Squirrel Hill was something I got a thrill out of, having helped her when she was in England. It was another part of my horse life and a different side to an Olympic Games. Eventing's a sport I've always enjoyed watching and being part of, and that hasn't changed.

When I first started looking back it seemed to me that 1996 was a real 'in between' year. While in Atlanta, I'd watched our dressage team: Vicki Thompson, Jane Bredin (later Gregory), Richard Davison (who was highest placed, seventeenth on Askari) and Joanna Jackson on Mester Mouse. Impy was wild, he never coped with that sort of atmosphere and then Cupido tied up in the middle of his test – the heat got to him – which was awful for Jane. Though I wasn't involved in any of that, I was competing a lot nationally. I loved what I did and I loved my work. I enjoyed getting stuck in and I was highly motivated. I had wondered whether I would be able to continue after Dr B, but in that situation you either keep going or you sink. I worked and off I went. I'd also found an apprentice in Jo Barry, who'd won the Scottish Talent Spotting Final, for which the prize was six lessons with me.

After Marcia had brought Democrat for her *Horse and Rider* prize lessons, she kept on coming. Marcia ran Donnington Garrison Saddle Club near Telford in Shropshire with Alan, her husband, and while Doob (her pet-name for Democrat) was only competing at elementary when we all first met, it was through Marcia's work at home, keeping the training going, that he was up to the small tour mark and learning piaffe. The intention was that Marcia would compete on him. Her original aim had been to get to medium level, and she saved up for those training trips. Then she had a lot of problems with arthritis – as she put it: 'everything went wrong, bodywise' – and as I'd lost the ride on Gershwin because the Oldhams were returning to the US, she asked me to compete Doob.

We'd made our international debut at Hickstead CDIO for fourth and seventh in the small tour classes and qualified for the nationals, then at three days' notice we were invited to compete at the Horse of the Year Show. It was a small tour competition alongside the only World Cup qualifier ever held there. We all trogged up to Wembley not knowing what would happen. As I rode Doob into the arena, it felt as if eighteen hands-worth of horse was about to turn round and make a sharp exit, but he didn't, he gave me a terrific ride. Then he did it again. We'd won the prix st georges and the intermediaire I. The trouble was, we had qualified for the freestyle.

I hadn't thought for a minute I was going to get placed, let alone qualify for the music so I had nothing prepared. I had to rush home and put some music together. While Christmas shopping at Bicester village I'd heard this drum music coming from one of the shops – *Thunder Drums* it was called – so I'd nipped in and bought it at £3.99. It was brilliant music, really strong and so different then when everyone either had classical, synthesised or Abba.

I think that was the longest intro I or anyone else has ever done. There weren't any rules on timings then – and bear in mind I'd had to make this using the stop-go button on a cassette recorder – I literally stopped at C outside the arena, walked all the way down the centre line, all the way down the long side and halted at G before we actually did anything. I'd never ridden Doob to music, nor had I ridden the test. In fact it must have been my first ever music, so it was a case of shut your eyes and get on with it. We didn't do the treble; Doob's right pirouette was usually his best one but I oversteered a bit so we had to bow to Ireland's Heike Holstein on her young rider horse Ballaseyr Saturday Night, but it was still a fantastic experience. There's a picture Stephen Sparkes took of us thundering out at full pelt after one of the prize-givings, Doob looking like a great war horse and my legs not even reaching the end of his belly. It was a fairy tale for Marcia.

Marcia had a very good knack and such a strong bond with Doob that never broke, even when I was riding him. He adored her and she adored him. He learned his piaffe and passage in the long reins, because that's how Marcia found it easier. With me riding him three days at a time every three weeks while Marcia did the groundwork at home, that horse went international grand prix – and he did it the following year.

It was all possible thanks to sponsorship from top-flight commercial barristers Brick Court Chambers. Lawyer Bill Wood and his wife Tonia were friends of Marc's. Tonia rode and was at one stage a master of the Heythrop, but neither of them were particularly interested in dressage. But something about the story captured the imagination, and it captured Bill's enough for him to put it to his chambers and get a vote to support us. So 'Doob' became Legal Democrat and we could go travelling. For Marcia, who hadn't had a holiday in twenty years as she couldn't bear to be parted from her horses and who joked that she would only go on holiday if Doob went too, it was time to get a passport.

Our first trip abroad was to Schoten. I'm not sure where we finished, but because Doob's home in England was next door to an 'animal kingdom' he was perfectly at ease with all the zoo noises. It was during the journey home that we had the first big travel drama. We got stuck on the docks at Calais. There was a raging storm and in those circumstances they won't take horses on the boat. Marcia was practically throwing up she was so terrified of getting on the ferry and her friend Corinne wasn't much better. And in the lorry behind Emile was worried about Legrini, who'd been showing signs of colic.

We eventually boarded. You weren't supposed to stay below during the crossing but invariably one of the crew saw the sense in someone staying with the horses, which of course Emile and his groom did to keep an eye on Legrini. Bernie and I went upstairs to ring Katarina Ostborn, Legrini's owner, from the purser's office and ask her to have a vet waiting in Calais. As there was little more we could do, we went to the truckers' lounge for roast lamb – the truckers' lounge is by far the best eatery on a ferry and in those days it was certainly the only place you'd get real cutlery and proper napkins instead of plastic and paper. The roasts were always good. Then we went back downstairs to find Marcia and Corinne huddled in the lorry, frightened out of their lives. Fortunately Legrini was OK by the time we got to Dover, but this lovely, talented horse was plagued by colic.

Poor Marcia, for such an unseasoned traveller she never got an easy ride. She once put her hand into the lorry just as there was a gust of wind and the door slammed. Result: broken fingers, thumb wrapped up in a tail bandage. The only thing she could do was to take endless painkillers, so when we finally made it onto the ferry poor Marcia was upside down on the Luton, drugged out of her eyeballs.

Then there was the trip to Goess, right up in the north of Holland. The weather seemed colder in those January days and my God it felt about minus 300; it was so bad the lorry had iced up on the inside. Again the ferries were delayed due to the bad weather and we were there for hours, which I filled by watching *Titanic* on DVD.

At Hickstead CDI in July, Doob delivered what Marcia considered her best ever present when we won our first international grand prix on her birthday. We'd also done OK in Arnhem for seventh in the special so that year, 1997, I was back on the team for the Europeans in Verden, Germany. There was me on Doob, Emile on Legrini, Fiona Bigwood on Dance and Fly, and Kirsty Mepham on Dikkiloo. The whole trip was a shocker. It was incredibly hot, something like thirty-five degrees, and the trouble started when we had a puncture on the M25 and were stuck there for hours. We stopped overnight with Katarina in Kent, then set off for the ferry and Verden the next day. Emile and I drove in convoy, but neither of us had much idea (and my record was pretty lousy, remembering Wiesbaden) of how to drive lorries on German dual carriageways and autobahnen, nor were there speed limiters on the lorries in those days. I pulled out to overtake a truck that was going at what seemed to me a tortoise pace. Then I couldn't get back in; this queue of lorries on my right went on for about two miles and nobody would let me pull in. Emile was behind me, and behind him was about three miles' worth of cars all hooting and tooting.

We'd just driven for probably twelve hours and it was still hot. Our horses were so unprepared and when we arrived Doob was dehydrated. It was the first time ever Finland had fielded a team, yet they had a vet with them – we didn't in those days – whom Kyra Kyrklund kindly roped in to help Doob.

Our test was a disaster. On our final centre line Doob executed a perfect levade. He sat on his bottom, literally, like a dog. In *L'Année Hippique*, the big glossy annual we all wanted to be in, Dirk Caremans' photograph showed the top of my hat between Doob's ears. It was captioned 'Great Britain's Carl Hester and Legal Democrat performing a movement which would not be considered "classical" in dressage circles'. It was the only mention the Brits got. We finished eighth of the nine teams, none of us qualified for the individual, and I cheekily thanked Kyra Kyrklund, who'd been a star for years and was ninth individually, for bringing two friends to make up a Finnish team so at least we weren't last.

At the national championships Doob pulled out all the stops and gave me my second national grand prix title – he was the first horse ever to win the title in his first year at grand prix – and I was proud to be named Spillers Equestrian Personality of the Year again. It was hugely satisfying personally to prove wrong all those people who'd been so quick to put my previous win down to financial backing. We'd overruled (Bill and Brick Court didn't interfere but maybe something rubbed off!) the odds and that in itself gave me a buzz. Doob had fans coming up at shows and people who didn't know Marcia were ringing up, sending cards and enquiring after his welfare. It was a fairy tale. We had done it our way, and the story wasn't over yet.

Winning the national title on Doob had been the highlight, but the nationals as a whole had been a good haul. It was thrilling for Lizzie Henshaw, who worked part time for us, that Akkordion and I won the medium championship, especially as Lizzie had been furiously gulping Rescue Remedy to calm her 'owner nerves'. Donnersong had been advanced medium champion the previous year and unbeaten apart from one second when he spooked early in the season. That year he won the prix st georges championship, much to everyone's delight, with Nicky Barrett second on Cerruti (probably not to her delight!), but for us both that was a brilliant finish to the year.

I was training horses but I still needed training. We always do in this game, it never ends and it never will. My good friend Anni MacDonald-Hall was training with Bert Rutten in Holland and both Nicky and I decided to go. We had some wild times there with the horses. Nicky had Versace and Cerruti, and I went with Donnersong. We'd stay in a flat with a Canadian girl – Mad Marge, we called her – and the three of used to sit up in the evening playing cards and drinking wine.

Training abroad is something you should be honoured to be able to do, but by God it's a lonely life. It could be pretty desperate, just you and one horse for weeks on end, sitting around, watching and turning into a vegetable, and not knowing when your lesson would be as you'd be fitted in whenever the trainer could do it. I loved it though. Bert was a very good influence on my life then; someone I could talk to and get advice from on starting off again on my own. His dad, Jo, had ridden in the Olympics, and they'd bred some superstar horses. Jo Rutten was well known for his hat and cigar. Bert smoked cigars too, but when his dad came in to the school you'd just see a brim and a puff of smoke before Jo himself was revealed.

Until a few years prior, my job every day and what I'd become used to was a routine of structured riding on quality trained horses. Now there were no 'made' grand prix horses, I was training my own and feeling my way, and this was something I had never done unsupervised. It made me realise how long it takes to get established; thankfully, I started to get some young horses in myself.

I'd met Anne van Olst at the Barcelona Olympics but only got to know her properly during the Mondorf Europeans. She had suggested I visited her place, and at one stage she and her husband Gertjan asked me to come over so Anne and I could run her yard together. It was funny because after the Bechtolsheimers my first thought was that I'd have to take a job abroad if I wanted to stay in the game, and I had been in talks with Decia DePauw in Belgium, but my heart was in England. Anne and Bert Rutten got me into buying my own youngsters, which was scary at the time, but the thing about owning the horses yourself is that no one can take them away.

So I bought Fantastic Elastic – my name for him, not his original Dutch one – from Bert. He was by Clavecimbel, a stallion tipped for the competitive top until he was injured on the way home from competing with Bert at Goodwood, and I paid about two and a half grand for him as a youngster out of the barn. Then I bought Jaguar through Anne for about four thousand.

When you consider how many people buy million-pound horses these days, what those first youngsters of mine achieved, and the ones that came after, proved to be a really good success rate. Elastic was a project when it came to break him in. Igor Schechter had come to me for lessons at Stow. A great, tall Russian he was setting up a business breaking young horses in. I could see he was a calm, caring rider, which was why I sent Fantastic Elastic to him for breaking and later Donald. He'd set up at this place next to a country house with a walled garden arena and cottage – a beautiful setting and I didn't know it then but it was about fifteen minutes from where I am now. I remember going over to see Elastic, then on returning home hearing the news that Igor couldn't walk as Elastic had come over backwards on him. That Elastic, who turned out to be one of the gentlest horses you could imagine, was one of the most difficult to break in was I think partly due to me tying a dummy on his back. He went absolutely bonkers and it was one of the daftest ideas I came up with. I can't think now what possessed me but this straw dummy, more suited to Halloween, obviously possessed Elastic. He was so sharp as a youngster that I had no intention of getting on, so I thought it was worth a try. By the time Elastic arrived at Igor's to be broken in I'd probably done more harm than good and he nearly flattened all six feet four of Igor in the process, but he ended up the gentlest soul.

Early in 1998 there was a new four-legged addition to the yard. He made the national press and was on breakfast television. Kate always had a selection of canines around but the arrival of a 2lb puppy after a caesarean section to relieve the 12lb Jack Russell Meggie of her unexpected burden was a shock all round. The patter of not-so-tiny paws was the result of a secret assignation between Meggie and Kate's Rottweiler, Cutter, who weighed in at 133lb. Kate thought he must have got the relevant part of his anatomy through the wire of Meggie's run, to which she was confined while in season. The result, Dexter the Russweiler, has been my companion for fourteen years now and hasn't lost the opinionated legacy of his child stardom. I'd given Rupert to Becky's son Tom a couple of years before as Tom adored him and I was in the car too much. Becky later became the landlady of The Plough at Temple Guiting, the famous racing pub, when she married owner Craig Brown, and Rupert was resident terrier in The Plough until he died aged eighteen.

That winter was a lot more bearable due to the new indoor school we had installed. It cost most of the money I'd put by for a rainy day, but at least it meant I didn't have to spend my days riding in the rain. Kate's concentration on her breeding programme (horses not dogs) and the Donnerhall/Pastiche partnership had produced Donnersong, Donner Rhapsody – who was known as Madonna or 'Madge' for short – and Donner Dancer, who was bought by our friend Jackie Beaven. They all went on to international grand prix and Madge was later bought by my dear friend Anni MacDonald-Hall.

Otto was still a pain – or a prospective pain for me if I'd let him dump me again, which I was determined not to – and wherever we went I would always lunge him first. If you didn't, he'd get you. I learned that he would stop first and put his back up and that you couldn't ride through it, so I'd get off, lunge him and after he'd had a buck I could get on again. When he was seven we were guinea pigs for a Klaus Balkenhol clinic at Stoneleigh and my God he literally ripped me in half as I sat a particularly extravagant buck. Flamboyance has its down side.

I had lots to ride but one new ride, the lovely Maxwel who'd bag me both the small tour national championships later that year, was to lead to great things through his owner Roly Luard. I was also doing clinics in Jersey around that time and had met the Greens – Paul, his wife Jenny and their daughter Gemma, who wanted to go into pony dressage. We found Daphne for her; a gorgeous little chestnut aged five. Daphne was by Dressman, the legendary pony sire and one of the best ever dressage ponies who won six team and two individual golds for a succession of German pony riders, and she was extremely talented. With the small, neat and tidy Jo Barry up, we trained Daphne to pony international level.

The big event of the year, the World Equestrian Games, was to be held in Rome (that had been decided after Ireland pulled out) in October. Doob and I had a win at Royal Windsor; hard to imagine these days, I know, but it was on grass. Then Doob did something to his fetlock while out in the field and so had an enforced break on box rest. Marcia did all his re-fittening work and I only started riding him again three days before the national championships. I didn't know what to expect, it was a bit of an unknown quantity but Doob did one of the best grands prix he'd ever done and we took our second national title in a row. We'd missed Rotterdam as Doob wasn't fit enough, but despite the championship win we were not picked for Rome, which I was quite miffed about – and I wasn't the only one. Bless Simon Barnes who wrote with delicious irony that I was the brightest thing in British Dressage, which no doubt explained why I wasn't going! But I went to help the Kiwi eventers, who won team gold by a distance. Only poor Sally Clark had a bad run when Squirrel Hill spat the dummy on the cross-country. Blyth and Teddy won gold, Mark won silver on Broadcast News, and Vaughn and Bounce were fourth.

Those years were happy, fun times. I had met Spencer Wilton through riding for the Bamfords – he was working there – and when our relationship developed he not only moved into the cottage but came to work with me at the yard. Duncan Whitney-Groom, who had been working for me, went to the Bamfords. Spenny had evented mainly, as I had, but had a natural seat and plenty of talent. We were running the yard together, I was having successes, he was starting to make his way up and everything was good.

I was also working on my first book with Bernie, *Down to Earth Dressage*, which was born out of a whole series of articles we'd done for *Horse and Rider*, the magazine that had been such a support to me over the years. The aim was to produce a jargon-free book for anyone to be able to follow, with lots of lovely pictures. It was launched the following year and one of our favourite comments was from a lady who said she read it in the bath.

Doob and I were selected for the European Championships in Arnhem. He was brilliant and we got through to the individual final, my first on him. We were thirteenth overall, one behind Richard Davison and Hiscox Askari.

Doob missed Arnhem previously because of a bizarre mishap. I had stopped at Anne van Olst's for some training. Doob, as a big heavy horse, had always had a bit of a problem with his breathing and he'd been coughing for a while, and Anne suggested we put the ventilator on him. Anne's groom at the time was supposedly an expert with the ventilator, so Marcia and I agreed that he could go on it and obviously we watched her do it. But instead of the camomile that she was supposed to put in, the girl had put cleaning fluid in by mistake. It was horrendous. Fifteen seconds after she'd strapped the ventilator onto Doob's face, this thing began bubbling and then there were fumes coming out. Suddenly Doob started retching. We got the thing off him as fast as we could and took him out of the stable – he was doing these huge heaving coughs, coughing and coughing. The fluid had burnt his windpipe. It was the worst bloody disaster and Marcia understandably was beside herself, or least beside Doob as he spent the night outdoors in the sand paddock while Marcia slept on a camp bed beside him.

So Doob couldn't compete in Arnhem, but Donnersong did and

won the prix st georges there – his first international small tour win. And I beat Anky on Junior, which was quite a coup as she was at the height of her career with Bonfire, winning everything. But the Europeans were great for all of us and that year would end on a high.

We tried having Democrat at my yard but that was another pure horse story. Having been brought up by Marcia since she'd seen him over a stable door aged two and a half, Democrat was used to his routine and didn't thrive in ours. If he'd taken himself off to graze on the back lawn, as he did at home, Kate's mother Mrs Masek would have had a blue fit for starters! Although it seems unbelievable now that a horse could compete internationally and be as successful as he was with me riding him here just a couple of days a week every three weeks, which was the only time Marcia could get down and stay, is incredible. If anyone had said at the time of that *Horse and Rider* competition, 'This is what will happen ...' we'd never have believed it was possible. But it worked; obviously not to the standard of today, but it worked then.

Jo Barry had been on pony team with Duntarvie Edward and was the perfect jockey to train Daphne. The international pony test, at medium level, is quite a big ask for kids. Daphne had three lovely gaits and such a trainable temperament, so at the age of seven she went off to Pony Europeans with Gemma, both of them lacking in experience, and in 1999 they went on to win team silver in Sweden. It was an absolutely brilliant, a super-fast dream come true for Gemma.

The national championships that year were our busiest yet. We had eight horses there, so Jo took the less experienced young ones up to stay at Stoneleigh, to give them a bit of the experience they'd need for their international careers. The first win was Gemma and Daphne's in the elementary restricted, then I helped Henriette with her five-year-old Astonish, who won the open novice, and Kate was thrilled when Madonna and I won the medium championship. Spencer won his first national title on Elastic, the open elementary, then I'd taken the reins for the Blue Water Hotel Championship, for which the prize was a holiday in Antigua.

I had two shots at that, and the hot money was on a little horse I'd bought from Mette and Michel Assouline. 'Peanuts' had a lot of issues but would have been a winner in the show ring – we called him the 'show hack'. He got terribly anxious when away from other horses and wasn't much help with the holiday I was determined to win as he shrieked all the way through the test and only showed signs of his wonderful expression when going towards his friends. All the same I knew he had the makings of a top horse and that everyone would hear a lot more of Peanuts, or Escapado, to give him his proper name.

Carol and Paul Christie, from Newcastle, had bought a half-share in Elastic and I could see sun and sand on Carol's face as I went in on Elastic. The test was judged on training and way of going and Elastic's mature head seemed to sense the importance. We won it, we were off to Antigua.

The grand prix championship was in two parts and Doob scored his highest ever mark – 71 per cent – in the freestyle. He did a great grand prix the next day but when they announced the scores wouldn't be revealed until after the interval Marcia nearly expired of nerves. Bernie had to take her to the score tent because she couldn't stand the suspense. When the two of them returned, desperately trying to keep straight faces, I knew Doob had done it. It was a championship where a lot of dreams came true to round off a brilliant year.

Marcia, who didn't own a passport until Doob first went abroad, had found the trips a real strain. The thought of her beloved Doobs flying across the world, even for an Olympic Games, was too much. She'd also found the team regime very stressful. We all had, and it wouldn't change for a while. It wasn't a good approach to try to force her to sign a contract or put pressure on her to leave Doob with me full-time, which we knew was a non-starter in any case. But what a journey we'd all had.

Racehorse owner Paul Green told me that if I found a horse that was capable of going to Sydney, he would buy it. He wanted a stallion. He already owned Carvills Hill, winner of the Welsh National in 1991, Hors la Loi winner of the 2002 Champion Hurdle, and he'd had many other major racehorses in his life. We didn't have long, because Olympic rules on ownership said the horse had to be purchased by 1 January and registered. Time was running out when we found Gullit in Germany. He'd come over from Australia, having been produced by Matthew Dowsley who was reserve for Rome. We'd seen him at small tour at Schoten CDI with Matthew. Gullit, then eleven, was a talented horse but with stallion tendencies in the ring. He'd done a couple of grands prix with Hubertus Schmidt – and therein lies a lifelong lesson. Never underestimate the talent of some riders and how they can conjure up performances! Gullit was super sensitive at home and if you carried a whip you would have won a gold medal, but the minute that whip was down he knew what he was doing, or rather not doing.

I didn't have long to try and fathom out his personality. As luck would have it, my biggest success with Gullit came in Arnhem, the last show before team selection. I'd left him in his stable the day before his test, apart from literally just walking him – no training – and on the day of the test I rode him for twenty minutes, went in the arena and achieved the best score I'd ever got and one of the highest scores for our team, so we were selected for Sydney on that.

Gullit might have been clever, but we were now getting into team training politics. Conrad Schumacher, the German who had coached Sven Rothenberger, Holland's Ellen Bontje and other prominent names, had been employed as British team trainer. I will say he was a great trainer; Schumacher has fantastic training methods for the old classical basics and self-carriage, but there was no room for managing the individual. All my attempts in Sydney to get across that I needed to make sure the horse was super fresh for the day came to nothing. Olympics are exciting, but we went to Sydney for a month so by the time of the competition all the excitement had gone out of the main arena, all the excitement had gone out of the warm-up and all the excitement had gone out of all the horses. After three weeks they were used to it.

I was varying Gullit's routine – Mary King was rather surprised to see us out on the gallops – and my opinion was that the horse should have the day off before his test so that he would be fresh, but again I was told he must work the day before and do a bit of this and a bit of that, which was all training stuff. With hindsight, Paul Green, who had flown out with Jenny as a spectator, was absolutely right. They had watched Gullit the day before in training and after the test Paul said, 'Well, you won your medal the day before, didn't you.' And he was spot on, because the day before the competition Gullit was fresh and on the actual day he wasn't. I felt I was rowing not riding to get him through that test. And it was a disaster – the highest score was Emile's 66, then there was me, Richard and Kirsty on 65, 64 and 63 per cent.

The Games themselves were the best, and the Anky van Grunsven v Isabell Werth duel finally came to an end as Anky won the gold and Isabell's wonderful campaigner Gigolo completed his final championship with silver before both horses headed for happy retirement with ceremonies that year for Gigolo in Stuttgart and Bonfire two years later at Den Bosch. Sadly, I didn't even have Vaughn, Bounce and the Kiwi event team to cheer me up as the New Zealand team bubble had burst when two of their horses pulled out lame after cross-country.

Honestly, of all the shows I have ever ridden, that one was a complete disaster. As a team we felt broken and the worst thing was we returned home to a barrage of abuse.

With such a big build-up, as always with Olympics, plus the fact it was the first time we'd had lottery funding, well, it was purely embarrassing and took a dreadful toll on morale for all us I think. We didn't know where to go or what to do. Apart from Germany and Holland, most countries had their ups and downs, but the USA was then consistent in coming out to get medals when it mattered and they claimed bronze, the Danish and Spanish were thereabouts, and the Aussies had a great show on home ground led by Kristy Oatley on Wallstreet for sixth.

There'd been this whole hype that we were going to win a medal, a load of blah blah blah and trumpet-blowing, and it was misplaced – certainly behind the scenes the riders thought so. Too much hype, not enough reality. And basically we all fell for it. But we were used to heading home, or at least I was, thinking, 'That's it, we were always going to be making up the numbers.'

9

Stockholm Made Your Name,
or 'A Love Story'

For some reason back in 1998 I had said that I would give myself 'ten to fifteen years to reach the top' and was quoted on it. It was the late Pegotty Henriques who'd told me 'Stockholm made your name but the future will make your reputation'; Alan Smith, the *Daily Telegraph's* esteemed equestrian correspondent, had made a prediction along the same lines, and the message resonated. Alan was always such a support, but as he kept talking about retiring I felt I ought to get a wiggle on if I was going to give him something really good to write about.

Sydney had been a downer in so many ways, and I hadn't even been able to restore my spirits with a raid on the national championships as we were away while they were on – unlike Vaughn, who won the three-star event at Puhinui later that year for a swansong on amazing Bounce, who at eighteen would enjoy a long and happy retirement until he died at the ripe old age of thirty. Gullit would go on to be a schoolmaster for Gemma and be part of the victorious Young Rider Euro Cup team at Addington and the highest-placed British combination at the Saumur young riders' international. In 2003 they were members of the British team at the European Young Rider Championships where they finished just out of the medals in fourth. Gullit retired four years later and lived until he was twenty-two.

On the young horse front, things were definitely starting to come together. Suzanne Davies (now Lavendera) had been training with me for a while on her stallion Keystone Favoriet, then DiMaggio came into her life. One highlight of 2000 was when Suzanne and I went off to the World Breeding Federation Championships for Sport Horses in Arnhem. DiMaggio was already British four-year-old champion, but that a British-owned and ridden horse could triumph over the might of Europe at what must have been one of the first of these World Championships was unheard of! I rode her other horse, Keystone Waterford, and came seventh. Henriette was there too on the six-year-old Astonish, who would be such a grand prix stalwart for her, and I also had Brad, Legal Hotshot, who should have been a hotshot given his talent, but a weird tendon and a ridiculous and avoidable accident while he was at a rehab centre put paid to that. He went to enjoy the quiet life on Sark and now lives near home with Claire.

Claire had been one of my carriage-driving colleagues on Sark and unusually for a seasonal worker had stayed on. She returned to the mainland when I was at Dr B's and we rekindled our friendship, but eventually she went back to the island. Mum and Jess had separated and divorced before I went to the Bechtolsheimers' and Mum had moved away. I had a telephone message from Claire one weekend saying she needed to speak to me. I was out partying and didn't get round to ringing her back until the Monday. What she wanted to tell me was that she had married my father, Jess. Although it was a weird thing to have happen, the positive side was that Claire was to prove instrumental in reuniting me with my father. She helped us rebuild our relationship, which had fallen by the wayside since I left. Although the marriage didn't last it is lovely that we all get on and that Claire and Jess get on; they worked together, they built things together and were a great team. So we've been friends all those years and Claire now lives nearby.

Dolendo, known as Donald, had come into our lives via a phone call from Sandy Phillips. He was with Christian Heinrich in Germany and Sandy told me although he had some issues I should go and take a look at him. I didn't, I bought him over the phone, unseen, and picked him up and brought him home with us from the Arnhem Europeans.

Well, over the years Donald has had more operations than any horse I've ever met and is a prime candidate for a place in the Natural History Museum when he dies, but right now at the age of twenty he's still sound and going well as a wonderful schoolmaster for Julia Hornig of Classic Dressage. Yet veterinary opinion when Donald was five was that he would never go international grand prix. Donald had massive splints, dished badly, had grown an extra lip in his mouth so he couldn't breathe properly, had bone chips in his hocks – and that's not the end of it! He was also very nappy and was eliminated from his first competition – a young horse class – at the age of four when he refused to come out of the line. I'd given Igor the ride on him in those early years and sure enough, despite Donald being chucked out of a qualifier, they went on to win the Badminton Young Horse Championship. Donald was one of our important lessons, which is that some horses don't mature until they are nine years old, and until he was that age he was a walking disaster – and at times not even walking. The time and effort that went into getting him sound, healthy, fit and then keeping him right was worth it as he did win an international grand prix and was national champion. Then there was Peanuts, the little neigh-box.

Jo Barry had left us after Sydney to go back home to Scotland and set up her own business. Having initially joined us for three months she'd stayed four years, eighteen months of which was on 'notice' as I'd desperately wanted her to come to the Olympics with me. It's only now I realise it's like fledglings leaving the nest; Jo still returns for training, battling through snow to get here and back. As a youngster herself, Jo was proud to see Gemma do so well on Daphne, having done all the groundwork, and I feel the same way now about Jo and her quiet riding and talent for bringing on young horses. That talent was in evidence when she rode Legal Jaguar to third in the winter and national championships, and the young Brad at novice and elementary, among others. Suzanne Davies had loaned her first horse Keystone Swahari for Jo to do Young Riders and introduce her to small tour, but 'Hari' sadly went lame before the final team trial.

I'd advertised in *Horse and Hound* for a groom – the first and last time I ever advertised – and Caroline Dawson applied. Kate's husband Stuart Carter had been at the hunting yard where Caroline was working at the time. He'd gone there to sell insurance, but while he didn't have any luck persuading Caroline on that front, he caught her interest when he mentioned that his wife owned Donnersong and that I was based at his wife's yard. She asked him if there would be any chance of doing some summer work with us between hunting seasons. He told Caroline we'd be advertising for a groom soon, and she duly found the advert in *Horse and Hound* and applied. The rest is history, but even after all that effort, Stuart never did get an insurance policy out of her.

Caroline grew into her job and like Jo became a great asset, a horse-friendly, caring person who adored Peanuts in particular and was always there for him as a security blanket. She distinctly remembers the moment she fell in love with Peanuts. She'd not been with us long and in the build-up to Sydney I had my hands full without Peanuts' constant demands for attention. Quite often I'd abandon the school work and take him for a canter around the field to let off steam, but one day I got so exasperated that I brought him in and said to Caroline, 'Do what you want with him – hunt him, school him, show him whatever you want, he's yours. I've had enough!' Caroline relates how she began unsaddling Peanuts and he looked at her with those huge expressive brown eyes, 'almost as if he was crying', then thrust his head into her arms and snuggled up to her, and that was the beginning of total love. What none of us knew then was that Peanuts would take a starring role in the next Olympics. There were three of us in that marriage, Caroline!

The Stow days were great. Once we had the indoor school and

could escape the worst of winter weather it was merely a case of sticking to the outer edges of the fields to hack – if not, we'd incur the wrath of the farmer who owned the fields. Woe betide anyone who let a horse go on a bucking spree while hacking and left the track – or, more to the point, left tracks in the crops. The farmer's wrath would be delivered to Mrs M, Kate's mother, who would then deliver it to us, generally from a bedroom window as we walked the horses past the house up the track to the school. Amazing how deaf we could be.

We'd hack down to the water at Lower Slaughter, just as I'd done with Jannie, until the road became too dangerous with drivers not giving a damn about slowing down for horses – especially on the major bend at the bottom of the road – but while we did it the water was an enormous aid to Otto taking his first passage steps. We'd always take the young horses down there with the older ones who knew the ropes, and from the initial splayed front feet and askance look they'd go in and love it, just as the eventers had done.

Stow was very much Kate's mother's house and Granny was there too. It was a hugely convenient location in many ways and the Little Chef got a lot of custom from us for breakfast on Sundays after hacking. The garage next door was also hugely convenient and patronised by everyone on the yard for munchies, drinks and 'any other light refreshments' as they say on trains and planes. If I nipped up there and there was a queue, generally consisting of people I knew, I'd take the Julie Walters route in the *Wood and Walters* café sketch: 'Can I press by? I'm a diabetic.'

One day Kate informed me that the drains were blocked. I say 'informed', it was more a case of complaining and looking at me as if to ask what was I going to do about it. I probably looked blankly back. Anyway, we got the drain brain or whatever it's called and they found there were more empty packets of Walkers crisps in those drains than walkers on all the footpaths in the Cotswolds. It turned out that Granny, who was a diabetic, had been hoofing it up to the garage, buying her crisps – which were banned, due to her condition

– and flushing the packets down the loo to destroy the evidence.

Gemma was moving on from ponies to juniors, and there was the perfect horse for her in the yard: Maxwel. I'd better explain the significance of this transition, because getting to know Roly Luard, Maxwel's owner, was going to be of major importance in my life. It started when Roly had a horse called Elegant with Ulrik and Henriette. Ulrik was riding him for her. I'd come across them at an event and been introduced by Lizzie Henshaw, Akkordion's owner. Ulrik had been on the Danish Young Riders' event team, so we all had a lot in common. At that time Ulrik was the competition rider and Henriette was the back seat in the partnership. I had met Roly a couple of times through Posy, but I got to know her better through Henriette and Ulrik, as Henriette had started coming for lessons and we'd all been out for dinner a few times.

Roly was interested in having a horse with a British rider. She'd bought a horse for herself, which was Maxwel. Dear Maxwel was better known for the size of his hocks than his competition record. He had two of the biggest capped hocks I'd ever seen and no tail (or at least a very short one which offered no cosmetic cover-up to his hocks). He'd got a little bit backward thinking with her – he wasn't the most forward thinking at the best of times, but he had some real highlights such as a good extended trot and changes, so Roly asked whether I'd like to start with Maxwel and we decided I would take him out at small tour level. I was to win both the small tour national championships on him in 1998 – a poignant victory for Roly, as her husband Roger had tragically died shortly before Maxwel's greatest moment and she felt it was a fitting tribute to him. But Maxwel was never going to be a grand prix horse, so Roly suggested we find him a home and look for something else. He was a perfect schoolmaster and, as luck would have it, he was ideal for Gemma, who then took him to successfully make the transition to Juniors and Young Riders.

It was Roly who spotted Peanuts. Michel Assouline had rung her up about him; she had a look, then called me and said she thought she'd found a horse I might like. So, I went down to Mette and Michel's to meet Peanuts, or Escapado. I can't remember being wild about him when I tried him, but he had an excellent hind leg and a lovely trot, although he had a tendency to neigh all the time. I thought, well, it's the next thing to get stuck into, a good project.

Kate and Stuart had decided to move deeper into Gloucestershire, to Eldersfield where Hooze Farm offered more land for the breeding stock (and more space for their growing twins), and we moved the entire operation there in 2001. Hooze Farm was such a great place; it had 108 acres and a gallop track, as it had formerly been a racing yard, and plenty of hills. We probably had the fittest horses we've ever had there as we used to spend all hours going up and down the gallops, and it was a brilliant place to bring horses up with all that outdoor riding. Once again we had to start building the outdoor and indoor schools, so Kate and Stuart got to work. It was a cosy little yard. We put six stables in the indoor school; the rest were outdoor stables in a semi-traditional courtyard. The downside was that it was on the flight path for jets – they'd come over full and fast out of nowhere in the summer. One day I was riding Donnersong 'Otto' up on the hills and this jet came so close I swear I could see the whites of the pilot's eyes. Otto turned tail and ran at what seemed like a hundred miles an hour, giving me as much G-Force as the pilot and carting me until he ended up in a hedge head first. I got groin strain and could hardly ride for two months. I suppose the only saving grace was that I had that sucked-in cheeks look for a while. It was an ongoing risk when we were at Hooze Farm. I never worked out where the jets came from, but I think they were heading off to Wales. We did, however, have the most incredible views as the yard and house were right on the pinnacle of a hill.

Gemma was still at school and based in Jersey. In Stow there was a bed and breakfast next door to Kate's and the yard was run by a lovely couple who had literally taken Gemma in as their own, so she would stay with them in that B&B at the end of the outdoor school. That meant her parents could rest assured Gemma was in a little family unit when she came to stay with us for training. Gemma was fifteen or sixteen at the time of the move to Hooze Farm and it would have been unsettling for her as there was nowhere for her to live as family there, so I suggested that she and her horses move to Henriette and Ulrik to train.

It had taken quite a while for me to make the decision to move – there was no question about the yard but plenty about my social life. I considered staying near Stow and commuting, but being practical that was never going to work. So Spenny and I rented a bungalow in Staunton and also moved into deeper Gloucestershire. I suppose it was the biggest move since I left Sark in that I wouldn't now be ten or so minutes' drive from all my friends, the after work *soupçon* (our phrase for a glass of wine) with Bernie, Jamie and others. It was a wrench but the best thing for the horses. If you believe in star signs, which I'm not sure I do (although horoscopes used to be a lot of fun to read and I would relentlessly read friends' out loud from the daily paper while improvising furiously when it looked at all boring), but I'm a home lover and as a Cancerian like to have my shell around me, so that bit is true to type.

The following year I finally took the plunge and bought a barn conversion in Corse, outside Hartpury and not far from the yard. It had just two rooms downstairs, a kitchen and sitting room, but both were huge. It was the most fantastic house for parties and we'd have brilliant fun there. I bought it at the right time but I don't know how I managed it. I certainly mortgaged myself as high as I could. I should have been looking at a one-up, one-down, but I saw this barn and thought, 'I love it, I'm having it.' There were no ifs nor buts when I looked round the barn; it was a scary decision, but to see a place that makes you want to be there, in it, that minute – well, that's how I think you should feel about buying a house, there and then when everything's right.

Dear 'Fanny Elan', as I called Fantastic Elastic, was another who was not going to be a grand prix horse. But he had a temperament and outlook as fantastic as his name so was ideal for Gerald Bloomer, an Irish young rider, to take on and be selected for the Young Rider European Championships. He then went on to one of the Paralympic riders – I saw him at Hartpury – which was a lovely story for a lovely horse, so kind and magnificent looking.

Hooze Farm was the turning point for Peanuts. Spencer competed him at novice and elementary, as I couldn't ride at the lower levels due to having ridden internationally, and we'd shared the ride at medium level. What made the difference for Peanuts was living out during the summer months. He found the grand prix work in training extremely easy, but his tension was the element that needed managing. It always would, but after a summer living out he was rideable and relaxed enough to win the 2001 advanced medium national championship, and a year later he'd win both the small tour national titles for me.

In fact, the farm made a difference for several of the horses; Madonna didn't work in the school at all that summer, preferring the springy turf which seemed to give her a sense of freedom, while her brother Otto loved to survey the grandeur and majesty of the landscape from his own special stallion pen positioned on top of the hill. A couple of hours was enough for him though, and if it rained he'd squeal furiously, demanding to come in.

Otto was combining his competition and training with stud duties, and his first children 'the chestnut girls' – one out of Lady Bamford's Garbo that I had competed at small tour level and the other out of a thoroughbred mare of Kate's – were being broken in. But the 2001 outbreak of foot-and-mouth disease restricted stud duties and, to some extent, all other shows and outings. It may have been inconvenient for us but it was a terrible, devastating year for the farmers involved. In the meantime, especially with Peanuts' advanced medium national title and Donald winning the medium title for me, the horses were all clearly enjoying the playground that was Hooze Farm, while we were enjoying the perfect party place that was the barn. At the nationals I had won a return trip to Antigua thanks to Trish Andrews' Toblerone. They'd changed the prize to the intermediaire I freestyle, probably to stop me winning it, but Toby came up trumps and we got another spell in the sun.

Trish and her husband Peter were then neighbours in Stow, very into their racing and great fun to be with. Her Toby loved his music and while the previous year we'd come in second (no holiday involved) it was to another Trish, my old team-mate Trish Gardiner, and her beloved Moon Tiger, so I didn't mind a bit. We're all neighbours now and Trish Gardiner, well into her seventies, hacks Valegro once a week.

It's funny how Danish people have somehow ended up being a big part of my life; Anne van Olst, Anne Cohn, Henriette and Ulrik, and of course Kirsten Gill. I'd met Kirsten when I was at Dr B's; she had introduced herself to me at a show and asked if she could come and watch me ride one morning, which she did. Kirsten was another surrogate mother, such a warm person with a family-orientated outlook on life. She had two sons my age and found it somewhat odd that I was in a country I wasn't from without my family around me; I think she decided I needed taking under her wing.

Kirsten and her husband David owned Woodredon Riding School on the edge of Epping Forest, but they also had a cottage in Cold Aston, which was near Dr B's, and when I'd moved to Stow it was even closer. After I'd left Dr B's she'd suggested I might like to come and watch her training with her Danish trainer, Nils Valdemar. In need of a bit of inspiration, off I went to Woodredon.

It was the funniest thing I have ever seen. Goofy, Kirsten's nickname for her horse Kingsize, was the most unconventional dressage horse in the whole wide world and I will still put down as my greatest success winning the intermediaire II at Hickstead with him, together with the joy that it brought.

The lesson seemed rather 'old style' to me; the horse had to be almost above the bit. Goofy was an upside-down eighteen-hand chunk of a horse anyway, and he had the biggest hips – bigger than Nigella's. He was quite something to look at, but he did have an incredible engine and incredible piaffe and passage. Nowadays he would be considered a banana, because he was doing all the right stuff but in an upside down shape.

I ended up taking him on because Kirsten decided that she wasn't cut out for competition. He was my first grand prix horse after Dr B's. I'll never forget that morning at Hickstead. To get that horse on the bit was hell as he hadn't been trained to be round in his outline, and coming from Dr B's I knew the horse needed to be round, working from his hindquarters over his back into the contact. These days I'm way more savvy after years of teaching and learning and could explain the athletic stretching we do, as any athlete or dancer does, but this isn't the time. The point about this much-loved horse was, I could 'kid' him round but not ride him round – you can't make a horse that hasn't been trained in that way and isn't built to do it, do it.

That morning at Hickstead was Kirsten's greatest moment as an owner, a role she loved. I've still got the photo in my office of Kirsten in a floral dress and a straw hat. I was drawn first to go at 8.15 in the intermediaire II, a national class at the international show. We'd all had a heavy night before, off to bed at 2 a.m., absolutely tanked up I seem to remember. When I woke the weather was hot and there was a heavy early morning mist – which was to be my saving grace.

The mist was such that no one could really see at that stage what was happening at one end of the arena, so the judges couldn't properly make out his outline or my efforts to get Goofy's head down, but they could see his brilliant piaffe and passage, which at that time you did down at A in the intermediaire II so that was a stroke of luck. Anyway, he won, which was a glorious moment for Kirsten. Then I did my first grand prix on him at Solihull and won that, but tragically those wonky hips made Goofy a tricky horse to keep sound, so we decided to retire him on a high.

Peanuts was nearly ready for his first grand prix but he had become notoriously difficult to teach sequence flying changes to because he was so hot. I used to try and take four weeks a year to train in Holland with Anne, and had gone over this time with Spencer, Donald and Peanuts. I'd bought a new phone in Dubai (I went there quite a few times, either to visit Mum, who was living there at the time or for dressage shows run by Nereide Goodman whose Wellington Laska I rode for a while. He was so kind and had a distinctive blaze which replicated the Wellington logo). Anyway, this phone was a fancy little red flip-up number, one of the first of its kind, which Anne alighted on, insisting she must have it. She got a sharp response from me, I can tell you. 'I'm not giving it to you,' I told her; 'it's mine, I bought it in Dubai and wouldn't find another one in Europe like it.' I'd been commuting and was going home for a week to try to earn some money. Anne bet me my phone that by the time I returned Peanuts would be doing fifteen one-time changes. And when I got back a week later, there was Anne on Peanuts doing fifteen ones. They were the smallest, shortest ones I'd ever seen and covered all of about ten metres of ground, but he did them and I had to give Anne my phone. Anne of course was gleefully delighted to receive it.

The sunshine tour in Spain was the perfect place for Peanuts to make his international grand prix debut. I did the intermediaire II first, which he won, then in his first grand prix Peanuts gave me the highest international score I'd ever had at top level, over 69 per cent. I was more over-excited than he was! For once he actually let go in the arena instead of tightening up and he scored eights for his piaffe. The second week he was even better, winning the grand prix special with over 70 per cent in a unanimous verdict from all the judges. He was tense and ready to run in the next grand prix, but he still came second, then I hacked him before the special and it worked. It caused a lot of excitement. I'd been dropped from the World Class Performance programme a month before we left for Spain, not the best New Year's present, but by May I was back on.

I also had the ride on Sara Timpson's Celestial King, who was king of the small tour in Spain, and as there was space on the lorry I borrowed Polly Hodges' Santas from Spencer to take with Peanuts down to Italy then on to Lipica in Slovenia. The advantage would be in getting to Italy early enough for Peanuts to settle in as I was convinced he would improve as the show went on. And so he did, only missing a win in the special by a whisker with over 69 per cent, then in Lipica again the second test was his best and we notched up another special win. I knew there was a lot more to come from Peanuts, but having top judges tell me I had a top ten horse was pretty gratifying.

Peanuts had whinnied all the way through his first elementary championship and he screamed like a girl through his first test in Athens – you can hear him on the recording! His personality was very needy and his insecurity came from being on his own. Even if he was only a hundred metres from another horse he cried like a girl, and that was the sweetest thing, that squeaky neigh. Several people came to me and said they couldn't believe how a horse could piaffe like that, not moving his head, yet keep neighing at the same time. It was ridiculous but divine! I understood him, Caroline understood him, but many didn't – including the selectors.

The European Championships were at Hickstead that year, 2003. There were the obvious choices of Richard Davison, Emma Hindle and Nicola McGivern, who had been out getting the international scores, but the fourth place for the team had been swinging backwards and forwards all year. Escapado had got those scores at smaller shows but there was still the worry about how he would cope at the bigger events. Emile was also in contention for the fourth place and got the nod.

The week before the championships we went to the Fry's international where Peanuts and I won the grand prix and beat Nicola and Walero. Then I was told I was on the team and Emile was told he was the reserve. We arrived at Hickstead to be told we would have to do a ride-off. It just couldn't be done nowadays – and thank God for that; that sort of not-very-merry-go-round is unfair, it's unsportsmanlike and a totally ridiculous and utterly pointless pressure to put horses under. I can't remember who was responsible for it, and that's probably a good thing for them, but as chair of British Dressage, I think Desi Dillingham had to accept some responsibility for this mess, and although I have always loved Rosemary Herbert – or Vi Sherbert, as I called her – I could have cheerfully punched her that day.

We didn't exactly 'ride off' – there were no lances and no jousting tilts involved – but we both had to ride through the grand prix, as I remember. We were told that the selectors were going away to discuss what they had seen, and then we would all gather in the lorry park for a meeting. Well, to be fair to Emile, it was a pretty rough way of doing things; he'd been put on the team, he'd been taken off the team, I'd been put on, then we were told we would have the ride-off. So at about six thirty we all turned up. It was one of the most uncomfortable moments of my life. There we were, sitting in the lorry park with the three selected members, so it was fairly public and whoever failed to win the place would have to grin and bear it. They turned to me and said they were sorry but Emile was back on the team as fourth member and I would be the reserve.

No reason, just their decision and that was that. Caroline was desperately disappointed, as she would be for Peanuts, and Roly, well she was typical Roly, saying 'Never mind, darling', which is why she's always been such a fabulous owner. I wanted to stay and support the team, that wasn't a problem for me, but if the whole thing had been embarrassing up to that moment, it was about to get a damn sight worse.

The stands were full for the Hickstead European gala evening and there was to be a team parade. We were all seated around this table and a buggy arrived at the tent to pick us all up and take us around the arena. The five of us got up. 'Not you, *daawling*, you're the reserve,' drawled Desi Dillingham to me as she swept the others off, leaving me sat at this table all on my own while the team went off to parade in front of the crowds. Considering I had dressed up with the team, come in with the team, if I could have crawled under a stone I would have. It was a weird, weird evening.

That Hickstead episode could have finished me, but I was determined to turn it round. I thought to myself, 'Right, I'm going to get this.' I believed in Peanuts and I knew that if he was given the days to be at a competition venue, to get settled, he would be fine. Everything started gathering steam then, coming together, and Peanuts went from strength to strength. I really do think that it was my belief in him, and the conviction that we could do it, and that he sensed that and believed it too.

So Olympic year came round and again I took Peanuts to Spain for the sunshine tour as I thought – well, I knew – that psychologically for Peanuts to be in one place for three weeks, being plaited every week, doing shows every week, it would get him to realise it was no different to being in a training arena. It was all about getting his confidence to be the same away as it was at home. That, I felt, was what would make him, and by the final week in Spain he completed a hat trick of grand prix wins, including the freestyle. It was a lovely trip as Anni MacDonald-Hall was there too with 'Madge', Donner Rhapsody.

The big problem in 2004 was Aachen. Everyone involved in selection said Peanuts had to go to Aachen, and my response was an emphatic 'No, that's not the show for this horse'. It meant a long drive and then competing the following day, and Aachen's a huge, buzzing show, the biggest show in the world atmospherically. I knew Peanuts was not going to manage that. Needless to say everyone argued that if he was going to the Olympics he ought to be able to cope with Aachen, but my argument was that heat would be a factor at the Olympics – we knew all along Athens would be hot – and I wanted to be there for a week before the competition because that would suit Peanuts. Instead they insisted I rode at Aachen.

We came last on the first day. Peanuts totally freaked out, he was so tense, and while he wasn't unrideable it was as if he had regressed to being a baby again. I was back on a baby grand prix horse. The atmosphere terrified him. For the team place it was a battle between me and my old friend Peter Storr, who was also in the running on Gambrinus. I don't think Gambrinus would have been a horse for the heat, but he performed quite well in Aachen and there was a lot of talk afterwards – in fact, that's an understatement; there was a huge furore. I thank God for David Trott and give credit to him as he had the foresight to see – and actually believed – what I was saying, which was that I knew Aachen had been a bad show and knew why.

With Emma, Nicola and Richard we had a strong team that had taken team bronze the year before at Hickstead. I was confident I could pretty much trust Peanuts to do the job and David took that on board and selected me and Peanuts for Athens. So I went as fourth member, which is always the slot people have the lowest expectation of, but there was a lot of flak going around: that as I hadn't performed at Aachen I wouldn't perform at Athens, why was I selected and so on. So when we went to Athens, I realised I had a lot to prove.

I did an interview with *Horse and Hound* the week before we left. It contains one of my most famous quotes. I told them that I would take this horse to Athens and 'stick two fingers up in the air at all the doubters'. The magazine came out the day before we were competing and I remember seeing it and thinking to myself, 'What on earth have I done? This could go completely tits up.'

Richard Davison was a huge support to me as was Ferdi Eilberg, who was then team trainer. Ferdi went and recruited a few muckers to go round stamping on seats and generally making a noise while I had my ride in the main arena. That is what a team is all about, everybody helping out and pulling together for the cause. Ferdi helped stage it, Richard helped stage it.

We had these round lunging pens on site and I said I was going to turn Peanuts out in a pen as I wanted him to be loose and I want him to let rip. Everybody said I was crazy, but I turned him loose and he did let rip and he pulled a shoe off, which gave everyone, me included, something to freak out about. But he was absolutely fine and it got rid of all the tension he was obviously feeling. We managed him every step of the way for that Olympics, and naturally he had his security blanket, Caroline, caring for him all the time.

As the fourth member, I was drawn first. Peanuts was tense in the grand prix and he did neigh, but he was so rideable and did some brilliant piaffe and passage. He was wonderful, he didn't make a mistake and when we came out I punched the air with delight. We scored over 70 per cent, which was the magic marker in those days, and were fourth individually after the first day with the team in bronze medal position. I was over the moon. Peanuts had done what I had said he would do if they would let me manage him. Bernie was commentating for the BBC with Mike Tucker and told Peanuts' story – the BBC website got loads of supportive responses.

Sadly the rest of the team that year did not get the performances they had wanted, and there was no medal, but in the special Peanuts was magnificent. He was only eleven and for that level of his training, a little over a year and a half at grand prix, he really did his utmost. I practised my halt before entering the arena and Peanuts waved his front paw, which was not a good sign, but that test was one of the best rides I can remember having. Even though the scores didn't match the levels I'd reach and the sport would reach in years to come, it stands out because of the feeling of total adoration for Peanuts – I was ready to lie down and die for him – and what he had overcome to have achieved that test, and ninth place overall.

I was sorry that my mate Richard hadn't reached the freestyle after being the second highest placed British rider in the grand prix, but it was to lead to an extraordinary act of generosity and quite possibly madness. We were in a restaurant having dinner and celebrating how well Escapado had gone that day when I said to Richard that I didn't think my 'Here Comes the Sun'/'Isla Bonita' music was up to Olympic final standard. I hadn't in all honesty thought much about getting that far, only about reeling in a good grand prix score for the team, and it wasn't a difficult programme either as the music hadn't exactly been a priority for Peanuts. Richard turned to me and said, 'Use mine – you've got forty-eight hours to learn it.' Richard had been extremely successful in the World Cup – the international winter freestyle series – and I'd seen him ride to that music loads of times. He says now he was being facetious, but I thought it was a terrific idea and was deadly serious.

Being an expert, Richard gave me a quick lecture on freestyle. The thing about freestyles is that you have to remember to include every compulsory movement or else the judges give you a zero for anything you miss out, therefore each freestyle is choreographed and timed to ensure the horse performs every movement exactly at the right part of the music. Freestyle programmes are totally individual for each horse and the rider has to know the plan and music well – intimately even! The time allowed according to the regulations is quite tight when it comes to fitting in all the compulsory movements so, contrary to what some people think, you cannot simply float around and make it up as you go along, as I had done with Doob at the Horse of the Year Show all those years ago.

Richard's freestyle had been specifically choreographed for Ballaseyr Royale. Known as 'Big Bird' she was a large mare with completely different movement and rhythm to Peanuts'. Every beat of the music had been edited to match the rhythm of each of Big Bird's steps. But over a glass of wine we laughed and joked as the imaginary scenario became more and more hilarious and ridiculous. For a start, the judges would think there was some mistake as Richard's music – which was familiar to the judges – started up as I made my entrance into the arena on Peanuts; this would result in much confusion and odd looks between the judges while they tried to work out what was going on. Then, to counter the all-too-real possibility that mid-test I might suddenly forget where I should be or what movement I should be doing, we set about engineering a series of secret signals so Richard could prompt me.

Over a few more glasses of wine we dreamt up a whole code of discreet signals that involved sideways head nods to turn right or left, downward head gestures to indicate slow down and upwards to go faster. By the time it came to conjuring up a head signal for a pirouette our eyeballs were spinning out of their sockets. Outside assistance is not allowed, so we then considered the danger that if Richard was spotted signalling by one the judges it could get me eliminated, or worse still, from Richard's point of view, the judge might interpret his nods and winks as a proposition for a date. It was a hilariously silly conversation.

So then, over a few more *soupçons* (wine to me, if you remember) we thought about what would happen if I forgot my way when I was at the end of the arena without Richard in sight. There were a number of riders in the restaurant and as they got wind of our conversation they all began joining in and suggesting alternative signals, so I ended up being directed around the restaurant, from one table another, in a mad frenzy. It was a great evening and very special as a result of my result with Peanuts in the special.

Richard thought it was all just banter, but at breakfast the next morning I told him I wasn't joking. It took him a while to realise I was serious, then he debated whether he should go along with it, bearing in mind he was meant to be the responsible 'elder' of the team. 'Trickie', my pet name for Richard, was told to get his skates on and finish breakfast. We were going to give it a run through and see how it worked.

I wore Richard's headset so I had the music playing in my ears while, reminiscent of scenes from the restaurant the night before, he ran around waving and shouting at me, directing me and Peanuts where to go. We attracted a crowd of other competitors and trainers as they gathered in the corner of the indoor school and tried to figure out what on earth we were doing. As the answer dawned on them we were greeted with a mixture of horror and laughter.

We caused even more confusion when it came to the official

sound-check, where each rider has the chance to set the volume levels that best suit his horse. Richard, being the World Cup expert, had to explain all this to me; while I'd done freestyles until then they had always been a bit 'on the hop' – famous last words in this case.

During the sound-check each rider is allowed to hear a part of their music for a couple of minutes before the sound technician notes the levels required and moves on to the next rider's music. Richard told me it would be quite a casual affair as riders and trainers mill about in the middle of the arena on foot, awaiting their turn or chatting with each other – bear in mind this was my first Olympic freestyle. When Richard's music struck up, he directed me to run around the arena while exclaiming this mantra-like commentary: 'canter-canter-canter-flying change-flying change' and so on. I duly ran around like a demon and everyone fell about laughing, thinking yet again we were up to our old pranks from the night before.

But when Richard, on the controls, insisted that the sound engineer play the music all the way through for the whole five and a half minutes, their amusement turned to disbelief as it sunk in that we were serious.

The final was the following day and we'd done all the practice we could. Richard and I then spent every minute of the rest of that day – in transit on the coach, playing tennis, lying by the pool or over dinner (fortunately in a different restaurant) – going through every beat of the music and the floor plan. Richard says it was the one time in my life that I didn't allow myself to be distracted by other people or take any phone calls, and that he'd never known me so totally focused. But the bottom line was we both knew we'd be in for an almighty bollocking from the team hierarchy if it all went wrong.

Bernie was in the BBC commentary box with Mike Tucker and aware both of the plan and Richard's music, so Richard – who was up on the trainers' stand, colloquially known as the 'kiss and cry stand', praying that his telepathic communication would keep me on course – had a TV camera trained on his face. I knew the programme and I felt confident with it even if nobody else did. Peanuts was hot going round the edge of the arena. I tried to halt and he did his trademark pawing with that front foot. This was a bridge too far, a wing and a prayer. He didn't really walk – he was crab-like and looking for the exit and feeling nervous as by then the stadium was packed, the flags were flapping, the music was loud and the wind was blowing. But in by far his biggest test to date, Peanuts did the best he could. I knew he was trying to get back to the other horses, he was desperately lonely, insecure and so nervous and yet he gave it everything he could. We completed the programme, we were on the mark all the way with the music, there was nothing more to ask from Peanuts. To me it showed the growth of the horse because he coped. Richard's Rodgers and Hammerstein theme was 'How Do You Solve a Problem Like Maria?' Well, Peanuts had solved his problems, or at least learned to deal with them. Bernie said something on the BBC commentary like 'Never mind Maria, here comes Peanuts!' and to me that was it: Peanuts had arrived.

Sometimes it isn't just about winning, nor is it about the best score. That day I felt that me and my horse had won. He was so shy and nervous by nature, but Peanuts did his best and that was the top of his game at the time. He'd come last at Aachen the month before, and to show up at the Olympics and do that, score over 70 per cent all the way, finish best of British and thirteenth at the Olympics, that was a huge moment. Peanuts was on the rise and that's where he took off. That Olympics made him what he became. Then he came home and he performed out of his skin at the National Championships, which he won. He deserved national recognition and praise, and he got it. I was on one hell of an all-time high and those two fingers had been firmly stuck in the air at all the doubters. We'd also given Alan Smith, Jenny MacArthur and the other 'dailies' something to write about at last.

Although some questioned my management of Peanuts' lifestyle, I never allowed it to bother me. I felt totally natural and comfortable

Kirsten's proud moment –
'Goofy' wins at Hickstead

(Author's collection)

Perfect unison: Vicki
'Queenie' Thompson
and I reprise our
winning pas de deux

(Author's collection)

Dexter takes centre stage as we open a new wing at the Blue Cross

(Author's collection)

Dear Doob won me three national titles – here we are in Levade at Verden, 1997

(© Dirk Caremans)

Enjoying the Blue Waters Hotel, Antigua – won that holiday three times!
(Author's collection)

With my father, actor Anthony Smee, my half-sister Vivien McCaig (née Smee) and
Mum, Brenda Hester, 2001 (Author's collection)

Always flamboyant – Otto at Hickstead (Author's collection)

Peanuts in
Hagen,
Euros 2005

(© Arnd Bronkhorst
www.arnd.nl)

That lap of honour,
Windsor, 2009

(Sara-Jane Lanning)

Dear Lenny and my first
team medal after 19 years,
Windsor, 2009

(© Jon Stroud/Jon Stroud Media)

Me, Polly, Jess, Jesse and Corey on Sark, 2010 (Claire Hester)

Watching Charlotte and Valegro, Rotterdam, 2011. The pictures say it all!

(© Jon Stroud/Jon Stroud Media)

First gold and my first
individual medals – I finally
caught my dream, or was
it my hat? Europeans,
Rotterdam, 2011
(©Thomas Bach Jensen/Ridehesten)

Talking to the media after it all:
part and parcel of the job
(©Jon Stroud/Jon Stroud Media)

Me with Marc, who's still supporting me and hosts a box at the National Championships 2011
(Claire Hester)

Peanuts and Donald, home to enjoy retirement, 2011 (Julia Hornig)

doing what we did; I knew my horse, I'd brought him up and I knew what he needed. Of course there was an element of risk, but I don't take uncalculated risks and I was certain that if he'd been stabled all the time that horse would never have become the star he did. When he was stabled we couldn't do a thing with him, he was too tense and too hot, but once he started living out he learned everything and could cope with doing it, even if he was in a scary environment. I don't think we would have got to the point of him learning all he had to learn, let alone being relaxed at a show, if he hadn't been relaxed at home. He had to find that first.

Erik Theilgaard – yet another Danish influence – had helped me with Peanuts. Erik has a calm temperament and was very good for me in those early stages of Peanuts' grand prix work, soothing his nerves and acknowledging that his development had to come in slow, gentle stages. I'd known Erik, who's now Development Dressage Coach for World Class, and his assistant trainer Stephen Moore, since they were based at Kate's, back when I first met her. Erik wasn't about 'technical' but he was very good at keeping the lid on! In Athens we managed to record the highest score ever by a British Olympic rider, even if we hadn't topped Chris Bartle's highest place: sixth on Wily Trout at the 1984 Olympics. But there were less competitors then, Chris!

Back at home we had a move to make. Kate and Stuart felt they wanted more of a private life with their family, Otto had been retired from top competition, and all this coincided with Anne Siefert-Cohn buying Court Farm, five miles up the road. I'd met Anne at Hickstead some years before and we'd become friends. She'd bought a stallion, Finesse, at the Vechta auction and I'd ridden him while we were at Stow. As Anne was moving from Surrey to make a new start in Gloucestershire, and didn't know anyone, it would work well and establish her in the area. Kate, Stuart and I have always been friends and still are, it was the right time to leave and the right time to move on.

I knew Peanuts was going to be sold. Roly and I had discussed it.

She had been so behind us and believed in us, and she'd been there in Athens to watch with her two children, Harry and Isabella (I still have the lovely 'Good Luck' card they sent us, the three of them looking over the stable door with Peanuts), but it had been a business arrangement from the start. I'm sure some people will find that hard to understand, especially with the bond I'd built up with him, but it's the nature of the business. In the meantime, though, there was yet another adventure in store for me and Peanuts.

I'd never done the World Cup series before but I guess some of Richard's enthusiasm must have rubbed off. First we went to Maastricht and opened our points account with fourth place. Shortly before Christmas we went to Olympia, the London Horse Show, where I had to revert to my 'Isla Bonita'/'Here Comes the Sun'/'Fame' mix as Richard for some reason wanted his music back! I had tweaked mine into a more grown-up programme, however, and I had the best ride ever on Peanuts that night. It really topped off my year. Spain's Beatriz Ferrer-Salat, a great friend, won it with her Olympic bronze-medal-winner Beauvalais, scoring 79 per cent, and Richard flew into fourth on the legendary 'Bird' Ballaseyr Royale. It's always an evening performance. I wasn't on until after ten o'clock, and although I'd tried to resist having wine with my dinner had ended up drinking about a bottle! I've never been so relaxed in a test in my life, nor had Peanuts (who obviously hadn't had a *soupçon*). The way Peanuts coped in that atmosphere – indoors, in London, at night under the lights with the crowd so close and not a blade of grass in sight – was bloody amazing! It was the first time I'd winched in a big score – over 77 per cent – and I couldn't have been prouder of my squeaking show hack.

The World Cup Final was to be held in Las Vegas that season, and although it was far removed from anything I'd ever planned before for Peanuts – I'd never thought of him as a horse for indoor shows, let alone for freestyles to music – Athens had opened a new chapter. It had been the making both of the horse and my confidence in him.

At Olympia it was a dream to ride him in such an atmosphere without that initial panic he'd given me at every other show. You'd have thought it would be a big gamble, but Peanuts was to continue like that through all the world cups. Off we went to Mechelen, our next qualifier, which starts on Boxing Day. It wrecked Christmas, but in Athens the cracks had already started to show in my relationship with Spencer. I was beginning to realise that perhaps things weren't going to work, although we didn't actually separate for another couple of years.

Anne van Olst and I had both decided to aim for that World Cup Final in Vegas, so she had taken Peanuts home after Olympia so he could spend Christmas in Holland with her and Gertjan, and I went over on Boxing Day morning. It was bloody freezing – minus 12 in the daytime – and it was snowing. Anne and I both got flu, so we were sniffling all the way through the show. I don't know how we managed it, because it's one of the most notoriously difficult rings to ride, with the crowds so close, plus as it's Christmas everyone's absolutely slaughtered so there's no peace, no relaxation, and everyone's out for a jolly. Anyway, Peanuts was brilliant and I won my first World Cup qualifier, the first Brit to win one since Anni MacDonald-Hall won in Germany at Neumuenster in 1991. Peanuts stood like a rock as they played our national anthem, although he watched closely as the flag was raised, his eyes following it all the way up. I'd booked a flight and had to leave immediately after the prize-giving, so I left Richard, who'd had a brilliant ride for third on Bird, to do the honours and collect my trophy, rug and prize money.

On we went to Amsterdam, where the atmosphere was like a pop concert. Peanuts' forefoot wave sent the crowd wild – sweet of them, but not terribly helpful – and mistakes in the one-time changes in a class as hot as the atmosphere left us seventh, but we had sixty points and were standing second in the World Cup League. We did one more qualifier, Indoor Brabant (dear old Sloggenbosch to me), got our Vegas ticket and finished equal fifth with Holland's Edward Gal in the league. I was only sad that Anne didn't get through to the final with Dexter, but she was coming to Vegas anyway.

Vegas was like arriving into a parallel universe. We were staying in the Paris Hotel, which you can't miss as it's got a stonking great Eiffel tower outside. The gambling life dominated inside and out; on my way home one night I saw someone being shot at over four lanes of traffic. Another time I was going up an escalator when a large lady on the down escalator fell – everyone else on there just stepped aside and let her roll all the way down to the bottom! It is sin city and it is crazy. In the mornings people would be lined up playing the slot machines – they'd probably been there all night.

The competition was at the Thomas & Mack Centre and the World Cup Showjumping was held at the same time so they got some phenomenal amount of people watching – over 90,000 for the whole show. It was the third time the jumping final had been held there, but a first for dressage. One of the two partners who enabled the centre to be built was Parry Thomas who, with his wife Peggy, owned Debbie MacDonald's Brentina, who was retired right there in 2009 after an iconic career for the USA. It was lovely to have Debbie visit us years later in her role as development coach for the USA.

I remember we were drawn very early for the grand prix and I think we did OK, ninth on over 71 per cent. Defending champion Anky van Grunsven on Salinero and Edward Gal, whom she was training at the time on Lingh, were the high fliers though on over 78 per cent. Those were whopping scores then. On the night of the final we were drawn among the first to go. The warm-up was in a tent at the top of a long sloping ramp and you had to go down the slope and through a tunnel into the arena. To warm the crowd up in true all-American style they had fireworks in the main arena, followed by an appearance by the entertainers and magicians Siegfried and Roy. They'd been famous in Las Vegas for their shows using white tigers and Roy had been partially paralysed after one of the tigers attacked him on stage two years before. They were bizarre-looking, all purple hair and fur coats and a nurse holding Roy's hand up to wave.

Anyway, despite the craziness out front, behind the scenes it was all nice and quiet, and Peanuts and I were having a good warm-up. Then as we made our way down the slope a big pink Cadillac came past with these two characters in the back. Peanuts was starting to light up and I could feel him coming to the boil like a pressure cooker. As we entered the arena I heard them announce my name, but I couldn't see much of anything because the smoke from the fireworks was still very heavy. As we were going round the edge, poor Peanuts started sneezing and I thought straight away, Oh my God, am I in for a rough ride here. But Peanuts being the horse he was then, he did it. He was tense, he was tight, but he did it and I was happy.

I was glad to have Anne there. I could see her peering through the smoke at the side as I was going round; my eyes were popping out of my head, her eyes were popping out of her head, but it was OK, it was fine and it was a really good final. We were tenth. Edward and Lingh did this amazing test with amazing choreography, although Anky won in the end.

It was an unbelievable trip; there was a fabulous party in beautiful gardens with the desert as a backdrop and we had a few days by the pool and did some shopping. Bernie was there, and Nicky and Richard flew out to watch, loads of friends came. But you don't get over the jet lag! Sure it was a week of no sleep and a tense atmosphere, but it was an unforgettable week and as the only World Cup Final I've ever done it was a brilliant experience, considering that the music's not my thing.

Our music was the first I'd had produced by Theo van Bruggen and it was fine, but because Peanuts was still a nervous horse I hadn't constructed a difficult programme, just concentrated on keeping the lines as straight and fluent as possible.

There's no question that journey from Athens, through the qualifiers to Vegas, set Peanuts up for the future. Of all the horses I've lost, nothing came close to what it felt like losing him. But I had agreed it with Roly and knew that was the way forward. Being a dressage competitor doesn't pay the bills, don't forget, and Peanuts was, without a doubt, a top horse and as such he was something that other people desired. Roly and I kept our heads together about it. We'd had a lot of fun, a lot of success, and she wanted to do it all over again with another horse. That was the deal and I couldn't go back on it. If I could have found someone who would have bought him, or her share, that would have been ideal, but Roly was right, our job was done – or it would be after the European Championships. Our wish was that I could ride him there.

The German rider Nadine Capellman tried him before the Europeans – three times, in fact. I don't think she quite understood my management, that Peanuts did four days a week training, hacked the other two and spent the rest of the time in the field. Nadine rode him well and I thought she would buy him, but in the end maybe the deal wasn't good enough, I don't know. I have to admit I was relieved when she didn't buy him because the regime was so different in Europe, or it was then at any rate. If a horse has been brought up as one of theirs, that's fine, but for one of mine to be brought up how I do it, then go into one of those regimes – well, I would not like it. I felt strongly about that, as I still do.

Then Hans Peter Minderhoud came along. He rode Peanuts brilliantly and so the deal was done. Again, Hans Peter had tried him before the European Championships. It was all top secret, but when he rode the horse I thought there and then that he would be great for Peanuts. We discussed Peanuts' lifestyle; Hans Peter and Edward Gal, his partner, took it all on board, agreeing that he would be turned out and so on, and the icing on the cake was that we made that deal where I could have Peanuts back after his competition life.

It was nevertheless an extremely tough decision and a sad one, but it was the right one at the time. I went to the European Championships in Hagen knowing that when those championships finished on Sunday night Peanuts would not be coming home with me. Even so, that European Championship was fantastic. I didn't think 'Oh my God, he's not coming home', not in any of my rides. I just rode Peanuts like I always rode him.

Seventh in the grand prix, he led the team to fifth place. Then we were third in the special and Peanuts earned his and my first ever ten, although sadly not a medal as at the time there were no separate medals for special and freestyle. The freestyle was difficult for him as it was raining and umbrellas were going up among the spectators around the arena; he didn't really walk, but the two of us finished fifth overall. Again he did his best and again he was the top British horse, the team leader.

Then on the Sunday night Peanuts went on the lorry to Holland. It was very hard when the lorry came back to the yard without him on it, so very sad. Later, Hans Peter took him out to Florida and they were second in the freestyle, and then they went on to win the freestyle in Aachen, of all places, along with a host of other wins. I realised then that my pleasure was in seeing him do that. It gave me a big boost to think, 'We've trained him, we've brought him up and there he is, being an international star.' Hans Peter made the transition to grand prix on Peanuts and gained his first international successes after many successes internationally with young horses.

It was all especially sad for Caroline, his groom, who had been an intrinsic part of that journey Peanuts took from nervous 'show hack' to top dressage star. She adored what he was, she adored what he became, and it's wonderful that Peanuts is with her now, hacking out and looking a million dollars.

It shows, as it was to later with Lenny, the importance of the trio. When it came to Peanuts, well, Caroline would have slept on the floor of the stable for that horse. She never left his side, which is the best bit of the story because he has ended up with her, ten miles down the road from me. At that time Peanuts needed the person he knew really well riding him, the person he knew really well looking after him, and that combination is what took him to the highest level. That trust triangle helped the horse reach the peaks he did. Peanuts came home aged seventeen. We picked him up on our way home from Hagen in May 2011. He was one cool horse in the end, and he still is.

Kirsten had continued to be a big part of my life and she often came to Hooze Farm to watch. Her favourite saying was about getting the trapezius muscle working – the one and only muscle she ever thought about, but what an important one. She was always there for me, a kind lady and an amazing cook. Kirsten was well known for her baking and could whip up scrumptious dinners like no one else.

When Kirsten became ill with cancer she didn't want me, or anyone for that matter, to see her. That was terribly sad. But during the times when she'd had treatment and felt better David would drive her over to watch the horses. She was finding it difficult to walk, yet she'd always bring one of those marvellous cakes with her.

After having been in remission for a while she then got very ill again. I was at Hickstead, ironically, when David rang to say Kirsten wanted to see me. David warned me that I would need to prepare myself, that she would not be as I remembered her. I left Hickstead on the Sunday night and drove to the hospital at Bourton-on-the-Water. I was trying to picture what she would look like; David had told me she didn't like to wear her wig so wouldn't have that on when I got there. He'd also warned me that Kirsten wouldn't want me to be upset and that if I didn't think I could handle it, it would be better not to go. I'd thought to myself, no, that's ridiculous I'll be fine. But as I went in to her room I was hit with shock, I had to gulp as the realisation of what David had said came home to me.

Kirsten was very frail, thin, and she had to sip water every few minutes as her lips were dry and hurting – she was having more chemo then, I think – but I chatted away to her as normal, told her all about Hickstead and the horses, all the things I knew she'd want to hear about. She so wanted everything to be normal; we didn't talk about her illness. It was a lovely summer evening as I walked out of the hospital. I got into my car and cried. I couldn't believe what the cancer had done to her.

She made one more small recovery, even getting back up and about for a while, but I was glad I had seen her at Bourton because it made the next time easier. You can't get used to it, but you're more accepting, and I did the only thing you can do in these situations, which is carry on as normal, and for us that meant talking about the horses.

I was going to visit my mum in Dubai, flying out on a Monday for a week. Kate had been to see Kirsten, who was now in Cheltenham General Hospital, and told me the view was that she wouldn't come out this time. So I went to see Kirsten on the Sunday and although she still looked frail her colour had improved and she seemed to me to look better. We chatted, and she was happy I was going to Dubai to see Mum; being close to family was so important to Kirsten, it meant so much to her and she always wanted it for me. I asked Kirsten if she would like me to get her anything from Dubai – the designer fake shops were a bit of a draw then – and she asked would I get David a wallet for her. She died the following Sunday, the day before I got back. Kate broke the news to me. It was hard to take in; she'd been in a private room on the Oncology ward at Cheltenham and we'd held hands as we'd chatted. It was a lovely time, that last day I saw her, and to me it hadn't appeared that she was going to go so quickly.

Her funeral was in Cold Aston. David asked me to read something. I'd never done it before – I certainly couldn't have spoken at Jannie's funeral – and I remember sitting in the church, staring out of the window, unable to think of anything except how on earth I was going to do this. But it's amazing what you can do for people; you know you can't just break down. I thought of all the nice things we'd shared and just pretended she wasn't dead. And I got up and did that reading for Kirsten, and it was lovely.

The funeral finished to 'My Way', and that was Kirsten all the way. She was a very strong-minded lady. I used to call her Dame Edna as she wore huge glasses – she loved that. She laughed a lot and was striking to look at with wonderful skin. Those great big spectacles suited her.

That Nicky was pregnant had come as a big surprise; she and Richard had been trying for twenty years. The sheer delight was all over Richard's face and the utter 'undelight' clear on Nicky's at the thought of having a baby at that stage. After Vegas I didn't see Nicky again until Hartpury. Naturally, being pregnant she had put on weight, but when she told me she'd put on three stone I responded that she must be carrying the most enormous baby! Poor Nicky had a terrible time; she got pre-eclampsia and was rushed off to hospital where she stayed for twelve weeks and the baby was born premature. But as he had come out at 3.4 pounds I ribbed Nicky mercilessly for blaming the rest of the three stone on this little boy. Despite this, I was blessed to be asked to be Milo's godfather.

10

On and Up, Up, Down and Up

I had been thinking for a while that the outlay in renting a yard wasn't the greatest investment in the world, and Richard Davison, who is brilliant at the business side, kept on at me about buying and investing in property, so I got to looking around. A ready-made set-up as I imagined it was way beyond my price range, but then I came across a sixteenth-century Gloucestershire mill house with thirty acres. As I had done with the barn, I fell in love with it and knew I had to have it. Having gone through what amounted to an interview process with the mill's outgoing owners, I'd got the call during the World Cup Final in Vegas that it was mine.

Kate's husband Stuart took on the project management and planning applications; he'd got the experience whereas I hadn't much of a clue except knowing what I wanted. The only outbuilding was an old barn sitting on the highest point up the hill from the house. That, I decided, was where the stables would go. They had to really as the lower fields are on a flood plain. But there was a shock in store when we discovered three springs around the barn. The bill for putting in the land drains was an even bigger shock, but at least the yard has never flooded and while I might have not just touched wood but grabbed a tree trunk to say this, neither has the mill. I could claim King Canute-like talents as water had literally come to the mill's front door but in all its history floods have held back from invading the house.

It was some time before we could move in but when we did,

talking of invasions, we threw a housewarming party. I'd met Robert Oliver in 2000 when *Horse and Hound* asked me to go and ride one of his show horses for the 'Dream Rides' series. Having initially been underwhelmed at the thought I had a fabulous day and a fabulous gallop on Irene Susca's lovely middleweight champion Jamaica Bay and plenty of laughs with Robert, who is a big character. The party had kicked off around eight. Unbeknown to me about a mile away as the crow flies my new neighbour Robert was having a barbecue. His wife Claire, a contemporary of mine in young rider days who won gold on Another Fred and was on the eventing young rider team with our mutual friend Vanessa Ashbourne, swears she tried to stop him after a heavy night of drinking but shortly before midnight on what was a beautiful summer's night I was sitting in the garden with some friends when we heard a hunting horn. Where on earth are we living that there's midnight hunting? I thought as hooves thundered down the then gravel drive accompanied by hounds in full cry. Everyone ran through to the front of the house to see Robert on a great big cob, two girl grooms, bareback with blonde hair flying, and hounds milling about. We spent half an hour chatting and laughing until Robert suddenly sounded his hunting horn and off they went. As Robert planned, 'Hester' did indeed find out what sort of neighbour he had!

I wanted a haven, heaven even, for the horses, and that's what they have here. The stables are in a courtyard so the horses can all see each other, enjoy fresh air and have their own space and quiet. When they're working it all starts in the 'changing rooms' at the end of the indoor school where the horses are tacked, untacked, groomed, washed down and warmed under the solarium. Nothing to do with work goes on in their boudoirs. That's their space. And I love being able to look out of the kitchen door and see horses in the fields. But it did take a while to get it all as I'd dreamed. Stuart was brilliant, even buying reclaimed bricks from an old hospital in Gloucester for the stables, as were all the local tradesmen he got involved in the project. The one import was the horse walker from New Zealand, which

Mark Todd recommended. It took time but it was so exciting and all about building for the future. It wasn't the only project that fitted those criteria.

I had been staying with Anne van Olst again in Holland when she suggested we go to the stallion show and grading. Gertjan, Anne's husband, is a renowned stallion producer and stands both dressage and showjumping stallions at stud, and at the time Anne was riding this fantastic black stallion, Negro, who looked as if he would set the world alight. So off we went to Ermelo in the north of Holland.

I'd never seen anything like it. The grading is remarkably fast; the two-year-olds are let loose in a pen in the middle of the arena where they walk, trot and canter, then they are sent down a jumping lane. The marks are snapped out and the decision made whether the horse is either passed or not passed – it's literally that quick. Gertjan would have presented a group of maybe seven or eight youngsters and probably only one would have got through the grading, those are the odds. Anyway, the day ended and we went round to the stables at the back to meet Gertjan who said he was going to sell the group that hadn't graded as stallions. I looked over one of the stable doors and said, 'I like that one.' He already had that physique of his, as we always said 'the head of a duchess and the bottom of a cook', that strong little stamp and although there wasn't a lot to see in his free movement he had a great hind leg in canter and a great outlook. He was also a very cheap horse. So I said, right I'll have that one, and two-year-old Valegro came home with me.

Roly and I had bought a new prospect as a three-year-old through the Verden auction – Christian Heinrich had tipped us off about her – and despite the fact we were looking for a dark-coloured stallion we ended up with a chestnut mare. At six I took Dea to Royal Windsor where she won the young horse class for her age. Katherine Bateson was here training and looking for an up-and-coming horse. She fell in love with Dea, and called Jane Clark, who has been such a supporter to equestrian sport and to Katherine. I knew that Dea would have a wonderful home and that I'd still be involved, so they bought her. Dea was US small tour champion in 2009. She proved not to be physically strong enough for grand prix so she is back over here to be a mum nearby. I love that they come back like hot pennies. Katherine's become a good friend. She groomed for Robert Dover for all those years and when Robert retired for the fifth time and actually meant it, Jane Clark kindly gave Katherine the opportunity to become a rider – and what a rider she's turning into. She comes over for a few months every year to train and she will hopefully be on the US team.

I'd been helping Sasha Stewart, an event rider who had competed for Ireland in Athens. We met on the last day as she was going round the stables inviting swaps on Olympic clothing – the nations' swap and the Olympic pin swaps are big Olympic traditions. I had a spare GB shirt but it was massive so would probably have looked like a dress on her if she'd worn it, while she gave me a pair of green shell-suit bottoms which I accepted with grace and didn't risk wearing. As they were about to start a family, Sasha's husband Andrew had said he'd prefer it if, having done an Olympics, she would concentrate on dressage in future. I found a lovely old grand prix schoolmaster of Rebecca Greenwood's, Falco, for Sasha. He was difficult but she competed him at small tour. She'd also decided she would like to find a young horse. I'd told Danielle Van Tuyll, who is one of the selectors of Dutch horses for Brightwells sales, that I was on the lookout and she had organised a few for me to see in Holland.

The first horse I saw was a bouncy little dark bay stallion that had been placed sixth in the PAVO Cup, the prestigious Dutch young horse championship. At four years old Uthopia was on springs but he had this tiny walk. He rode, however, like a giant, considering he was so tiny and that he wasn't fully developed. To sit on him always has been like sitting on a springboard. He had this lovely suspension and bounce and a lovely canter, he had this lovely personality and he'd had a lovely life. Ivonne Lawrence, his then owner, had done a good job on him. He was nice to ride, he had a normal life as a stallion, and he was in the field all the time. It was the perfect package.

Sasha was competing in Holland at one of her last events, so I said that while she was there she should go across to this yard near Amsterdam and have a sit on this little horse, that I thought him wonderful. I was also looking for a horse for myself but decided I'd let Sasha have him and look for something else. After Sasha had ridden him she rang me up squealing with delight, she loved him, so Uthopia came to England. He did go to Ireland for a few months with Sasha, but he bucked her off in the school – which I can't ever imagine him doing. Afterwards Sasha rang me, laughing, to tell me Uthopia had bucked her then galloped off and jumped a huge hedge with all his tack on. 'I think you'd better have him back, he's quite a handful,' she said.

In March that year, 2006, we'd gone off to Spain again for the sunshine tour taking Pro-Set, who'd won the intermediaire I title for me at the National Championships, and Michael Mouse, whom I'd found as a two-year-old for Liz Mackenzie from Scotland. Spencer was driving me to the airport – Luton 'scareport', to be precise – for the flight to Gibraltar. Richard and Gill Davison were on the way too when they had a puncture and limped to Gill's parents, so we diverted to pick them up. After a mad rush through the airport and pleading with them to re-open the gate which had just closed, we all fell into our seats all hot, sweaty and in Richard's and my cases probably with longer noses due to the Pinocchio factor of talking our way into being allowed to board.

Halfway through the flight a large person in front of us started to have what appeared to be a heart attack, or at least convulsed and passed out. I was in the aisle seat with Richard in the middle and Gill obliviously dozing in the comfort of the window seat. As they put a call out to see if there was a doctor on the plane the stewardess ran down the aisle shouting, 'Someone help me.' Well, I looked round thinking, 'Someone help her,' but she was looking directly at me as Richard elbowed me in the ribs. I have never picked up anyone that big in my whole life but somehow I managed to scoop my arms under the shoulders of what by this time looked like a lifeless body and in, according to Richard, 'one fluent manoeuvre that would be the envy of any judo black-belt', lifted the floppy body out of the seat and into a (very) prone position in the aisle. We got out of our seats to give the doc and the stewardess more room to do CPR and went to the back of the plane. Richard saw me starting to sway and look a bit pale so he grabbed another stewardess to fetch a glass of water as he could see I was close to being second man down. Fortunately the CPR worked, but the funny thing was Richard recalls the victim as a corpulent fifty-something bloke while my memory is of a large black lady. I don't know where our heads were on that flight, but it gave me the freak-out of my life! Then we got to Gibraltar and into the airport. I'd overdosed on cigarettes in the duty free so they scanned me and pulled me over. I'd had a trauma on the flight then got my wrists smacked in the airport and all my cigarettes, which I desperately needed by that stage, were confiscated.

It was just one disaster after another. Later into the competition, around the second week, the three of us were in a restaurant having what we thought would be a nice quiet dinner. All of a sudden a man at one of the adjacent tables, dining on his own, fell backwards off his chair and hit his head on the tiled floor. There was blood everywhere and he'd fainted, so while I held his head Richard was mopping blood up – then he starts going through the guy's pockets! Contrary to my first thought that he was planning to fleece the second victim of being anywhere near us, Richard was actually looking for some ID. In the end the guy was taken off by ambulance. I can't remember what his name was, but I called him Pudsey. It turned out he was staying in our hotel. We recognised him at breakfast as he was the guest with the big plaster over the left side of his head. He gave us a bottle of sherry as a thank you but followed us round a tad too much for comfort. We came to the conclusion that we were not supposed to be around people that trip.

Despite it being labelled as the 'heart-attack tour' the horses were great. Pro-Set was small tour champion with a string of scores over 70 cent, Michael Mouse won his debut prix st georges – his debut competition, in fact – and Richard achieved his objective of settling his new grand prix prospect, Hiscox Karachi, with some high placings. But sunshine tour? The weather was ghastly.

I'd had Valegro broken in to ride at the age of three and a half at Sandra Biddlecombe's. Her yard is just up the road and geared to getting the babies fledged. Valegro hadn't grown much and at about sixteen hands high he was rather a squat horse. But under saddle he was like a professor from the minute they got on him. He walked, trotted and cantered and never put a foot wrong. He was, to be honest, quite common-looking. He had a cobby trot action in his trot, a normal walk but an excellent canter and a very good character. So he came home. He was four and he rode like a pony so I said to Suzanne Davies, whom I was still helping with DiMaggio, that I thought she should have this horse as he was too small for me yet he had this amazing canter and she could have him cheap. Suzanne said yes, she'd have him, unseen. But about a week later she rang me to say her tax bill had come in and as a result she couldn't afford to buy him.

That was fine, and as I was off to Holland to a show I decided to put Valegro on the lorry and drop him off at Anne's to see if she could sell him for me. On the way back from the show I stopped off again at Anne's, where she told me that I should keep him as he was going to be all right. I've always trusted her opinion so I put him back on the lorry. It was fate really, Valegro wasn't meant to go anywhere except home with me.

The next bridge to be crossed was that he was a head-shaker. It's an almost inexplicable condition and there is no cure for it. Sometimes horses grow out of it, but it affects some so badly they can't be ridden. There are several operations that can be done but they involve cutting nerves in the face, which was not a road we wanted to go down, so the question was what to do? One sunny day in spring I took five-year-old Valegro to a young horse class at Hunters Equestrian Centre and he was virtually unrideable. Because he had such a big canter, every time his front feet landed dirt and stuff would fly up and he would head-shake violently. He didn't like anything near his face. So I enlisted the help of an acupuncturist, who felt it was a matter of breaking the habit. The fact was, if the weather conditions were OK we could get away with it, so we muddled on for a year trying homeopathy and the acupuncture. I had spoken to the surgeon about the operation and decided I didn't want to do that; the success rate wasn't 100 per cent and I thought it was too drastic.

Despite all this, Valegro won the Shearwater national championship that year and plenty of other young horse classes. One of the best was when I put Lucy Cartwright, another protégée who came to me at sixteen and after six years went on to set up her own successful yard, up on him for the Badminton Young Horse Championship. It was Lucy's biggest win to date, and as she is from Badminton it was a hugely popular one. Uthopia and I were second and I didn't mind a bit.

I had been asked to be on the panel for the 'start and potential' sector of the World Class Performance programme. We were looking to spot those future stars that might make future teams and would benefit from the support. At the assessment day Emile Faurie and I were the riders; he took one group I took the other. Then there was a panel to watch and assess.

The horses and riders came into the arena in pairs to demonstrate what they could do. Charlotte Dujardin came in on Fernandez, who was a normal-looking horse and a 'nice' mover, nothing spectacular but he did look very electric, sharp and well trained at only six years old. There was a bit of 'that's not good enough . . . doesn't look international' chat going on with the panel, so I suggested that they let me have a sit on the horse and see what I thought. So on I got, and not only was this horse really well trained but he also had the qualities to be a good grand prix horse: he wanted to piaffe, he wanted to collect and he was very forward-going. I got off and insisted to the rest of the panel that we had to put this horse on the programme, that he did have what it takes to be a grand prix horse, I could feel it. So thankfully – and that's the point of having a rider on those sort of things – Fernandez was put on the programme and we would see him again in a year's time.

When we had finished, Charlotte and her mother came up to talk to me. Charlotte, whom I'd never met before and didn't know, was buzzing with delight and 'oh, he looked fabulous' comments, but even more so with questions on how did I do this, how did I do that? She asked if I would consider giving her some lessons, but I was too busy riding and with the pupils I had already. We kept in touch, however, and eventually she came for a lesson the following year. I liked what I saw and I liked her questioning attitude, so I suggested that, as one of the staff was going to be away for ten days, she might like to come and work, fill in, ride and bring Fernandez with her. That's how Charlotte started.

You get good days and bad days with any horse, but if it is just you riding a horse things can become quite a worry – and the head-shaking was definitely a worry. Sharing can give you a better perspective, and I put Charlotte up on Valegro.

I don't know whether this worked or not, or if it did quite how, but Valegro was a really strong horse. He was strong in all sorts of ways; he was strong in his body, he was strong in his mouth. One day I suggested we try a double bridle on him, as the acupuncturist had said to me that the curb chain of a double bridle lies on an acupuncture point. Anyway, the head-shaking virtually went away. It has diminished with each passing year, but it has affected him in some ways even at grand prix – you could see him reacting in the extended trot at Hagen in Olympic year when the dirt came up – so his head-shaking was more related to things around his head than sunlight, which is one of the possible causes, because he's happy to be in the field all day long in the bright sunshine and he doesn't do it at all.

That was the interesting factor with him. It was flies, dust, and dirt – anything around Valegro's head – that would make him head-shake. It's understandable for a sensitive horse. He doesn't like flies now, he won't tolerate them, so we always put him out in the field covered in fly spray and dressed in his hood and his jacket. We've learned to manage it and it's gone away as he's got older.

It's another management journey and it has been a good journey for him. Although it's a frustrating thing as a rider, you know intuitively it's not the horse being difficult and you'd never punish him for it – you can't suddenly tell a horse off for a head-shake as it's obviously uncomfortable for them – but Valegro (or Blueberry, as we call him) grew out of it, learned to cope with it, and we learned how to manage it. It was a crucial part of his journey.

At that stage Charlotte hadn't ridden grand prix, so as part of her training I said I would put her on some of the advanced horses to give her a feel for what grand prix riding – the movements, the feel and most of all putting the movements together – is like. The idea back then was to train Fernandez to grand prix. We both knew he'd got it in him, she was determined and looking back, hasn't he been brilliant? He and Pro-Set, whom I also took to grand prix, now comprise half of the Norwegian team. It wasn't planned, so how interesting that those two horses who were together at the yard both then went on to Norway with those two good riders. Charlotte and I love seeing them on the team with Cathrine Rasmussen and Lillian Jepsen, who both live in Denmark. We saw them at the Europeans in Herning, which was special for both those girls too.

Along the way, Fernandez suffered what was almost a career-threatening injury. The little toad escaped from his stable, ran off and fell over. It took a long time to find out exactly what damage he'd done to himself, but eventually we learned that he'd torn a meniscus. Essentially that's a hind-leg injury which can mean the end of a horse's competitive career. Once the diagnosis was made – and that took a while – he had to undergo an operation. Charlotte's mother, Jane, took Fernandez home after the surgery as he had to be walked in hand five times a day. Thanks to her, Dez had the best rehabilitation and he came back better than ever.

It was clear from the start that Charlotte would ride anything. She had the 'treats' of riding the older horses, but at that stage I needed a rider who would get on any of the young horses. Spencer and I were riding the main horses – Spencer had made his grand prix debut with Dolendo (Donald) – and there were a lot of up-and-coming horses in the yard, but what was special about Charlotte was her enthusiasm to ride, all the time, seven days a week. It was that enthusiasm I needed, especially when Spencer was at the point where he only wanted to ride certain types of horse. Charlotte had my own work ethic, she was exactly like I had been at the beginning, and she understood that the horses wouldn't learn and get better if we gave them endless days off or stopped riding them. I was still having to go away a lot doing clinics so I managed to get a rota set up, and it was good to know the horses were kept on track at home.

Charlotte was also adventurous. I didn't have to tell her at each stage 'this one needs to learn this now, that one needs to learn this', she would get on and want to teach the horses. Most people have to be spoon-fed on that, or they're too worried about the 'when' to try a flying change or any new movement. But Charlotte's mentality was the same as mine: yes, it will take time – years maybe – to perfect a change, but if we don't start now we'll never get there. Even if it doesn't feel right, or it's wild, you've got to keep going.

We'd always had a good grooming team, led by Caroline and Jo before her, but finally the riding team was beginning to take shape. In addition to Charlotte and Lucy, we had Rosie Moreton-Deakin. She'd done Young Riders, and Enfant – Queenie's Olympic ride and Mondorf partner – was a great schoolmaster for her in the small tour and for her first grands prix. After Rosie had been with me a few years and the time had come to move on, she went to work for Anne van Olst before deciding to start her own business; and Lucy would be with us for another couple of years before she too set up her own business nearby.

I'm so proud of everyone who has worked with me. Each has their different strengths, like Jo who is fabulous with young horses, and Lucy who is already training young riders herself. There are so many factors involved in influencing the decisions that will shape each individual's future, and it's rewarding to see them go on and achieve success.

Charlotte chose to stay and she saw the opportunity that was there for her. She had ideas of being on the GB team, in fact she knew she was going to be a team rider, an Olympic rider. From day one it was 'I want'!

She has a rare talent for teaching a horse the collected movements. At the time Charlotte came to me the trend was for people to make a team on bought, made horses. That was never going to be the case with Charlotte; there was no financial backing, no wealthy parents, it was about learning to do it. But she had a gift, the ability to teach horses the most difficult movement and the one that makes the difference between small tour and grand prix – the piaffe. She had watched my DVD on how to teach a horse to piaffe and how to teach a horse to really move in trot. She had been inspired by that to take her horse at the time, a thoroughbred, and teach it to piaffe. Charlotte had the instinct and the inquisitiveness to learn how to do it; that was her gift and it's a God-given gift. What I had to do was channel it. How many days a week to ask questions of the horse, when to give the horse a rest, when to do stretching work and when to bring a horse to the peak again for a test – these are all the things you have to learn as a young person, and you can ruin your career or you can ruin a horse by not having a mentor to take you through that. Charlotte had that natural ability but she didn't have the structure. Helping her start the process of learning all that was the one beacon in 2007, a year I still regard as my 'annus horribilis'.

The year got off to a good start, with another trip to the sunshine tour and a new grand prix ride, Sasha Stewart's Lecantos. Anne van Olst and I had spotted him at the World Games. He was ridden by a Polish rider and it wasn't his score, poor horse, that made us notice him but his piaffe and passage. I knew Sasha was looking for a grand prix horse so made some enquiries and sent Sasha to Poland to look at him. She fell for him – mainly, I suspect, because when she asked the groom what his name was the reply was that he didn't have one. She wanted to give him a name and a hug. So Lecantos arrived and went straight into rehab: dentist, farrier, back man, physio. They were all amazed he could work as he did with the problems he had. He'd never been out in the field so we turned him out and shut our eyes as he lapped that field. During the three weeks in Spain, Lecantos won everything, apart from one second place, so we were immediately in the spotlight for team selection for that year's Europeans in Turin. We weren't destined to get there. Lecantos knocked himself, probably in the field, and was off the team.

I'd been doing demonstrations or commentating for Badminton radio on the dressage days for years and I always love going. Spencer and I hadn't been getting on for a long time and on one of the dressage days Spencer announced he wasn't coming home. It didn't really register, or at least I didn't think that would be the end, but we had some squabble – there had been plenty, so I can't remember what it was about – and he went away for a few days. When he eventually did come home it was clear that he had decided our relationship was over. We muddled on for a while, and Spencer lived on and off in the flat as he was still riding here. If I'd been stronger I would have called time on it there and then, but I suppose part of me thought things would somehow work out, so it alternated in spates between getting on and fighting. Six months later it was obvious that things weren't going to improve. I felt then that Spencer was staying simply because his career was here but his personal life wasn't. It would take six months or so before I finally came to the conclusion it was impossible go on living like that. Recalling the Bechtolsheimers, you might say it was my second divorce at Badminton.

I was very fortunate that, thanks to his daughter riding with Spencer, I had got to know gastroenterology consultant Manny Srivastava. Manny popped his head round the door of the indoor school one day and said that he had heard I'd been suffering indigestion problems. He recommended that, given my age, I come to see him for a colonoscopy and a gastroscopy so he could check me out. Then he asked whether I had cancer in my family and I replied yes, so he stressed that it was doubly important.

I made the appointment as Manny had pushed me to do. My friend Jackie – Rosie's mum – came with me. As we drove down to Newport to the clinic we were laughing and I'd joked to Jackie that wouldn't this just top the year if I were to find out there was something wrong with me. I didn't feel anything was wrong, I wasn't in pain, and I'd always had a funny tummy which I put down to nerves.

At the clinic they sedated me. When I came round Jackie was in the room. I felt very woozy. One minute I was laughing, the next dozing, but I do remember complaining to Jackie that I was absolutely starving – I'd had to fast beforehand. Then Manny walked into the room. He is the most lovely man and both he and his wife Luba have become friends, the pair of them have been incredibly supportive and come and watch me at competitions. Anyway, Manny sat on the bed and held my hand. I was immediately swamped by this feeling that he was not going to say what I wanted him to say. He told me, 'You are very lucky, extremely lucky that you've come here.' He explained that I had developed some polyps, which I had probably had for a minimum of four years. If hadn't come to see him, if I'd left it another year, he didn't think he could safely say I'd be here at all.

Once you've got bowel cancer it's a difficult thing to treat and I was at a prime age, forty, and a prime candidate with a history of cancer in the family for that to happen. While I had been under sedation Manny had not only carried out the investigations but removed all the polyps so I was indeed fortunate. All I had to do was continue with a programme of yearly check-ups. However, even though you're told that it's out, that you're OK, it was – and especially with how emotional I was that year anyway – extremely frightening. I was relieved but at the same time it really did shake me. In the car on the way home with Jackie I just cried. I don't know why; relief, I suppose, but also the realisation of what might have been. It was a difficult episode to deal with and I was, and still am, so grateful to Manny.

Lecantos was all we hoped for in one respect; he was a talent albeit not a medal-winning one, and his character was showing, despite his being a good horse in a naughty horse's body, as I described him in an interview. He bruised a tendon two weeks before the Europeans. Game over. In hindsight there was something wrong from the day we bought him; he was fragile from day one and it was clear he'd had a hard life.

My old mucker Doob had a good life and a great retirement with his devoted owner Marcia. He was put down that July, aged twenty-two, following a colic attack. Doob had made fairy tales come true, not just for us but for all those thousands of people who'd followed the story of a horse bought for £2,500 who had gone on to be a superstar, our 'people's prince'. I was having a shit year, but I could only feel for Marcia, who'd lost the equine love of her life.

Needing to get out, do something on my own, I accepted an invitation to a seventieth birthday party in Devon. This wasn't your average seventy-year-old though. I first met Sara at Hickstead – I think it was during the Europeans, actually. A few people said they could smell dope, but no one realised that the source of the aroma was the elderly lady sitting on the grass smoking a joint. Sara was 'Granny Gange' to me after that. I took myself off to Devon wondering whether I was doing the right thing – what would a seventieth birthday party be like? But it turned out to be a lovely evening. Sara and her husband have a gorgeous farm on the edge of the Dartmoor National Park and they're part of a relaxed hippy extended family. Harriet, Sara's daughter, whom I'd first met years before when she was married to her first husband, an eventer, was there with her two kids – godchildren of mine – climbing trees barefoot and running riot round the place. Everyone was invited, and the guests all walked from the village in Holne down to the farm, where there was a wonderful marquee sat at the edge of the garden looking down over the valley. It was a fascinating, fabulous evening.

Sara had come to Britain from Canada – she was one of the first supermodels there – and there were pictures of her on the front pages of the newspapers when she arrived in England to be married then to Noel Harrison, who wrote 'Windmills of Your Mind', which they sang together that night, Sara dressed in red and looking fabulous. There was a real 'good to be alive' feeling, and that night marked the start of me getting myself back together.

As the year drew to an end, with Olympia coming up just before Christmas, I made the decision that I would take Dolendo on. Call it revenge, call it satisfaction, I don't know, but I felt it was my last grasp on what I'd had. Spencer had become national champion that September and I felt I had pushed the boat out as far as I could for him to achieve that. I did it because I had still hoped and wanted it to work. It broke my heart when I finally told Spencer that October that he'd have to go, but then I thought: he's gone, why should he take my horse? Donald's mine, I want to keep him and I want to be responsible for how his life ends up. I wasn't about to let go of Donald's future, especially after all he'd been through. So Olympia was difficult that year. I knew Spencer would come to watch, that he'd be in the crowd.

And then there was Donald's half-owner, Ann Cory. Ann came along back in the early days when I was at the Fortune Centre. After the national convention with Hans Erik Pederson I got invited to do a two-day course with him in the New Forest, and Ann's daughter Sarah was on the same course. We were both doing junior eventing trials but we only met properly there. I think Ann could see I was quite a lost little soul as a seventeen-year-old and she made me a sandwich for lunch and invited me into their lorry. They were probably the first people I met outside the Centre, they were lovely and we kept in touch. Until she gave up horses, Sarah and I were good friends; while I was at Dr B's I used to go down to their place at Normandy near Guildford to teach and it was as if I became a part of their family. So when Helen Owen decided to emigrate to Australia and wanted to sell her share in Dolendo, I thought of Ann. By this time Ann had sold her house in Normandy and moved closer to us; she didn't have a lot of money but she'd always been interested in dressage and I thought it would be a good way to keep Donald in the family. She and Helen came to an agreement when Donald was about seven, and after that there was no way Donald was going away.

I was worried about how he would go for me at Olympia and terrified he would not go well. Thankfully, I had the wonderful support of Georgie Lloyd. I had known Georgie for years, had taught her when she was a kid and I enjoy spending time with her. Jamie Reynolds and Dan Greenwood were a huge part of what was probably to be a year of picking me up and saying, 'Come on, you've got to get out.' They'd persuaded me to come and have dinner, get a bit social, and that's where I'd rekindled my friendship with Georgie. It was Cotswolds revisited, and it did me good. Georgie offered to come and support me at Olympia. She's an incredibly warm character. She literally slept in my room for however many nights we were there and kept telling me, 'You can do this, love' – she made me feel that I could do it. And we did do it. Donald and I were fourth in the freestyle just above a combination with a very exciting future ahead of them: Mistral Højris and Laura Bechtolsheimer. Donald was wonderful and I left Olympia feeling elated, only to be back in the doldrums again at Christmas. My first Christmas alone maybe, but that sort of low can be the start of rehabilitation, especially with 2008 looming, and with it the Olympics.

I decided to put Donald on that road, and Lecantos. It was a fresh year and I would try for the Olympics with both. A group of us had rented this fabulous house on the beach as our March home-from-home in Spain and Richard Davison had come up with the idea of hiring a cook. Gareth and Rebecca Hughes' nanny had recently finished her job with them and Gareth suggested I ring and see what she was up to. When I sounded her out on spending three weeks in the sun, cooking for us in the evenings, basically a paid holiday, she accepted. We met her at Gibraltar airport for the first time and all piled into the car to drive up to Vejer de la Fontera, find the house and move in. Then I met Yvonne Losos de Muñiz, who is lovely and a real laugh, at the show and she came to join us in the house. The first night we were there I said to the girl, 'Pop to the supermarket, get a couple of chickens, stick them in the oven and we'll have chicken and salad for dinner.' Her response was: 'How do I do that?' Ignoring the potential for discussion on how to visit a supermarket, I cut straight to it and asked her outright if she had cooked, to which she replied, 'Just basics.' There was no point arguing that roast chicken and salad was basic, I just thought, 'Oh my God, we're here now.' Fortunately, Georgie, who is a brilliant cook and takes gastronomic catering in her stride, arrived two days later. Even though she was supposed to be there for a holiday, Georgie, bless her, took charge in the kitchen and taught this girl, who I think learned more in three days than she had in the whole of her life. We had three weeks of glorious sunshine and for once it really was a sunshine tour.

Donald and I were getting to know each other again. He scored a heap of nines, which I hadn't scored at grand prix since Peanuts, and over 72 per cent to win the final grand prix, but he, Lecantos and me would be on and off all year.

The main campaign for Donald got under way at Hagen. I was having a tough time with it all, I didn't feel focused and I didn't feel right. The night before the grand prix I'd had a huge fight on the phone with Spencer. The reality of it finally dawned that he was now with someone else. I didn't sleep a wink. The test didn't go well – we got a miserable 65 per cent – and apart from feeling spooky, Donald didn't feel at home on the surface. I didn't do the special and when we got home he really wasn't right so Donald was signed off for another six months.

I took Lecantos to Outdoor Gelderland in June. He went quite well and improved from the grand prix to some 68 per cent in the special and fifth place, so was looking a team prospect. Then we went to Rotterdam where he passed the trot up, but one of the judges came to me afterwards and said that horse didn't look right in his opinion and that he'd like to see him again the following morning. It was highly unusual, a precedent even, but the next day the ground jury came, we trotted Lecantos up and the vet just said to me, 'No, he's not right.' It was fair enough, we all felt in the team camp that he wasn't right but I'd had to trot him up. I couldn't start him, so we couldn't get selected for the team. Poor Lecantos, his hard life meant he was never as good as he should have been but he got a happy retirement in Ireland with Sasha.

Two horses in the running, both went wrong, so 2008 as an Olympic year was over. But the good thing, the plus side of that year, was that Valegro and Uthopia were starting on the road to grand prix and we knew that in the wings we had these two very talented grand prix horses.

It was in September, before the national championships where Sarah Tyler-Evans' TMovistar swept the small tour board for me, that I'd got a telephone call from Donald McTaggart. He owned Liebling II, who had been on the 2007 team with Anna Ross-Davies. Liebling had by all accounts been quite a difficult horse but had come good at the Europeans. I didn't know Anna, apart from in passing at shows, and I didn't know Donald, I had never met him. The phone call was to introduce himself as Liebling's owner and to tell me that since his relationship with Anna had come to an end he was looking for someone to take the horse on. He was hoping I would consider it, but if I wasn't interested he would be sending Liebling to Germany to have him ridden by a German rider.

I asked for a day to think it over and promised to call Donald back. I did think, long and hard. Taking a ride from another rider has always been controversial. In showjumping and eventing it happens all the time with no consequences and no questions asked, but when it came to dressage it was a different matter. I knew this from experience, as although Dolendo was my own horse there had been some snide comments and remarks about the fact that 'I had taken him back'. What people didn't know was that I'd never given him away; I'd produced the horse with Spencer and had made it clear that if he left my horse stayed behind. Why would I let him take my horse? So here I was, faced with a dilemma. Even though it wasn't the same scenario, it struck a chord.

My first thought was that I should speak to Anna direct. As sorry as I was to have to ring her in that situation, I made the call. And I told her exactly what Donald had said to me, I didn't know what else to do. Half of me thought that people, if they heard the story, would be glad the horse stayed in Britain. I knew there'd be some who'd feel sorry for Anna, which I would totally understand, but having slept on it I thought I might as well see how I got on with Liebling; he could be a future team horse and it's what any rider would do. I didn't know the reasons behind the split and I still don't to this day. I never asked Donald, he's never discussed it with me, and I never asked Anna. Their relationship had broken down, the horse needed riding and riding is my job, that's all there was to it.

So I phoned Donald to tell him my decision. He requested that I pick up Liebling immediately and asked if I could send a lorry. There was a bit of bother, and I had my first taste of dealing with internet trolls, but the decision was made. You have to get on with these things. A couple of weeks later I took him to Saumur and Liebling, 'Lenny', was fantastic. He came third in the grand prix and won the special with over 70 per cent, so we went on to Olympia where it was wonderful to be back.

Lenny was to be a good part of my life. He was not made for

dressage; it may seem weird to say that after such success in grand prix, but in his confirmation – that is, the way he was built – he had a dropped back and wasn't ideally designed for the job. He also had a difficult mouth; we had to watch out to get his noseband and the curb chain on his bridle settled 'just so' to make him comfortable. Lenny was also a hollow horse, it wasn't easy keeping him truly round as he had a tendency to carry his head and neck high. I'd always have the feeling that he was above the bit when riding him. In that sense he was tricky, but he was very brave and he has wonderful eyes – like two walnuts, those wonderful brown eyes – and he has the biggest character. Out of all the horses, even Uti and Blueberry (Uthopia and Valegro), Lenny was the character of the yard. He'd eat cucumber sandwiches, and bananas were his absolute favourite. He was a worker, he was always happy and I loved having him here. The following year brought the change of fortune for British Dressage, and Lenny was to be a part of that.

11

Gong Ho!

We all arrived at Windsor – Emma Hindle, Maria Eilberg, Laura Bechtolsheimer and me – knowing that this was the start of something big. Hopefully we would have the home advantage on our side. Of course that brought pressure too, but we were all feeling positive about it. Maria was to kick off the proceedings as we were going in order of our standings that year. She and Two Sox put in a solid score of 68 per cent, then it was my turn with Lenny. I had felt quite stressed beforehand knowing how much was at stake but I'd taken our team manager Richard Davison's advice to have a break beforehand, so Lenny had had three days off. He did his best grand prix ever at that point for me, with only one mistake in the one-time changes. As we halted and I gave my final salute the crowd went wild. We'd been a partnership for barely ten months and this was our fifth international show. A score of 72.085 these days wouldn't look too exciting, but bearing in mind expectations must be realistic for each horse, that score was well beyond our expectations for him. At the end of the first day the team was in bronze medal position.

Laura was beginning to peak with her beloved 'Alf', Mistral Højris, and despite copying me and having a mistake in the one-times, scored a personal best and the highest mark a British rider had ever achieved in an international grand prix: 76.638 per cent. As incredible as it seemed looking back at my past championships, we finally had a chance to beat the Germans. The Dutch team with Totilas and Parzival had won gold before Edward Gal and Totilas even started, but Emma had to score 71 per cent or above to nail a British silver. She and Lancet did it with 72.936 and we had won team silver, on home ground.

Kyra Kyrklund's owner Yvette Conn had organised a party for everyone at her husband's polo club nearby. It was fantastic. Yvette had planned to throw a party anyway for all the competitors, owners and supporters, which was incredibly kind of her, but the fact we'd done so well and had something to celebrate made it pretty monumental. I think it was one of the first times, if not the very first, that all the GB riders had got through to the individual round of a championship and qualified for the special. My friends Anne and Gertjan were there – the Danish team was fifth – and as Anne had helped me with Lenny for three weeks prior to Aachen she was an honorary member of my team.

I found myself then in the top fifteen to go through to the music with Laura, who'd bagged individual bronze in the special, and Emma. The freestyle was a sell-out and it was the most unbelievable night. Riding dressage to music at night is always a thrill and very atmospheric, especially when it's outside with Windsor Castle all lit up behind us. I rode to my Tom Jones programme. It was one of my first Tom Jones freestyles and was absolutely made for an evening performance. I was under no illusions about getting a medal, but I had an absolute ball riding to it. Theo van Bruggen put the music together for me and I still think it's a work of art. When people first heard it, they either loved or hated it. Fortunately, most loved it – I certainly did. It wasn't about winning a medal it was about creating an atmosphere, and that's what the music did that night; it created a fun, party mood. Lenny was in great form and we finished tenth, as we had in the special. Windsor was a real celebration of British Dressage; for the first time, the crowds were right behind us and it was brilliant.

The grooms partied that night – well, they partied until about six in the morning! The grooms are such an integral part of our teams; they too were winning a medal for the first time in ages, and on

British soil, so it was one huge party. Caroline, my old head groom, had gone on to work for Anne in Holland so she was there to share it all. Catherine Owens, who had taken over, had come to me from Zara Phillips. Catherine and I had a unique relationship in that she was brilliant with me and with the horse. She may not have been everyone's 'people person' but Lenny was a special needs case and she understood him beautifully. She adored him and he responded, as he was such a people horse.

For the first time in my career I came back from Windsor feeling it was a job well done. After nineteen years of international competition I had my first medal, and the entire team had ridden at our maximum, so there was none of that awkwardness you get when one member of the team succeeds but the others fall short of expectations. Instead we all felt this delicious euphoria because we'd come away with a team medal, we weren't the afterthought any more, the whole country was behind the team and everybody felt involved, a part of it. Winning an individual medal is great for you and for your fans, but you want that team medal because that's what motivates your country. When you get four people from different backgrounds who come together and produce that result, you know everybody in the country is going to relate to at least one of those four people. That's why I felt that medal was such a huge success for our country. Plus, in winning that silver, we'd beaten the Germans for the first time. That was historic in itself.

The funniest thing about Windsor was that they had decided to do the prize-giving without horses, so I found myself at the age of forty-three having to run round the arena on foot with these three girls under the age of thirty who seemed to have a lot more spring than I did. And that was after we'd been jumping up and down on the podium as we couldn't contain ourselves. I kept going until the bitter end though!

Donald, Lenny's owner, didn't make it, although he'd tried to get back for the freestyle. He was in Greece and I'd phoned him with all the news. But he was absolutely delighted. And as Donald was behind Patchetts Equestrian Centre, which is a long-standing institution and which had supported Lenny all the way, it was a cause for celebration for them too. It was really was good for everybody.

Dear Lenny. The lift didn't go straight to the top with him; he was forever thinking of ways out, but he delivered the goods when it was needed. I am so grateful to him. Even when he moved on, I kept in touch with him. The young Dutch rider, Jonna Schelstraete, had him as a schoolmaster and did really well with him. She agreed that when the time came I could give him the retirement he deserves. Four years on from Windsor and there was Lenny taking Jonna to international success – third at CDI Perl. He has taken Anna, me, Yvonne Losos de Muñiz and Jonna to international success and was unlucky not to go to the Olympics with Yvonne.

After a couple of weeks' holiday, Lenny went to the National Championships and gave me my sixth title of National Champion and my fifty-first national championship. He then gave me a personal best at Olympia of over 78 per cent. It was my best year in twenty years!

The World Equestrian Games in Kentucky was the big diary date for 2010. I had Uthopia in the wings, so Donald and I had agreed that as Lenny was not going to be the star of the yard – although he was in our eyes, having done so much – it was the right time for him to move on. Lenny had done everything Donald had wanted him to do and more, so he agreed that if I could find Lenny a suitable home, now was the time and that would be an ideal solution.

I got a call from Canadian rider Cheryl Meisner who had heard Lenny was on the market. Robert Dover was then training the Canadian team and gearing them up for Kentucky. Cheryl duly came over to try Lenny with her sponsor and supporter John Risley. She got on with Lenny instantly and loved him, so the deal was done there and then, Lenny was vetted and sold to Canada. My job at the time was to try and put these two together for the forthcoming World Equestrian Games. Cheryl based herself with me and after only two weeks with Lenny went to Addington to do her first grand prix on him. She did a great job. I helped her understand the ropes; how the warm-up should go, that sort of thing.

Generally, when it comes to forming a partnership you're looking at a year at least because you have to adapt to the horse and the horse has to adapt to the rider, even at grand prix level. So for Cheryl to go out after only two weeks and achieve 66 per cent at her first international, especially considering she didn't have a huge amount of experience, well we were all delighted. But Cheryl's competition plan meant she went then to a base in Europe and we lost a little of the communication. It was nobody's fault, she wanted to be with her trainer, Bert Rutten, so the base had to be Holland. What often happens in these situations, however, is that you hit a bit of a lull. Things didn't go to plan for the next few shows, and I think Cheryl suddenly realised that this was a tall order for her to get ready for a major championship in a matter of three or four months. So, when she decided to return to Canada John rang me and generously asked would I like to ride Lenny at the World Games.

Uthopia had just started grand prix. He'd won his first few grands prix in Spain on the sunshine tour but with the offer of Lenny on the table we decided that, from the point of view of experience, Lenny was probably the better bet. Uthopia hadn't done any big shows at that stage so we thought, let's take Lenny. I had one show to qualify him, Hickstead, where he was fourth in the grand prix and won the special, for which I have to thank Adelinde for choosing the freestyle. As I had ridden at Olympia we were qualified from two grands prix, and the decision was taken that I would be selected for the team on Liebling rather than Uthopia. Richard as team manager was keen Uti shouldn't be rushed as we had the Olympics in mind, so with six weeks of match practice I had to get back on and get myself organised.

But that wasn't anything new. It had been the case with a lot of horses I've had and I felt I knew Lenny so well by then. It was great for me to be able to ride him in Kentucky. I had Uti coming up, which was exciting for the future, but I knew Lenny would be the solid team member that would hopefully deliver the same sort of score we'd had at Windsor. And he did.

Lenny was a well-travelled horse, he flew comfortably, he settled in comfortably and I had Anne van Olst's help in Kentucky to polish up the rough edges, and again he delivered a solid performance and scored 72 per cent. Laura had blossomed that year with Alf. They needed to score 78 per cent to secure the silver; in the end they not only smashed the 80 per cent barrier but by scoring 82 in that atmosphere and showing the new level of control she had achieved led many people to feel she should have beaten Totilas in that test. What she did was brilliant. Thanks to that huge score, plus Maria as our anchor, and Fiona Bigwood who had re-joined the team scoring a personal best, 72 per cent, on Wie Atlantico, there we were at the world games taking a silver medal.

It was ideal experience too, because at that stage there was a bit of swapping round as Emma had dropped out of the picture. That meant there was a chance for different people to come into the team. As always when you have a big scorer, as happened when Valegro came along, it's that big scorer enthusing the other riders that lifts all our game. Kentucky was a long trip, we were there for two weeks, but we went to visit the famous studs and enjoyed touring the sights, so it was a real holiday as well as having to deliver for the team.

I don't remember feeling pressure, maybe because it all happened in six weeks, but I trusted Lenny and I knew once again I was not up for an individual medal. Lenny was a real team horse, the sort of horse you want when you're going for a team medal. He may have been the most unathletic dressage horse I have ever ridden, but he was an experienced campaigner and such a trustworthy soul. With those wonderful lion eyes and that big heart he was dead safe and he was bold so he never spooked. We all made it through to the special again, but Lenny did feel tired in that test and we finished sixteenth.

Only the top fifteen went through to the music. Laura and Alf bagged individual silver in the special and Fiona was fifteenth so got the last slot, and I can honestly say it was a relief. It was the first time I'd done a major championship and thought thank God I'm six-teenth. I felt I couldn't go any further, we'd reached our limit. Lenny was never a three-day championship horse, he was always at his best when he was fresh, before the boredom of dressage had time to kick in as it does with some horses – after all, he did start life as a show-jumper – and he was already a bit flat in the special.

That year, as the Totilas hype had come massively to the fore, I was glad of the opportunity to sit and watch fifteen of the world's best. I really wasn't in it for myself in those days, I was only in it for the team and I was delighted to come sixteenth in such an amazing competition. For most people I'd imagine coming sixteenth – one place away from being in the final – would be the biggest disappoint-ment of their life – but for me it was an absolute joy. I did get a lot of tellings off for that from team management, but I loved being able to watch those tests. Laura went on to win second individual silver with Alf, Fiona did a brilliant job and finished twelfth, and then there was Totilas and Edward on over 90 per cent for gold and the home team's Steffen Peters winning his second individual bronze on Ravel – the first individual medals for dressage for the USA since 1932, I was told. Poor USA had to wait longer than us!

Fiona and I get on brilliantly and we had a great laugh. We're kin-dred spirits and we tease each other unmercifully. As we both like diners we couldn't believe we'd landed in 'diner heaven' and were sur-rounded by places where we could eat as much as we liked all for one price.

At the end of the world championships our GB star was begin-ning to rise but in the back of my mind, although I was delighted for Laura, I kept thinking about Uti and Valegro and how the next year was going to be very special indeed.

For the first time ever, I think, I hadn't ridden at the national championships. I had sold Supernova, known as Neville, to Jen Goodman for Spencer to ride and Neville left us the week before we set off for Kentucky.

Charlotte and Valegro had won the novice championship in 2007 and the elementary and medium championships the following year. In fact the only time they ever lost a championship and came second was at advanced medium. They'd won the winter championship at that level, but at the nationals where we didn't ride him twice, which was our usual strategy, he was very hot and he was early to go in the morning. Something clattered in the walkway, he lost concentration, she lost a movement and that cost them the championship. Aside from that one blip, the horse has been a champion from the off, Charlotte's confidence grew with every championship, and so they both grew up and came up together all the way through.

Jonathan Rippon from Horse & Country TV had called me up and said they wanted to make this exciting new series. We had a meeting and off we went: *At Home with Carl Hester* was launched in 2010. I doubt Jonathan knew at the time, and I certainly didn't, that it would run and run, but it has been wonderful for us to have the opportunity to look back, as anyone can through the DVDs, at all those moments caught on camera, such as the year Charlotte won the prix st georges championship. Even though she won, she came out of the test and went on and on at me: 'He did this, he didn't do that, he felt too this, he felt too that . . .' I let her go back to the stables, turned and looked at the camera and said, 'This is not his final goal, the London 2012 Olympics is where I want him to be, it is not the end of his road.' I didn't care what she said that day; they'd won the championship and I was on record stating that's where we wanted to end up. Charlotte meanwhile had to get into a Jacuzzi with a bottle of champagne – fully clothed, of course – having made a bet with photographer Kevin Sparrow that was what she'd do if she won.

12

The Road to Greenwich

In January 2011 we also had Fernandez about to launch his GP career. We made an early start at Zwolle in Holland with me on Fernandez to do his first grand prix and Charlotte getting her eye in at small tour on Valegro. That was when people began talking about Valegro and recognising his potential as an international horse. He didn't actually win, he was second to Voice and Edward Gal in the prix st georges, but there was a buzz of 'wow this looks like a potential star' and Wim Ernes, the Olympic judge who went on to be the Dutch team coach, came up and said Valegro was one of the best young horses he had ever seen at small tour level. He should have beaten Voice there but on home ground in Holland as a new contender it wasn't going to happen. Fernandez did his first grand prix. He made a few baby mistakes but he was third.

What I wanted us to achieve was that I would qualify Fernandez (or 'Dez' as we called him) and Uthopia, so that when Charlotte had a bit more experience I could put her back on Fernandez and she too could qualify on him and Valegro. That way we would both have a team horse each plus a spare. The next step towards achieving this plan was Addington, where I rode Dez and Charlotte rode her first ever grand prix on Valegro. It was hugely exciting for all of us when they won with 74.62 per cent. But I wasn't going to let Charlotte have it all her own way; Dez was mistake-free and second with 74.26.

Valegro got his first ten in that very first grand prix test. I had been working with Charlotte for a whole month preparing them for the test. We realised with Valegro that, as he was so intelligent, there was no point in using exercises to catch him out – to get him not to anticipate, that sort of thing – which would be on the agenda for a lot of other green grand prix horses. Two weeks before Addington we decided specifically to try and teach the horse to do the test and we just did the test movements with him. That has always been Valegro's way, he needs to know where he's going and that suits him. He was pretty much ready though still pretty green and it wasn't enough time for him to know where he was going. But we were excited. Those 74 per cent scores were the highest for both of us at grand prix, for Charlotte in her first test and me after twenty years! I was excited about Dez too, but he always carried on like a horse who had been doing it his whole life.

My plan was designed to progress in a gradual way, start at the bottom and work our way up to the European Championships in Rotterdam that coming August. Our next stop was Vidauban. By that stage I had decided to give the sunshine tour a miss. We'd had fun there, especially when Angie Rutherford was competing as she and Mike laid on entertainment at their house, turning the trips into holidays; but much as I appreciated what Spain had done for me and the horses in the past, I decided that Vidauban in the South of France, just north of St Tropez, would be the next best thing as it was one day's travel closer. The point was, and the showjumpers knew this way before we did, that getting the horses competing outdoors was a great start to the competitive year as of course all the championships would be outdoors. We went off with Charlotte to do her first international grand prix and my second international with Dez and it turned out to be quite an exciting show.

The first thing was that we didn't get the weather, which was sad. It was an absolute wash-out and I didn't want to run the horses but Charlotte was determined to try to get her scores. Anyway she won everything – two grands prix and two specials – so Valegro's and Charlotte's international careers were launched. I knew that Charlotte was going to be a cool competitive customer, but bearing in mind that Valegro was extremely green, even in those early days he was doing mistake-free tests – without polish, sure, but he could miss his one-time changes outside the arena twenty times yet in the test he would not miss a single one. That in a horse was astonishing. Dez was runner up to Valegro in the first week, then in the second I ran him in the freestyle grand prix, which he won, then he duly won the freestyle with 77 per cent, which was a super score for him. We brought them home with the job done. I had qualified Fernandez, Charlotte had qualified Valegro. It was time for the second stage of the plan to swing into action and for us to start swapping round.

Charlotte took the reins on Dez for Addington CDI, coming second to Laura Bechtolsheimer on her national champion, second string Andretti, then we went straight off a few days later to Saumur CDI with Valegro and Uthopia. It was Uthopia's first outing since he'd won there the year before. I hadn't competed him while I'd been concentrating on Lenny and he'd been busy with his stud duties. He was never a horse to compete a lot. But I was back on him for Saumur and that was when the rivalry got under way between Edwina and Grandad.

Charlotte started calling me Grandad when she caught me out being sensitive about my age one day and of course it stuck. I wondered how much she might be induced to pay me not to tell the story of why I call her Edwina, then on consideration realised it would never be enough. Besides, Charlotte herself had already told the *Daily Mail*. The full title is Edwina Scissorhands, because she was quite strong with the mitts when I first took her on.

Saumur was where we suddenly started to find ourselves in the unfortunate position, which has carried on throughout our careers with these horses, of being on the same scores and the same placings. What it meant was that we came into the world rankings at the same level at the same time, and this was to make life more difficult as we went along. Valegro was nine, Uthopia was ten and there they were, at the top of the leader board at that show together. In his first test for a year Uti won the grand prix on 74 per cent with Valegro one per cent lower in second. Then in the special Charlotte beat me by some ridiculous 0.08 per cent. Valegro was looking one very exciting young horse and Uthopia was relaxed and so cool with being back in the arena.

Within days of getting home came tragic news. I had known Jane Gregory (née Bredin) since for ever, but as with most competitors life means you tend to catch up at the odd social event or at competitions. Then the previous January we had all gone on holiday to the Maldives: Jane and her husband Aram, Nicola and Harvey Buchanan, Ulrik and Henriette, me and my then partner, James. It was a wonderful ten days with the icing on the future cake brought by the announcement that Henriette and Ulrik, who'd been together such a long time, were engaged. Jane had always been to me and to a lot of people the epitome of a hard worker, she'd made it from being a groom – she was the lynchpin of David Hunt's yard for many years – and was always someone to admire. One of the most open-minded riders in the sport, she had such an enquiring mind and was a terrific ambassador for dressage, someone everyone enjoyed being with. We had talked a lot about Golly on that holiday. Jane and Aram had bought Golly, Dances With Wolves, at the Vechta Auctions and I'd seen Jane at a couple of shows with him. He was an impressive horse even then but he was a handful. Jane told me about this big horse she reckoned was going to be a real prospect for the future but admitted he was so hot that she struggled with him. When we got back home she brought Golly up to see what I made of him. I had a sit on him and golly was Golly strong. She had really worked on his submission but Golly wasn't having much of that, so we discussed him, I gave her some ideas and she'd already said on holiday that if she found she couldn't ride him she would like me to ride him, that she thought I'd love him. But when I watched her riding him I laughed and told her I didn't think I could do a better job than she was doing anyway.

The news that Jane had suffered a massive heart attack and was with us no more was unbelievable for so many of us and devastating for her family and Aram. She had been walking back to the stables on Golly when it happened and she never regained consciousness. It was so typical of Jane's generous spirit that she donated her organs to help others. Everyone who had been part of her life came to her funeral; Anky came over from Holland. There was a beautiful picture in the church of Jane on Lucky Star, whom she'd ridden at the 2008 Olympics, with her typical beaming smile.

As shocked and sad as everyone was, the funeral could have been horrific. Instead it was lovely, and afterwards we all gathered at Jane and Aram's home. Jane's mother Bunny is the warmest, nicest person in the world, she was just gorgeous to everybody. She, Aram, Jane's sisters Clare and Mary and her stepfather Martin were the ones bearing the biggest loss, yet they were so welcoming to everyone. Clare had delivered a wonderful tribute at the church and Mary read that oh so apt poem 'Horses She Loved'. Despite being in a state of shock, Aram held himself together. It was a day of stoicism but also about celebrating Jane and her life. So many lovely stories, so many people telling them and remembering this wonderful rider and wonderful woman.

Naturally it took Aram a bit of time to decide what he was going to do, then I had a phone call asking whether I would be interested in coming down to Wiltshire to see the horses with a view to taking some on. It was an unusual situation and one we all hope never to be in, but I went down there and I rode them. Sirius Black I realised there and then wasn't one for me but he went on to be very successful with Peter Storr. Peter had, in horse career terms, grown up with Jane so it was wonderful Peter took on Sirius. I decided to take Douglas and Golly. I got on with Douglas, whom I'd later team up with Sam Thurman-Baker to make the Young Rider team, but with Golly I didn't get on and think 'wow'. What I thought was, 'My God, feel the power! I don't know what I'm going to do with it, but I am going to do this for Jane, and for Aram.'

For Charlotte the next big step was to go and ride at Aachen. As Richard Davison puts it, Aachen is the 'Wimbledon of dressage'. I needed to know, she needed to know and the selectors wished to know what her temperament would be like on a team and at a big show. Fernandez was the one for that test.

At the beginning my conscious plan was to get these two horses, Uti and Blueberry, to the Europeans with a spare, and to build up to these big scores. So we needed to plan the bigger shows as we were going along. I realised that to take Charlotte with me on this journey was a pretty big thing to do as I was not only trying to produce Uthopia but also trying to produce her to have confidence as well. I needn't have worried on that score, however, as she's as competitive as the most competitive person you've ever met. Everything I seemed to throw at her, including Aachen, she always did her best. I thought we'd save Valegro and Uthopia for the big pot, so Charlotte took Dez to Aachen, where they did a brilliant job to score 71 per cent. It was there that Dez was spotted by Cathrine Rasmussen.

By that stage we were in July, and Charlotte had a big decision to make. I advised her that the decision would be a life-changing one for her and it would be her first lesson in being a professional rider. Obviously Valegro and Uthopia would be the horses to go to the Europeans. Dez was never going to be our star as long as we had Valegro and Uti, although he was good enough to be on our team and would have been in reserve should anything have happened to those two horses. It was better to take the money and let Dez be a star. Although it's incredibly hard to part with a horse when you've spent so long building up a partnership with – and Charlotte got him as a three-year-old – it is rewarding to see them go on to be successful and have a good life; that's what you want for them. I'd done it many times before, but this was a first for Charlotte. Dez was still our reserve when we were selected for the Europeans, and he went to Cathrine in September after our big adventure. He would be the highest placed horse for Norway at the 2013 Europeans and has taken Cathrine to numerous World Cup shows. They came to Olympia that year.

We were lucky at that stage in that I planned what I wanted to do and I was experienced enough that the team management and selectors let me get on with it. As with all these things, selectors are there to select in case the team does not select itself, but on results the team should be able to select itself. I don't think anyone knew how phenomenal these two horses Uti and Blueberry would turn out to be – I think even Laura got a shock, having happily been sailing along as the queen of British dressage – but I'd gone on record as saying I thought these two horses were destined to be the best in the world, that there was going to be a shake-up that year.

Once I got to Hickstead and Uthopia beat Parzival the writing was already on the wall that Uti was getting to his peak, then Valegro reached his peak the following year. It was interesting that Charlotte, at that stage, was hovering around the 75–77 per cent mark because of her greenness and Valegro's, whereas I'd managed to get my mitts on Uthopia and get the accelerator working better. Uti was so excited about dressage then, when he didn't know what he was doing.

Off we went to Rotterdam, the Europeans and that magical moment. The funny thing is I won the grand prix which was amazing for us then, and Charlotte was to win the grand prix at the Olympics, so they truly were the best horses in the world for a while. Uthopia's grand prix was bizarre because we'd had this moment when we were warming up and I was about to go in where the horse suddenly became so, so light in my hand – scarily light – that I became absolutely convinced that something had happened. Had he bitten his tongue or got his tongue over the bit? As we walked up to the arena I literally had nothing in the reins and I was starting to panic, thinking something must be wrong, he just didn't feel the way he normally did. Then there was a slap on his arse and it was a case of get through those gates and get on with it. As I went round the edge of the arena

I was still thinking he was suspiciously light, but he was on his twinkle toes. When I watch that test now it seems to me one of the most effortless tests I've ever seen him do; I think it was Richard Davison who said on the commentary: 'the horse just looks as if he's out for a stroll in the park.' It was unbelievable. Bearing in mind I was always going to be up against his walk so everything else had to be as perfect as possible to get a score anywhere near 80 per cent, that day he did everything absolutely beautifully and I got 82.568. All seven judges gave Uti ten for his final extended trot. And I gave Richard Davison a ten for delivering that slap on the arse.

With Adelinde behind me, then Totilas and Matthias Rath, Charlotte was fourth and Laura fifth with 78 and 77 apiece. Suddenly the team had moved up to fielding four members who scored over 70 (Emile made it) and one over 80, and we won with an all-time record team score. And then there had been the huge hype over the German team with Totilas now ridden by Matthias Rath after Paul Schockemohle had bought the stallion. Isabell Werth and Christoph Koschel didn't have great rides but Germany got the silver and the Dutch bronze. While Adelinde scored 81 per cent for the Dutch, the other three riders only scored 70 per cent each.

Before we knew it we were round at the back of the main arena. The stadium at Rotterdam is huge. The Dutch want to bring the riders to the people and when we won, after our press conference, we were driven round on buggies. It was like going out into a pop concert. We were at the back of this stage and you could hear this wall of noise coming out of the front of the stadium. They were taking the teams round individually and as you'd expect the crowd had gone mad for the Dutch, and then for us to step up there it was completely wild. We walked up the stairs and we'd been given bottles of champagne with which we were expected to spray each other and of course we did. It was like Formula One racing, it was one big party and that was just after the one team competition.

It was a huge celebration for us – pivotal moment, monumental, mission accomplished – but not only did we win with an all-time team record score that beat the Dutch record set at Windsor, we won by the biggest margin ever. And the questions! Someone asked me if I had anything to say to the Dutch people and I replied yes, first of all I'd like to thank the two most stupid Dutch people for selling me Valegro and Uthopia. They loved that! It's been remarkable all the way through how much the Dutch love these two horses and how they feel part of the story as they bred them.

After a day off where Uthopia had a relaxed day, walked and grazed in hand, we moved to the individual competition. That's where things started to go tits up, because Charlotte, for the first time in her career, was left without me. We had to work in together and so I couldn't fully concentrate on her. That show was only six months after her first grand prix and Charlotte wasn't quite mentally ready to cope on her own, so she and Valegro slipped a bit down the placings. However, when I watch her two individual tests now, the special and the freestyle, I can see they're full of highlights but littered with mistakes; she went wrong in her music, things started leaving her brain – it was an experience she'd never had before.

It was a departure for me too. Watching her grand prix was terrifying – I could hardly hold myself upright and I've never cried so much in a test in all my life. I started when they announced her name, so it was even before she went up the centre line. It was beautiful to watch but oh my God, the strain, the stress. Even after twenty years of competing these were things I wasn't used to; I'd never had that much pressure or had to worry so much about somebody else. Meanwhile Uthopia romped his way through the special, and all was going well until it came to my effing one-time changes, which I messed up when he decided to go for a poo in the middle of them and stopped doing the changes. I couldn't believe it, that line was a total mess. Then although Parzival didn't make a mistake Adelinde went wrong in her test (for which you lose two marks from each judge). I could so easily have won the gold if it weren't for that poo. But that's life, and life is full of what ifs and if onlys. And Adelinde's a great sport and she's not one of those people who makes you feel bad about coming second, we both know the perils of being a competition rider. It was a fabulous podium finish with Laura in third with Mistral Højris, and I had my first individual medal.

The freestyle was the following day and as there were separate medals for special and freestyle, more medals to be had. Theo van Bruggen had put together my freestyle and I'd got it the week before so this was a debut performance. I'd decided at the last minute to ditch Tom Jones and do something different. Theo had carefully constructed a chorus which had my name in it which I found really funny, very 'Ankyfied', although thankfully for all concerned unlike Anky's Athens freestyle I stopped short of singing on it myself. Despite only a week to learn it from a DVD we ended up at the right place at the right time and while Adelinde aced the gold, there I was popping up on the podium again next to her.

We came home triumphant. It was fabulous, it was the end of a superb campaign, and while my ambitions have always centred on team medals those two individual silvers, which have pride of place in my kitchen, were an added bonus.

Then shortly before Christmas the three of us rode at Olympia. Laura set another record becoming the first British rider ever to win Olympia. She did it by a nose as we all had 83 per cent scores – that was Laura, Charlotte and me. I'd like to say I was being polite by letting the ladies go first, but the truth is there wasn't much more Uti could have done, it was that close in the freestyle. He was ring rusty in the grand prix, but Charlotte and Valegro's 81 per cent win was the story there. The year had set the path for 2012 and we were all thinking about London gold and whether we could make that a reality. I had more than one medal in mind, and that was looking more achievable as the year drew to a close.

What seemed totally unreal was what happened on the way home from Olympia. I was driving when the phone rang. It was Sasha.

They'd had an unexpected phone call from some people who, she said, would like to make an offer on Uthopia. They want to come and try him, she told me, adding that she thought we should, must even, consider the offer.

Having just left Olympia where we were all on a high, having done so well, I suddenly felt crushed. It dawned on me that I had a desperate situation here because whoever these people were they would want this horse in the next ten days. The FEI rule is very clear that to be ridden at the Olympics a horse has to be in the ownership of the country he's going to be ridden for by 31 December of the year preceding the Games.

I got home. I was supposed to go to a party but I felt so sick about the whole thing that I just wanted to be at home on my own, so I didn't go. Then the next day, as luck would have it or whatever destiny had decided, Uthopia was lame. He had literally gone from doing this amazing test at Olympia to limping out of his stable the next day. It's something we've had to keep an eye on with Uti since. He has ultra-sensitive feet and we have had to manage him carefully because of that.

Anyway, this situation had arisen so I sent a message to say Uthopia was lame so nobody could come and try him. But the situation was desperate because of the timing issue. Uti was highly successful and I think the offer on the table was for many millions. The following night a local friend was having a Christmas party and she had invited everyone from the yard, but someone had to remain on duty and so I told everyone to go and enjoy themselves and that I would stay home. I was quite looking forward to a night in.

At about a quarter to eight I was sat at my desk in the office, by the window, on the telephone, when the outside lights came on and a car turned up, heading towards the yard. The next minute there was a knock at my front door and unbelievably there at the door were the potential purchasers with their trainer, who had flown in that night. My heart literally felt as if it had hit my head I was so shocked.

I managed to ask them what they were doing here. We have come to see Uthopia and would like to try him, they said. But I told you the horse is lame, you can't try him, I responded, but they insisted they wanted to see him. Sasha and her dad were there too. I felt desperately sorry for Sasha as I knew that her father was under a lot of pressure to sell the horse. It wasn't Sasha's decision and although I maintained a half-share in him I couldn't magically summon up someone at such short notice to buy out the other fifty per cent, although we did go on to try that.

Anyway I had no choice but to make my way to the stables and get Uthopia out. I walked up there thinking, 'Please God, Uti, don't be sound!' and sure enough he literally pottered out of his stable. He was extremely sore and it was obvious straight away that I had been telling the truth and that no way could they have ridden him. Because we knew Uti we realised it was his foot, but I could see from the way they were looking at his leg – and in fact I could hear them saying – they thought it was his suspensory ligament. I remember thinking to myself, 'Fine, if you want to think that, but it's not his suspensory it's his foot.' So there were a lot of quiet moments and embarrassment on their side and it was a bloody freezing cold night – I was standing there in pyjamas and wellies – and they had to drive away. They did not come back the next morning as they had said they were going to and I never saw them at the yard again.

The next stage of the operation was to try and raise the money to buy out Del, Sasha's father, but unfortunately it was going to take a lot longer than the ten days – and this was over Christmas don't forget. Thankfully the dreaded 31 December deadline passed in the meantime; it was better to make a decision on what to do without that pressure. By that stage it was clear that his feet had taken a bit of a pounding, so we decided to give Uti a holiday, let his feet settle down and not start working him again until February, bearing in mind he was going to have a heavy year ahead of him with the Olympics.

Uti was still on the market but there was no rush for anyone else to buy him as they could not have ridden him at the Olympics anyway. I had everything crossed that no one would come forward, but rumours are rumours and sure enough the rumours started that Uthopia was not a sound horse.

It was a question of getting him fit and competing him again and the Olympics were coming up at the beginning of August. Sasha and her father gave their word that if he was going to be sold we would try and persuade any potential buyer that they could have him after the Olympics. Theoretically, someone could have bought him to keep him out of the Games, thereby weakening the British challenge, but they didn't, thank God.

We'd got through the deadline and into 2012. The World Dressage Masters organisers had invited Charlotte and me to compete in Florida. I didn't think Uti would be suited to that trip but Valegro is a good traveller. As it happened, Fiona Bigwood had asked me to ride Wie Atlantico while she was pregnant so I ended up taking him to Florida. If you've never done it before, Wellington is an amazing experience: the polo clubs, the show venues, the winter residences, it's where anyone who is anyone in US equestrian sport spends the winter, plus a good few foreigners as well.

Both horses had flown beautifully, which was a huge relief, but as the competition kicked off we had a problem. When it came to doing the draw I got a phone call in my hotel room to ask whether I realised that I was not qualified. The criteria meant I needed to have completed two three-star events with over 64 per cent. I hadn't done a single show on Atlantico. It transpired that there were three of us out of fifteen starters who were not correctly qualified. An emergency meeting was held and, thanks to the generosity of the other riders, Stephen Clarke and Thomas Bauer's solution that the show be downgraded to a four-star from a five-star was accepted. And the sponsors generously agreed to keep the same prize money. I did feel pretty stupid having gone all that way, but I had made it clear when the invitation came that I only had Wie Atlantico to ride and that I hadn't competed him yet – I'd only had him a few weeks – and they had said fine, bring him over. I've never been one for knowing the rules!

Atlantico did a nice grand prix for a little short of 70 per cent. This was irritating as that's all I wanted to get on him and we always seemed to be just shy of it on 69. Valegro and Charlotte were second to Steffen Peters and Ravel, who were the home favourites. It was close but Ravel deserved to win. This was a big show centre and Valegro was hot and made a couple of big errors. There were a lot of people but they were welcoming and the Americans were thrilled to see Valegro as they'd heard he was one of our up-and-coming stars. Charlotte and I starred in the programme. We'd taken part in a special photo shoot which produced some super-model-style non-horsey photographs. My favourite was of Charlotte about to kiss a frog, which she clearly must have done as she looked like a princess in the photo.

When it came to the music I dragged out Tom Jones for another airing. That music must have accompanied more horses than any other music in the world, but everyone loves it and I knew I wasn't going to win so it was about being competitive and having a fun time. Fiona couldn't fly out, but all the excitement brought on early contractions and she ended up having to ring the hospital for advice. We finished fourth while the battle engaged again between Valegro and Ravel.

It was another example of how a single judge can affect the placings. There was a minuscule difference in the final scores. Steffen thought Charlotte had won and graciously congratulated her, but the US judge placed Steffen highly and Charlotte under 80 per cent. You have to take these things on the chin in this sport and we came home on another high because Valegro had turned a corner at Olympia and Florida backed that up.

Then it was on to Vidauban with Wie Atlantico and Golly for two glorious weeks of sunshine. We had rented a villa and Aram was there with us, which was lovely. He was also riding so I was helping him, Henriette and Ulrik. Poor Henriette had a nightmare trip. One horse sneezed through the test and had blood on him so got eliminated under the newly introduced blood rule, which meant any evidence of blood led to instant elimination. It was hot during the day and cold at night so there were lots of bugs about and the constant watering of the sand surfaces led to more than one white-legged, clipped horse getting chafed heels. The evenings were spent practising psychology in an effort to persuade Henriette that it was beyond the realms of anybody's fault. But all in all it was a good show, and Nip Tuck, 'Barney', had tagged along for another winter holiday too. Atlantico had been back a month from his Florida trip but he still felt a bit tired and didn't go at his best. With Golly I was still at the stage where I felt unsteady with him; one bad arena, one movement in the crowd at the wrong time, one judge rustling his paper and it could all be over. But on our debut together he won both his prix st georges tests, I couldn't have asked for more, and I am sure Jane would have approved.

When Golly and Douglas came here – and sometimes it is better not to know how difficult they've been and start from a clean sheet – I thought, yes, I'm going to have to adapt, but they're going to have to adapt to the way we do things here. For probably the first four or five months of riding Golly I found it difficult and he was tricky, I couldn't get the right buttons. He was quite nappy and so frustrated, but I kept thinking, 'I can't tell Aram I can't ride him, I've got to keep going until I find the buttons.'

Then one day somebody walked onto the yard, I think it was somebody who'd come to watch a morning's demonstration, and I was showing the group round the yard and introducing all the horses. We got to Golly and she turned to me and said that out of all the horses on the yard, who all seemed so happy and natural, this one seemed depressed. It was weird, I got this cold feeling. I asked her why and she replied she didn't know why, he just seemed very depressed, and she asked what had happened. I didn't know who she was and I still don't know, but she was a bit of a horse-whisperer and there was something about her that made me tell the story of how Jane had probably died on him, having suffered that massive heart attack on the way back to the yard. It made me really, really think as it was such a weird thing to say, but I suddenly had this feeling that I ought to spend more time with Golly, bond with him and get to understand him better. It was as if we turned a corner then.

He was a very strong horse at that point but we started to gel when I put him back in a snaffle bridle. My thought was that it would work doing it like that, so I took my time and Aram gave me all the time in the world anyway. Normally the girls here do the warming up and cooling down, but I spent more time with Golly and did this myself, and I added more depth to his training, more time, more exposure, and took him out to places where he didn't have to compete, perhaps riding him twice a day and generally fiddling about with him. Undoubtedly he had grand prix potential, it was never a question of will he or won't he, the question was would he cope with being submissive enough to do it at a show. But it worked and I suddenly started to find this suspension in his paces which I hadn't been able to get before. Both Fiona and Alan are very touchy-feely with the horses, they're pets to them as well and that's important in a competition yard and the reason why I have the high 'people to horses' ratio, so there's time to spend with the horses. That's what we did with Golly, we all spent a lot of time with him.

Aram said one thing to me which always stuck in my mind, something Jane had always said, which was when you ride this horse you always have to think lazy, so don't think of riding him with power but be lazy and then he starts to relax. A funny little saying, but it worked. In the beginning I couldn't do a flying change on him, he always used to run off when I put my legs on him. I knew Jane could do them because she'd told me and she'd competed Golly at small tour, but I couldn't get a single change without him running off. It was those words of Jane's that flicked a switch. Then when Golly finally came out at small tour we'd already got this relationship going.

The next stage on the road to Greenwich seemed like a good plan:

Hagen, Fritzens then Hartpury then the Games. Uti and Blueberry didn't need extra travelling. They were well known, we knew they went in any arena and didn't need acclimatising to different surroundings so we were going to keep shows to a minimum. Charlotte was having her new freestyle programme prepared – the Big Ben programme – which we were going to air at Hartpury as her one run before. In Hagen we were going to do the special so she would have experience in both tests, bearing in mind that for this Olympics the grand prix and the special would now count towards the team results. I was comfortable with the special because I always thought that was Uthopia's test of choice and my new music was the least of my worries – as usual for me with the music.

As it happened we were making a new show for Horse & Country TV called *Carl and Charlotte Dressage Superstars* so the crew were coming with us on the journey to Hagen. I thought it would be interesting for people to see the behind-the-scenes action and what it is like to compete at a big show as not too many people get that opportunity. So we were all in preparation for Hagen. My philosophy has been always to try and keep the horses in their routine with as little disruption as possible, whatever the approaching occasion. That included their daily turnout in the field, although I had cut the time back to a maximum of two hours a day so that they didn't get fat or bored. We were on a real fitness regime with the pair of them to try and get them to top fitness for Greenwich, and that programme would work if we started them in May at Hagen. We could then keep them for the three months at that high level of fitness rather than going up and down all the time. That's why we didn't start competing earlier.

Uthopia decided, literally a day or two before the lorry was due to leave for Hagen, to rip across from one side of the field to the other when he was ready to come in; he pulled a front shoe off. For a normal horse, that probably wouldn't have made a jot of difference, but Uti had pulled a small chunk of his foot off on one side. With him being the wimp that he is – he only has to look at a stone and he squeals 'Ouch, my toes!' – he had to be shod, then he was lame. It was a bit of a blow but at least we knew why. There wasn't a major panic, there didn't seem to be anything else wrong, so Haydn, our farrier, advised me to give Uti three or four days, after which he'd be all right. But it did mean we were going to miss Hagen. So that was my first trauma of the year.

It's easy to spend a lot of time worrying what other people think and my first thought was that people were not going to believe me. The good thing, however, was that the Horse & Country crew had been with us that day and had actually captured that moment on film. So if anyone had questioned me I'd have raked out the footage and said, 'There you are.'

There was nothing I could do about Uti, but we went to Hagen with Valegro. What an exciting piece of the jigsaw that turned out to be. Valegro and Charlotte scored 88 per cent to set a new world record for grand prix special. The BBC was also there filming, as they had started doing their short films on the Olympics and potential medallists, so I was strapped up to a BBC microphone for Charlotte's test. Even when I look at the film now I am surprised at how calm I was, standing at the entrance commenting: 'That's a nine, that's a ten, that's an eight, that's a nine.' It all flowed, somehow it seemed to last for ages, but from one movement to the other Valegro produced a flawless test, as if every moment was there to be savoured. He had won the grand prix on 81 per cent, then that special – nearly 2 per cent higher than the previous record score set two years before by Edward and Totilas – and the dressage world was alive with the buzz of Valegro.

Totilas was there, back in the ring after eight months away. He was competing in the other grand prix for the freestyle, which he won, and people were making comparisons. They were both spectacular, but in different ways. Charlotte's partnership was growing but Matthias to be fair was under this awful media scrutiny. Everything he did was picked apart. No way would I wish that on anybody and no way would I let myself be put in that situation. It was unenviable. Although Totilas must be a lovely horse to ride, who would want to have the world following your every move? On the one hand their connections had provoked a lot of it, they had 'over-gloated' themselves as I say, but when people were writing disgusting, vile things on Facebook and forums, well, it made me realise just how cruel people can be.

So we left Hagen, which is always an amazing show, brilliantly run by Ulli Kasselmann and his team, and sure enough when we returned home on the Sunday night not only had the place flooded but the whole farm here was flooded. From 'Horses and Dreams' (as Hagen is sub-titled) to wet reality. Thankfully, Uthopia was sound so every cloud has a silver lining.

The following weekend was Addington CDN, a 'friendly' international. Right, I thought, I'll go to Addington to get Uthopia through a grand prix. Firstly I wanted to show everybody he was actually fine and secondly I was looking forward to a run. I hadn't been out on him for nearly five months and I was beginning to feel that I was so concentrated on Charlotte I wasn't going to get the concentration for myself and Uthopia. So I took Douglas, who duly won the small tour, and Fiona's Wie Atlantico, who was second in the grand prix.

It was an indoor show but I warmed up outside and I felt as if Uthopia was actually on fire. I could hear him breathing like a bull and then he saw the bronze statue of the horse. It's unbelievable what some horses can get fixated on, and for Uti to be fixated on something other than food was unbelievable in itself. But he had clearly decided that this bronze statue was a living, breathing mare, so by the time I went in to do my test he was breathing fire and wild, and I got 83.29 – a British record for a grand prix at that time. Although it didn't feel like the ride he'd given me in Rotterdam the year before it was great to feel him flying, and on full form.

I had to go to an international show. We were half qualified for the Olympics from our Olympia result but I needed to do another show so I decided to take Uti to Fritzens. A two-day drive up into the mountains, it is one of the most beautiful settings of any show I have ever been to. The show is at the home of the Haim-Swarovski family, Schindlhof, 800 metres up in the Austrian Alps, and the arena is set into the most spectacular backdrop of mountain views. It really is Heidi-land. All that's missing is Mrs Swarovski milking goats and Mr Swarovski yodelling.

Seriously, the Swarovskis are the most fabulous hosts. For some reason Wikipedia had got my birthday muddled up, so first of all Mr then Mrs Swarovski, followed by some of the journalists who were at the show, started wishing me a happy birthday. I kept laughing and saying it's not my birthday, thank you, it's not my birthday, thank you, it's not my birthday yet (this was at the beginning of June and mine's at the end). The show is famous for the Saturday-night party which always begins in the indoor school under the Swarovski chandeliers hanging at either end. As it was a special Olympic year they made a real effort to introduce everybody, the riders all have their time in the spotlight, and we had opera singers performing for us for forty-five minutes in the indoor school – not that it looked like a riding arena that evening. Everyone was dressed up to the nines and all the local glitterati and Heidis from the surrounding hills had come alive to the sound of music and filled the school. Then we went through to the huge tent. Probably two hundred of us were seated for dinner.

I was sitting at the back where everything had been set up for a band to play later – or so I thought. Suddenly the lights went out the band started playing 'Happy Birthday' and Klaus and Evelyn Swarovski climbed onto the stage – I am sure they ascended gracefully but we were in the mountains after all. To my utter horror they called my name. I knew straight away that this was a big mistake but by this stage, on that stage, there was no alternative.

So up to the stage I went. I thanked everybody for a lovely birthday, said a big thank you to the show, added what a great show it was and told a few jokes. I was handed a lovely birthday cake and a present, then I had to walk off this stage with a huge cake in one hand and a present in the other with everyone watching and applauding. I had to walk across the entire floor to return to my seat, and I happened to pass the table at which Evi Strasser was sitting. Evi's a great character; she's competed in international downhill skiing, snow-boarding and wind-surfing events as well as representing Canada in dressage. As I passed, Evi put her hand out to stop me and wish me happy birthday and as she did my momentum came to halt and the cake, a glorious gateau-type concoction, tipped straight over. It slid down the back of Evi's chair and landed in a chocolatey, creamy mess all over the floor. It was a hilarious evening.

At the show Uthopia was a nightmare to ride, his concentration had gone. I think because he had started at their show the year before, Klaus and Evelyn had promoted him as a huge star, which of course he is, but everywhere I went to try and warm up people turned out to watch, inluding an Arab prince and all sorts of local dignitaries including the mayor. It became a nightmare, with hundreds of people and hundreds of cameras clicking and videoing. It makes it extremely difficult to concentrate. I was high on the hill with a fat chance of being a lonely goat herd.

I warmed Uti up inside, then moved to an outdoor arena, then we had to go down to the main arena to do the test. He was just off my aids and not concentrating. In fact, he was a goat. We won, and it was a high mark of 77 per cent, but because it was close to the Olympics they didn't have a huge top-level playing field. The win felt a bit of a hollow victory as I didn't have good rides.

I came home disappointed, then we had Hartpury looming. Hartpury had been earmarked as Charlotte's run-through for the music which Tom Hunt had been working on. I was going to have my run as well for the music – which as usual with the music filled me with as much enthusiasm as taking part in a marathon – and this was our last show. I thought at least it's local and I can go there and get a great score ready for the Olympics.

Again, a few days before we were due to go Uthopia didn't feel right, and yet again it was his foot balance. We'd all worked incredibly hard – not least Haydn the farrier – to maintain his foot balance but unfortunately it slipped again, so Uti didn't feel 100 per cent. Some people may say that at this point I should have kept him in, should have wrapped him in cotton wool, but that has never been my way. Horses should be allowed to be horses. First of all that is what they are and their star status as competitors is what they give us when they are allowed to be themselves. That's my view, anyway, that's what I learned years ago from Jannie and I would take what was thrown at me for it.

Charlotte was worried that she and I were going to be drawn next to each other and she wanted me to be there on the ground for the whole of her warm-ups, music included. So I decided, probably against my better judgement, that we would leave Uthopia ticking along at home so I could be there for Charlotte and there would be no compromise then with the draw. We only had two weeks between Hartpury and the Olympics. I so wanted Charlotte to have the confidence because I knew that she was going to be the one to pull in the fat score – you could see the trajectory Valegro was on – but I admit now that I felt myself under-prepared. I'd only done one international competition, Uti was still only eleven and while he was always fine in training, things can crop up in competition – and they had done.

Uti needed to get the right show and get the right amount of attention, not so much that he was bored and not so little that he didn't concentrate. The fact was, when we were rolling down those ramps and the horses were heading off to London, I had this awful sinking feeling that we were under-prepared for it. I hadn't competed with my music, I hadn't had a good ride in the last show and I was feeling really weird.

What I had sorted out was the starting order for the team – the 'order of go' as the Americans call it, which has always tickled me, but at that point it didn't. It was serious business now. In our case, Charlotte's and mine, it was vital. With only three of us in the team there had to be some degree of separation so that I could do my job and look after Charlotte. On results it was obvious what the order should be. Laura was not happy when I called her to tell her what I thought, but I wasn't going to move. This was about everything we had worked for; it was also about the team. I called Will Connell and explained the rationale. He got it. I put myself first to go, Laura second, then Charlotte third so that I would have enough time without running around after my test to be there for hers. I was also confident, knew in fact, that Valegro going last would do nothing other than work. Charlotte had already got the world record in Hagen and I was insistent that she would go last because she would get the score, whatever we needed.

It must have been difficult for Laura, but to give her her due she rang me back, said she'd spoken to 'Papa', my old mentor Dr B, and that they were happy to go with it. And we all were as we collected those historic gold medals on the podium at Greenwich. That first Olympic team medal ever in the history of British dressage, of course we wished it would happen, and there were plenty of times when we thought it could happen, but over those two tests in London, that was when we made it happen.

We had a day off in Greenwich before the music, the individual final, on the Thursday. I took Uti for a spin up the gallops as by this time he was well and truly over the Olympics. There was not a schooling session left in him, having done his bit in the special. The gallops had been put in for the eventers and went past the side of the stables and up a hill. Uti loved whirling up and down there.

Charlotte and I had a session which went well, but Charlotte still felt short of match practice as she'd only ridden the final choreography of the test once. We had to go for a high degree of difficulty but were still trying to figure out whether to put in the piaffe pirouette at the end. It was the one movement Charlotte fluffed and it turned out to be the fluff of her test. It was also the fluff of our training session.

Valegro was still only ten and things like that were all new to him, but we did want to put a couple of difficult moves in to show off his talents. He'd been programmed for the grand prix and the special things like piaffe pirouettes started coming to him early on in his career, but he does like to know where he is going. We had a good practice though, and went through that last line a few times and all was well. So we spent the rest of the day watching telly – you don't want to do anything more engaging when an Olympic final is looming – at the team house opposite the park. We could at least try to relax – this was another time when the logistics put in place by our World Class 'British Army' proved so valuable – and then we got an early night, if not early sleep.

The next day I just remember how much quieter it was; the show-jumpers had gone home with their team gold and all that remained were the dressage horses who had got through to the individual final. But while it was a bit of a desolate area out the back, out front in the stadium was the biggest crowd we'd ever seen, and the noisiest and the most excitable.

My main mission was to try and keep Charlotte away from the inevitable questions from the press, from everyone actually. What was she going to do? What if she won gold, how would she feel? It would have been easy to run away. For the first time ever in the special I'd seen Charlotte get nervous. That was because she'd had to watch me ride then go and ride herself, but there were a new set of nerves to contend with.

Anyway, I did my test and it was rather like floating in a feeling of wanting to get that test done and out of the way. I didn't think about winning an individual medal as I knew in the warm-up that Uti's fuel levels were quite low. Richard tried to instil me with that last bit of enthusiasm. He and Henriette on the sidelines tried their best to rouse me, but I know Uti so well. I knew what I had out there in the warm-up was what I was going to get in the arena. Uti was on day three and by day three he is in dressage snoozeville.

I'd already done what I wanted to do and knew that team gold was in the bag ready to go home, but what I enjoyed about it was the reception and my music, which I loved. Some people called it a mess of music, but that was only a few disgruntled music makers so from that point of view I didn't care. I loved it and Tom had put some fun bits of music in there from *Last of the Mohicans* to the final centre line's 'Zadok the Priest', which was brilliant.

Tom Hunt was such a find, in fact he found us. He emailed and said he'd like to do some music for us, would we be interested, and I thought why not? Tom is so different, he's young, he's fresh in his approach and he's got his finger on every bit of music going round the world. A really nice guy to work with, nothing's a problem and if there's a piece of music you like and you want he's never going to tell you that you can't have it. It's a lot more exciting to work with someone like that.

I enjoyed riding the programme, although it was a bit like rowing a boat round – dear Uti had got quite glue-like by then. I had a mistake in the one-times and he had a little walk in one of the pirouettes but other than that he was fine and he did so well, considering how he was feeling. I hopped off and got straight back to the warm-up – there was no time to talk to anyone as there was only Adelinde between me and Charlotte, who was all plugged in so I ran in and grabbed the microphone. To avoid bellowing across arenas we, as do many trainers and riders, use a system where the trainer on the ground has a microphone and the rider a headset. So we got stuck in and forgot about everything else except focusing on that music.

It was impossible to tell. I'm her trainer, I'm a perfectionist, I know how her music should be; looking back at that last line, for those of us that knowValegro, I think he gave his last little bit of presence and effort, but equally we could tell he was tired. Valegro had never been tired before at a show, but you could see he was slightly flagging.

Selfies: collecting our Olympic kit – not the official photos!

(Adidas/Team GB)

In it together – ready to trot Uti up for the vet check, Greenwich, 2012

(©Jon Stroud/Jon Stroud Media)

Uti nails that score in the grand prix: we were on the way to history at London, 2c

(©Jon Stroud/Jon Stroud Media)

Gold at London, 2012. We made it happen

(© Jon Stroud/Jon Stroud Media)

That amazing sea of fans – we all went bananas

(©Jon Stroud/Jon Stroud Media)

Who should I spot from the Olympic parade float? Parked outside my half-sister Vivien's workplace!

(Josef Fickler)

Winning the national championship with Uti – 2012, what a year!

(©Jon Stroud/Jon Stroud Media)

Back to Sark with gold, Charlotte, me, Richard (Davison). An incredible welcome! (August 2012)

(©Tom Tardif/Guernsey Press)

Nan's tellings-off in the early days paid off with a gold medal! With Nan and the Olympic torch that finally came to Sark

(Claire Hester)

Meeting the Duchess of Cambridge at Buckingham Palace – jolly nice canapés too (October 2012) (AFP/Getty Images)

Dances with Wolves, 'Golly' – very talented and very hot, Rotterdam, 2013
(©Jon Stroud/Jon Stroud Media)

Rotterdam is famous for Formula 1 prize givings – getting new team members
Dan and Gareth used to it at the Nations Cup 2013 (© Jon Stroud/Jon Stroud Media)

Uti and I together again on the way to the arena at Hickstead

(©Jon Stroud/Jon Stroud Media)

With Laura Tomlinson at Windsor Castle. Twenty-four years after
we first met, here we are! (Getty Images)

Grandad escorting Edwina, the new European Champion with Valegro, Herning, 2013 (©Jon Stroud/Jon Stroud Media)

For the love of a horse: Valegro 'Blueberry' and Alan, whose expression says it all, Amsterdam, 2014 (©Selene Scarsi)

Neither of us had watched Adelinde, but she'd scored a whopping 88 per cent. When Charlotte came out she looked at me and I looked at her and we both knew what the other was thinking; that last little piaffe pirouette. With Adelinde's score, I didn't think she could have made a mistake and we knew she'd ridden her programme a lot. For Charlotte there had only been a little mistake in the aids, admittedly – it was nothing and for the age of the horse it was nothing – and it wasn't disappointment, but it was simply, as usual, you know what I think, and she knew what I thought.

There was this massive screening around the backstage area but the first thing I remember was somebody leaning over right from the top of the stands and screaming, 'You've done it!!!' Then there was this massive wall of sound.

There were people piling in and the non-tactile, untouchable Charlotte got more kisses than she'd bargained for! Jennie Loriston-Clarke was in tears, Richard was in tears, everybody was in tears, but that was one of the happiest little gaggles of people you could ever find in one spot.

Charlotte broke down and sobbed, which was a relief, that finally it did matter. We all knew it had mattered whenever she used to say, as she did, 'It's just another centre line, it's just another arena . . .'. Yes, it's a great attitude to have, but this mattered, and she made it happen when it mattered.

It took another half an hour or so before the prize-giving and only the top three were to go in. Laura had come third to get the bronze, which was wonderful for her. Alf, that great championship campaigner, had again got better as the championship went on. Whereas Uti was relaxed at the beginning and too relaxed at the end, Alf was tense at beginning and spot on by the end. The crowd had what they wanted, two British riders in the top three, and Uti finished fifth which was my highest Olympic placing.

Funnily enough one of my ambitions, which Chris Bartle and I had been talking about for twenty years, was to beat Chris, whose record placing – sixth at the Los Angeles Olympics – only got broken in London. And that meant coming fifth or higher! So I knew that Chris would be smiling. As Chris said after the Olympics, he couldn't believe it had taken so long for someone to beat that record. I think he was glad to finally be relieved of his post. Having won Badminton and trained the Germans to almost invincible eventing success in the meantime, he has hardly rested on those 1984 laurels.

As I went to watch the individual medal ceremony I had to walk along the front of the stands to get as near to the podium as I could in case Alan wanted a hand with Valegro. So I ended up standing with FEI President Princess Haya and various dignitaries. Princess Haya was very sweet and just said what an amazing horse Valegro was and how fantastic for us and for Great Britain. Watching Charlotte get up onto that podium, for the first time I felt a little twinge of wishing I was up there. It had been the three of us all the way through and I think maybe for a minuscule moment I wished I could be up there too. Then I thought, hang on a minute, as I always do, there's my horse winning a gold medal, there's Charlotte who came to me as a groom and has become a star, and I've loved seeing that. I cried as much as anyone else did. It was fantastic.

Alan and I and Valegro went one way while Charlotte went the other way, still screaming at me to please come to the press conference in case she needed help, but by that stage I waved back with a 'Go on, off you go, time to be a big grown-up lady!' Those moments are not at all personal because you are literally ripped away as the media machine swings into action. The press coverage had been amazing and obviously with another individual gold dressage was going to be on the six o'clock news again.

Four months earlier, Roly, Claire and I had been talking about organising something, some sort of Olympic party. My first thought was that this could end up being one horrible huge commiseration party if things went tits up. Even then, London was booked out; everything was either out of our league financially or gone already, but we had the option of a boat so we decided to push the boat out. I said OK, let's do it, but please God, fingers crossed, this is a premonition that we're going to win so it turns out to be a celebration. And it was a wonderful, brilliant way to finish.

All the team, all our owners and supporters, family and friends from over the years, from Christopher to a smattering of celebs including Nicky Chapman, who had agreed to be an ambassador for Olympic dressage despite her falling off while making a TV programme here, which was good of her. It was brilliant, absolutely memorable, but by then I was so tired. I remember sitting on the front of that boat as we went under Tower Bridge, the Olympic rings it carried from its walkways lit up. Everyone was taking snaps on their phones and I was thinking, 'This is a moment in time that I will never forget.'

The following morning I just wanted to get out of there. Will was at breakfast and we all wanted to go. We had masses of luggage each so the idea of getting the train had Charlotte kicking off that she wasn't going to effing carry her bags across London on a Friday afternoon when the trains were going to be packed wearing her effing Olympic kit. We had to be in Olympic uniform until the end of the Olympics, and to be fair that would have made life a bit difficult. So Charlotte went on to Will along the lines of we fulfilled our end of the bargain and got you all those medals, can't you organise a car for us, blah blah, and Will said it was OK, he'd got a van. I seem to remember him doing an about turn and quick march out of range, but as he did he gave me a wink and said be outside the hotel at one o'clock as it was all organised.

Charlotte had to go off in the morning and do more press interviews, so when we all met up at the hotel Will took us round the corner where our carriage awaited – a big white Rolls-Royce with tinted windows. It was perfect. We bunged our stuff in and we were tightly packed; there was me, Charlotte, her fiancé Dean and her best friend Ian Cast (Charlotte's lady-in-waiting, as I call him). No one could see in and we had a real laugh on the way home. Being Friday, the motorway was busy and we ended up queuing for about three miles around Birdlip. Everyone was trying to look and see who was in this white Rolls and we were winding the window down halfway, showing glimpses of our Olympic uniforms then winding the window up again (well, it was electric, but you know what I mean). It amused us and amused the kid in the car opposite, but it took four and a half hours to get home.

Our home team had decorated the gates and put banners up – the place looked a million gold dollars – and I couldn't wait to go up to the yard then get in the house. In the morning, Katie, who was in charge that day, had rung me and said there were two newspaper photographers snapping away in my tack room, what should she do? All I wanted was to get in, padlock those gates and not talk to anybody outside. Your heart's been racing on adrenaline for two weeks, but the minute you get through the door into your own house and shut it – the feeling! It's the safety, that you can do whatever you like, that you can take that uniform off and sit down. It was bliss.

I'd planned it as a break, a trip straight after the Olympics. The Channel Islands are peaceful so I thought we'd get away to Sark, Charlotte, me and about forty friends. What I hadn't bargained for was that mentioning this on Facebook and Twitter and to the papers (I know, don't tell me) would lead to the phone ringing non-stop with requests. Everyone on Sark was proud and wanted to share in the celebrations, but I didn't realise what the trip was going to turn into . . .

The island held a *vin d'honneur* for me, Charlotte and Richard, which is an ancient tradition. It's an official reception for an honoured guest and included all the residents who had known me since I was a child growing up there. Then there was Uncle David, Jess and of course Nan. I'd had no idea while cocooned at Greenwich what was going on in the Channel Islands over the Olympic weeks, and while I'd done interviews with Guernsey TV and radio, Sark is a separate entity. It was overwhelming how they had all followed it. I'm only the second Channel Islander to have ever won an Olympic medal – the other was Percy Hodge in the 3,000 metre steeplechase in 1920 and that wasn't on a horse – and I was made an honorary life member of the Sark Sports Club.

There was also the fact that Sark never got the Olympic flame. It went to Guernsey but there were some people on Sark left very angry that the flame didn't go there. Dr Roger Allsopp, a retired surgeon who became the oldest man to swim the English Channel at a spry seventy and who had carried the torch in Guernsey, loaned his torch for the day so that was rectified.

It was probably the only weekend that year that the island had a burst of sun. It was Charlotte's first trip there, and she loved it. It was lovely to include her and Richard Davison in all the celebrations. All the school kids we met wanted to touch the medal. We stayed at the Dixcart Hotel, had dinner at La Sablonnerie, visited the Seigneurie, had loads of photos taken beside the gold post box and best of all, the annual Sark Horse Show coincided with the visit, although I didn't take part in the bareback race.

Charlotte had been totally off the idea of doing any more media, but I said to her please do it for me, they love the fact that you're here, that you're the double gold medallist, come on, get out there and talk to the kids. It was all good training for her, thirty children on a small island who want their pictures taken is nothing on a grand scale, but it is all training and it meant a lot to those children. Charlotte and I were really close to what had happened and I still felt like her protector, but it was also very peaceful for her. Dean, her fiancé, came too so she was able to have a bit of time with him.

Back at home it was more post-Olympic euphoria and the Olympic parade through London. The 'Our Greatest Team' parade was possibly the most mind-blowing experience of the aftermath. I'd never taken part before, but then we'd never won Olympic medals before, and as it was all about London it was massive. The float I was on happened to be parked outside the Swiss bank where my half-sister

Vivien works. Suddenly there was Vivien with her husband-to-be, David, so it was absolutely fantastic to jump down and spend a few minutes with them before the float went off.

In alphabetical order Equestrian was next to Diving, so we were on the same float. Imagine being on a float with Tom Daley when you know all the crowd want is Tom Daley! We could hear the crowd screaming 'Tom' from miles away. We didn't speak much but he reminded me of a sweet little elf. Tina Cook, one of my favourite eventing personalities, had not long split up from her husband, so I said to her, 'Tina, you are looking at millions of men here, so stand right at the front of this float and wave your silver medal aloft.' As we went past every building Tina and I were making a selection, 'that one – no, that one' and laughing all the way. Clare Balding was on our float at one stage near the end and I looked down to the end of the float – as we went through Admiralty Arch, I think – to see Clare crying. My first thought was that I hoped no one had been horrible to her, but when I went over and asked her if she was all right she said she was just so overwhelmed by the love that everyone was showing. That captured the whole day. It was an absolute feeling of celebration and everyone was thrilled for us, for London, for everything that had happened.

While Boris Johnson made his hilarious speech as we all stood up on the big stand outside Buckingham Palace I was pinned up at the back with Zara being jolly naughty and telling rude jokes. It was like a school photograph. As the Princess Royal made her speech, Zara was leaning over the edge squeaking, 'Mum, Mummy!' The other naughty children in the back row were Tina, William Fox-Pitt and Nicola Wilson, who is a real laugh as well. All the goody two-shoes – that's you, Charlotte – wanted to be at the front so they could hear everything, but us lot at the back couldn't hear a thing except our own repertoire of naughty jokes.

The national championships had to be done. I love it and the fact that Uthopia won the grand prix title for me and Golly won two small tour championships was perfect. There is a difference between a national and an international horse – a national horse can cope with turning up, doing his test and going home; an international horse has to be able to sustain his performance in a strange environment over some days.

We arrived at Stoneleigh on the Wednesday night and I didn't ride Golly until I got on to do my prix st georges test the next day. I can honestly say that although I managed to complete every movement without mistakes, it didn't feel like dressage, it felt like water-skiing. He was tense, he was hot and it was by the skin of my teeth that I got him round that test. There are many good horses who have a lot of temperament who need to be settled in a place before they are rideable and Golly, I realised, was one of them. He's like Peanuts in that way. With a horse like that you have to think about preparation. This was not the way to do it. Golly needed to be settled somewhere and absorb everything, then he would become rideable. On the Friday when he won the intermediaire I, he was already a lot better. He is a 'twice-a-day' horse; he needs to be ridden first with no pressure so he has a chance to look at everything, then he can come back out and be schooled. It's a full-time job, just as it was with Peanuts. But it made me realise that Golly was a true international horse, he was going to have to be managed.

I still hate public speaking. I'm told I am good at it, and you'd think with the amount of things I have to do I'd have got over it by now, but none of that makes any difference, I still dread it. One of the first such outings in 2013 was 'An Evening with Carl Hester' to raise money for the Fortune Centre at the Soho Hotel. I was told I would be interviewed in a 'small screening room downstairs'. Well, when I got there and saw all those people – including Martin and Philippa Clunes, and a guy from Pink Floyd – my throat went dry and I had this awful stage fright, thinking, 'Oh my God, people have paid to come and hear me talk.' I did get through it and I should always stick to the method that works best for me – no preparation whatsoever.

I have done some things that have pushed the barriers for me and the school reunion was one. I had been dreading the Old Elizabethan Association dinner at the RAF Club, but it turned out to be hilarious. One of my biggest dreads, not having kept in touch with many people, was the thought of walking into a room on my own and in a proper boys' club. Thankfully I got together with James, Pinky and John Bell for a drink in the hotel before we walked over to the club. Although it was nearly thirty years on, I recognised them all: Richard 'Pinky' Bellis, who was always bright red at school; John, whose father was a maths teacher so knew how bad I was at maths; and James, who was a boarder from England. We were all in the same year at school. They are all in finance now. It was great to meet up with them.

As the four of us went over to the club I was absolutely terrified. Naturally I had forgotten all the etiquette that goes with being at a school like that: grace before dinner, then the obituaries of anyone who had died that year. After that I was amazed there was anyone left in the room, but there were over a hundred of us. I had assumed everyone would be from my year, but it was a wide cross-section. Thankfully I sat next to Mr Cross, my Latin teacher, who drank copious amounts of red wine while regaling me with tales of things I did when I was at school. It was, as you'd expect, a black-tie dinner, and by the time the pudding arrived Mr Cross was so – well, let's call it tipsy – he dropped this concoction of Black Forest fruits down his white shirt and looked as if he had been stabbed. James was winking at me across the table to give me the heads-up that I'd be on in a few minutes, and as terror struck me I looked at that white shirt covered in berries and just couldn't stop laughing. It broke the ice for me. This is going to be fine, I thought. I talked about life and suddenly started to remember my past and off I went. The school meant nothing to me when I was there, but the friends I made are fantastic.

Despite my love of dressage and National Hunt racing I've got a soft spot for flat racing – both of the latter honed during the Jannie and Christopher years – so another of our rewards, an invitation to

Champions Day at Ascot, was brilliant, and to see Frankel win was pretty spine-tingling. And how good are they at hospitality in racing! We started off parading in cars then repaired to a big private box for all the Olympians and Paralympians, where we were hosted by former jockey John Reid, winner of among other big races the 1992 Derby on Dr Devious. With Nick Skelton, who is very involved in racing, and the lovely Tina Cook, who has racing in her blood, we were well placed for some good tips. We had a fun day of silly betting as the only safe bet that day was Frankel and that was a waste of money as we knew he was going to win so the odds were hardly favourable. It was a fabulous day and the night before we'd dined at Windsor Castle to celebrate Champions Day. Having been there three times now I can safely say I know where the toilets – I call them bogatories but probably should say lavatories – are at Windsor Castle.

Then there was the reception for all the Olympic and Paralympic medallists at Buckingham Palace, which actually felt smaller than I imagined it, but it has a superstar feeling to it with the crowd outside and people peering through the gates. Being a fan of *Downton Abbey*, Buckingham Palace did live up to my expectations – my own little piece of Downton in town: butlers with white gloves, lovely canapés, 'duck à la fisherie' and all that.

I later got my chance when I was invested with the MBE, but I so wanted to meet the Queen there. However we were drawn in lines and told where we should stand – and can you believe it, I was on the wrong side of the queue yet again! The Queen went up the other side of the room and my chance had gone. One minute she was there in front of me, albeit with her back to me, then she was off talking to people on the line opposite so I missed my chance. Two minutes later along came the Duchess of Cambridge who stopped to talk to Charlotte, me and Scott Brash, so we got to see how beautiful she is close-up. I was able to tell her before she managed to slip my grasp that we had something in common. She asked what was that, and I replied, 'My groom taught you to ride, ma'am.'

I must have the poshest groom in the world. Alan had dashed home from Saumur leaving us with the horses to attend the royal wedding as he was a friend of the Middletons, he'd helped Carole Middleton with her horse then started teaching the Duchess of Cambridge – Kate in those days – on a lovely schoolmaster ex-show horse he had, on and off for about three years. The Duchess didn't know Alan worked for me so it was nice to have a nugget of banter like that to throw in. I also had a little chat with the very pleasant David Cameron.

After the reception was over Charlotte and I climbed in the car to go home, I got a text message from William Fox-Pitt: 'You'll never guess what HM said to me – "have you sold your lovely black stallion yet?"' William claimed he replied something along the lines of 'I think you've got the wrong person, ma'am, I'm an event rider', but I'm sure his response was more protocol-polished in reality. I texted back: 'I can't see how six foot of me could be mistaken for six foot six of you!'

The Palace fun was followed by a lovely lunch party given by Roly to celebrate Harry's eighteenth birthday. His godmother Jilly Cooper made a speech in Harry's honour. Concluding, she said she would also like to toast Roly's success as the owner of the Olympic dual gold-medal-winning horse, so could we all charge our glasses and raise them 'to the wonderful . . . Viagra'. Classic Jolly Super!

It was fantastic to be honoured in the Animal Health Trust awards, as were all the Olympic and Paralympic equestrians. It was a real celebration of equestrian achievement and even Frankel got an award, although he wasn't at the dinner. As we were about to be called up to receive our award I said to Richard Davison, 'You'd better make sure you come up with us, that's an order!' Mike Tucker read the citation while I beckoned him up. I even got Mike to ask him up over the microphone, but Richard stayed sitting. I desperately wanted him to get up with the rest of us – and I thought he would – because he had stood up for me in the past and I wanted everyone there to realise that even though he didn't feature in the team medal, he was there, he was support and certainly he had my back throughout the whole journey. Laura has her own support group and Charlotte has my support, but Richard had my back and a lot of that I was passing on to Charlotte so, as far as I was concerned, he was two-thirds of our team planning and he needed to be acknowledged for that. I was sad that Richard was not up on that stage, but I was happy that I could stand there and point the finger at him. At the time I was only thinking, 'Hang on, there were four of us in these Olympics.' It was only later on that it struck me that ten years previously he had done the same thing for me. It was worth everything.

As 2012 came to a close we decided Olympia was going to be a Christmas finale for Charlotte, myself and the horses. With the thought still hanging in my head that Uthopia was to be sold I had made up my mind that this would be my last competition on him. I felt that Olympia would be an opportunity for some of those people who hadn't got to the Olympics to see the horses and I wanted Charlotte and Valegro's names on that board out the back which only the competitors see and which has pictures of all the winners. One of my dreams was that if it wasn't to be me it was going to be her and Valegro up there.

The horses hadn't had that difficult a year. Uti had only competed a few times and Valegro only had to go up the road to London. So we arrived at Olympia, which has the best Christmas spirit in the world, and the weather was cold, crisp and lovely. Charlotte wasn't well – she had flu – but despite feeling under the weather her grand prix was beautiful. Uti was a bugger, I was simply glad it wasn't the Olympics. I put it down to my thinking too much that he was going to be sold and I maybe over-tried, but I didn't put my concentration into it and he wrong-footed me on every movement. And I was constantly hopping off to go and help Charlotte.

When it came to the music I thought right, I'm going to get this and go out with a bang, and Uti did a great test. I was a little disappointed to be behind Isabell Werth but it was by less than a mark, it was nothing, and after all these years I don't really care about the marks any more. The fact was we went well and it was wonderful to ride the London music again, so it was all great. Charlotte won. It wasn't her best test but it was a reminder of the fact that we'd gone there thinking Valegro would just do it – and you think he's going to because he is the machine of the dressage world – but he still needs riding. Generally he never spooks, he never gets hot, he always does his job. Charlotte was the double gold medallist and winning was almost inevitable, but there were a few blips amid some absolutely flawless bits that left everyone gobsmacked. We did exchange a few words.

At the Olympics she'd gone into the arena with literally one second to spare – there are only forty-five seconds allowed to get in that arena after the bell to start has sounded – and at Olympia she literally went through the boards at A with the clock at zero. I was standing at the side shouting at her, 'Three seconds, two seconds – get in!!' She was slightly thrown by me shouting from the side and the test was a bit hurried, not the polished performance of previous tests, but she won and we both went into the prize-giving in the top three.

Isabell is my lifelong competitor friend. At the Europeans when I won my medal she said to me, 'It's about time, you've waited long enough, it's your turn,' which was such a lovely sentiment to hear from someone I admire. We're not bosom buddies but Isabell is someone I enjoy spending time with; a proper sportswomen, competitive but fair, never jealous or bitter, she just has what it takes. More than that she has grim determination. Whatever's thrown at her, her mouth remains shut and her focus is her riding. That's what it takes and she has produced one horse after another with hard work, yet she's fair and humble enough to congratulate someone else on a win. That is Isabell's greatness. She has been the best and has been up and down over the years but she is one of the few who always makes a point of saying, 'Congratulations, you deserve it.' The nearer you get to the top, the better everyone is with you, but Isabell has always been the same, always encouraging.

So that was that, my last duty of the year. It was a bit of a family Christmas with Claire and Corey, her son whom Jess brought up, and Jess came over from Sark. We went to our lovely local pub, the Kilcot Inn, with Dan Hammond, my old Sark pony adventurer, and Barry 'Baz' Mollet another Guernsey import friend who now looks after the place. They did us a great Christmas.

On New Year's Eve after dinner at home with some local friends I was probably in bed just after Big Ben struck. I have never looked forward more in all my life to a New Year's Eve, not because I wanted to party but because I wanted the year finished, for the full stop on that Olympic year to be put in place.

13

Perhaps in Another Colour?

On 1 January 2013 my feeling was overwhelmingly one of huge relief. I could now do what I liked; I didn't have to compete, or if I did, people wouldn't be having heart attacks if I were to score under 70 per cent. I didn't have to impress anybody. This year was going to be about me bringing out the young horses and enjoying competing again without any expectations.

The year before we'd had two weeks of glorious sunshine and 25 degrees every day, so Vidauban looked the ideal winter show; exactly how it should be for my relaxed competitive start to the year, I thought. Well, what a difference a year makes!

We were flying into Nice on Sunday, the same day Alan was arriving with the horses. Alan got in first and texted me a photo: it was a snowscape. I thought it was a joke. 'Fasten your seat belts, we're about to make our descent' came the announcement, and as we descended through the clouds it became clearer and clearer and that the whole of the coast was indeed covered in white stuff. Whether it's down to global warming, I don't know, but snow is pretty unheard of for the French Riviera; after all, it's where the rich used to come to escape the bloody winter.

It was absolutely bloody freezing at that airport. Eddie Stibbe and Debbie Brooks were joining us in the villa as Debbie was doing her first international at small tour. They took one car while Henriette, Ulrik and me took the other. Villas in the south of France are not designed for cold weather and this villa was absolutely freezing. We kept hoping the weather would improve but we woke up the next morning, teeth chattering, to find it had started snowing again. Eddie, Debbie and Ulrik, being adventurous, headed off to try and get some food and bits and pieces. But we were right up in this little mountainous area and it's bad enough negotiating those tiny roads when there's no snow on them, so they did need to be adventurous. By this time I was beginning to understand why it hadn't cost the five of us much money to stay there.

Ulrik was brilliant and got the open fire going. Being Danish he's not unused to snow and had the trick of using fir cones as kindling – they're brilliant and better than firelighters. Ulrik then got dispatched every hour to bring in the next supply of pine cones. One positive development was that for the first year out of three we were able to get the television going, and as it had satellite we were able to watch BBC1 and see how lovely it was at home.

While home was having not too bad a February, on the Côte d'Azur it was the worst February they'd had in years. We couldn't even get to the show on the first day so Alan could only walk the horses. And the poor horses were freezing as they were clipped out and in these tented stables, which were extra cold because not many people had got to the show and the tents were fairly empty, so there wasn't the warmth created by having lots of horses in them. Eventually the weather began to cheer up and the snow finally melted on the third day. Unfortunately, that left the arenas as lakes. It was nobody's fault and it couldn't be helped, but it was really difficult to work and train and I had to get Golly ready for his first grand prix.

I knew he needed the twice-a-day routine; hacking out, looking around, seeing the sights so he had a chance to chill out, all the things he doesn't do when he's left in too much. But he was great and I was so happy with him. You never know how ready you are for grand prix until you do that test. Golly was really good, really rideable. I just wanted him to get through the test without any big mistakes and he scored 72 or 73 in each of his grands prix. Nip Tuck, 'Barney', had come for his annual holiday. He is owned by Jane de la Mare, a Jersey girl whom I first met when she came to work at the Bechtolsheimers. I found Barney as a yearling and Jane bought him as a project. As one of my up-and-coming young horses who is also a hothead, Barney does the annual trip to wherever we're going as a 'long stay' so he learns to chill at shows. In this case chill was the operative word and Barney wasn't in the least bit amused to find it was snowing down there. I'd also taken Fine Time, known as Bruno, for Gemma Appleton, née Green. Gemma was pregnant and she wanted some help finishing Bruno off at grand prix and he'd been a bit problematic with the changes. He was great, but in the final week the weather had taken its toll, churning the warm-up into heavy waterlogged sand which caused his legs to swell, so we called it a day before the final freestyle. The new boys were great and despite the weather and the arenas the show's got a great atmosphere. Everyone's super friendly and there's the aptly named world-famous truffle restaurant Chez Bruno in Lorgues just down the road. A trip there was planned, which was nice as I'd never done it before. I will not, however, do it again after five courses of truffles. It was a case of truffle overkill and I'm truffled-out for the rest of my life. But it was fun.

Despite my wonderful rose-tinted New Year resolutions I had to take into account the fact that we had a European Championship coming up. All the planning for the horses for the year has to be based on something for mine, something for Charlotte's, so I can devote as much time to her horses as to my own. I had two young ones and they needed different shows to Valegro, so we were, as always, aware of the influence of the draw.

Saumur at the beginning of May was a good one for us, but dates change in the calendar and unfortunately for the first time in God knows how many years it meant I'd miss Badminton. I love the event itself, always have, but I've showcased many of our baby horses there, including Valegro, so that was a bit of a wrench.

Golly needed these smaller build-up shows and Saumur was one of the few I could go to – in fact I spent most of 2013 in France. His winning streak continued, his confidence was growing and I was enjoying the time I was spending with him. I was finding this friendship with him, we were becoming partners and he was starting to look for me when I came into the stables. That special level of communication you get to with a horse after a period of time was working. I felt at home on him, I knew he would be doing his best and that if he got nervous it wasn't because he was naughty, it was because he was genuinely a bit worried about a situation.

Golly's insecurity tends to be noise-related. Saumur attracts a big crowd on the last day, and they all came to watch him; he was a draw as he'd won the grand prix so he had quite a big crowd of people around for his special, and he coped brilliantly. He won and upped his score to 75 per cent.

There were ongoing issues over Uthopia's future but he was still here. I had hung my boots up on him at Olympia but Charlotte needed more match practice and we didn't want to overrun Valegro, so I decided she should come to Saumur and ride Uti. What fun it was for me to watch Uthopia with Charlotte rather than the other way round. It just shows how different horses can be; Charlotte was used to playing with Valegro, but here it was a case of Uthopia putting Charlotte firmly in her place. I'm quite sure Charlotte expected to go out and get 80 per cent, but that bond that you build with a horse over so many years was missing. And being a crafty little stallion, Uti gave her all the right signs outside the arena then did his own grand prix inside. Charlotte was furious after that grand prix and just couldn't believe that Uti didn't go on push-button mode. I of course found it hysterically funny!

She rectified it slightly in the music, riding Valegro's programme – which was brilliant for Uthopia, who had no idea where he was going at all. Charlotte caught him off guard on every corner as he said, 'We're doing this' and Charlotte was saying, 'No, actually you're not, you're going to do this.' As a result he was great and she got her

80 per cent. That was wonderful to see, and just as funny.

It was a fun trip. We stayed in the riders' hotel in Saumur, which is bliss as it is in the town centre, the hub of everything, with restaurants all around the square. When you've been there for as many years as I have you know exactly where to go and eat; where the best fish is, the pizza restaurants on the other side of the river and the wine caves where we stock up the lorry with wine. It's a gorgeous little town with lovely things to do – a visit there is not just about riding.

My plan then was to keep Golly on the road and keep him moving. I was really enjoying competing again and was relishing the challenge of keeping him relaxed, so we took him and Uti to France again, this time to Compiègne. With the Europeans in mind I was thinking Golly for me and Charlotte could qualify Uti as her second horse for the Europeans.

We got to Compiègne, got Uti out for Charlotte to ride and there was this lump on his back where he'd been bitten by a fly. He didn't seem too sore, so we saddled him up and she rode him carefully for half an hour, but the minute we took the saddle off we saw that the lump had started to go red. It was obvious he wouldn't be able to compete so Uti was withdrawn to enjoy *un peu de vacances en France*.

Golly again did a really good test. He won again, so I knew that if I could ever get his head round a bigger show he was going to be great. A couple of weeks later we had to turn round and head to Rotterdam. I knew this would be Golly's biggest test to date and I decided that Rotterdam would be my benchmark. If he could cope with that, I would consider him for the European Championships.

Rotterdam would be his first massive stadium. The show is held in the Kralingse Bos, a big wooded park on a lake just outside the city centre, and it is a huge show in all respects. The stables are a long way from the arenas and the walk between them is through avenues of trees. A lot of the classes take place at night so the avenues are all lit up and the place is full of ponies, carriages, showjumpers – it's full on.

Having done the French shows where Golly was so good and I thought I'd cracked it, Golly was on the edge so it became a case of the whole thing not cracking him. Riding back from the arenas every day he quickly learned where the tracks were to the stables and that's all he could think about. He would be walking in the arena and he would be fine, he would work fine and then the minute he left the arena to head down through those woods he was a nightmare – he would piaffe all the way to the stables. I realised then we were not out of the proverbial woods just yet, even if he headed through the real ones jolly sharpish.

Basically it was still a baby nap – he wants to go back home, he wants to be with the other horses, he's insecure. Again, that's a similarity to Peanuts, although Peanuts was not as threatening as Golly, who can lose the plot. Peanuts would just scream. With Golly you feel that you daren't breathe; one false move and he'll feel he's being corrected and then be upset.

Rotterdam is a CHIO – a show with Nations Cup competitions in jumping and dressage – and one of Holland's oldest and best-loved sports events. I thought Bruno (Fine Time) would be secure even though he might not be at the same standard as Golly; Bruno was more of a known quantity, so I would ride him on the team with Charlotte and Valegro while I put Uthopia and Golly into the three-star grand prix. As predicted, the three-star was held in the same place as the five-star, so Golly had his first go in a huge stadium.

He was hot, and I lost the one-time changes as he was getting stronger as the test went on. I could feel his nerves building, but he was fine. We scored nearly 72 and I always think if I'm getting those scores with mistakes I've nothing to worry about. Charlotte pipped me with Uti and Edward Gal won on Voice. Uthopia did a good grand prix there too, so it was mission accomplished from the point of view that Charlotte was qualified, Golly was qualified and I felt he'd coped fairly well with the situation.

Bruno was a star. He does it at his own speed but I felt it was another genuine test and he scored a few marks less than Golly. He'd only done his first grand prix in Vidauban, and here he was on the winning Nations Cup team. It was also Valegro's first start of the year. Because he'd had a long break although he was fit he definitely wasn't at full fitness. He hadn't competed since Olympia, so rough edges appeared. There were some minor blips, he wasn't in perfect self-carriage and I think he stopped on the last centre line. Charlotte thought he was going to piaffe and he stopped. As I said afterwards, 'You can't just think, you've got to keep moving your legs!' He did get a good score and won both the grand prix and the freestyle, but Charlotte and I both agreed there was a lot to get back again to get him to where we knew he could be. But that was the first step towards the European Championships for Valegro, and the first step to where we needed to go.

Then Charlotte and I did the special. Uthopia played with Charlotte because he knew that test inside out – which was fun for me as I get so much backchat from Charlotte it's hilarious for me to see her getting it from a horse – and Golly did a really good special. On the last centre line, however, he went to piaffe and he turned round. And I knew then, I thought at that very moment, matey, this is your nerves again. He turned back and he finished the test but when I got home I did some reassessment.

I had set Rotterdam as my benchmark for Golly but I wasn't 100 per cent convinced, thinking of how big the European championships could be. We'd heard it was going to be in a football stadium. Was it going to be windy? Would there be a lot of people making a lot of noise? I didn't want to push it if Golly wasn't going to be ready. He had all the talent but did he have the experience to handle it? He had done a lot of shows to get to that point and I actually felt that mentally he would be better having a break.

Hickstead was to be our next and final show before the Europeans. Charlotte and I had a talk and she suggested I get back on Uti. 'He's fit and ready to go, you know him, just get on,' she said. My first reaction was no, I've retired from him, but the next day she told me again, get on and ride him. So I did and of course he was exactly the same as when I last got off, I felt literally as if I'd got off the day before. Charlotte was right about me and Uthopia and I realised at that point, 'I know him, I know he'll go anywhere and do anything. Wouldn't it be better for Golly's future if he didn't go, and wouldn't it be better for the team if I took Uthopia?' I was qualified but I had to show the selectors we were back, so the decision was made that I'd take Uti to Hickstead and Charlotte would ride Valegro. That meant I had three weeks to get myself back in the saddle and get going on Uti. For the following ten days that's exactly what I did, until I fell down the stairs.

If I'd been doing something interesting like making a *Strictly Come Dancing* entrance to greet guests or extreme Pilates or mega step aerobics, that would have been fine, but I don't have a chandelier to engage for the former and having fallen off the back of my treadmill while on the phone, neither of the latter exercises was ever in the mix. I simply slipped, barefoot, slid to the bottom and badly bruised my coccyx.

I tried for a couple of days after the fall to ride Uti but he has so much movement it was impossible to sit on him. It was effing agony, and Charlotte and I ended up arguing the whole time as she was telling me to sit and I was yelling, 'I can't bloody sit!' In the end I got off and told her, 'You'll have to ride him all the way up to Hickstead. I'll get on him there and I'll be fine.'

Meanwhile my helping Charlotte with Valegro was rather calmer. He was going well and starting to look fit again. Both Valegro and Uti had been using the water treadmill twice a week at Hartpury and the pair of them were coming up to a good level of fitness again. Muscular tone is so important. Using the water treadmill means less pressure on their legs and no pressure on their back. And it helps lift the middle of the horse – like core and abs work. The water's cooling and soothing and it also provides a level of resistance. As they are working through the front instead of from behind as in normal work they're working different muscles. To manage a championship, those three tests, a horse has to be muscularly fit. The key is that their muscles don't get tired.

So off we went to Hickstead. I took Bruno as well as there were the two grand prix classes and I actually found him more comfortable to ride as he has less movement. But I felt completely underwhelmed as I hadn't been able to ride and I was still hurting a lot. I was riding on a seat saver, which was embarrassing. They look old and fuddy-duddy, so I couldn't wait to get my tailcoat on to hide the seat saver.

We did a reasonable grand prix, not quite up to our previous standard, but I benchmarked myself again. As Uti knows the test so well I wondered whether he'd try and catch me out, but my thinking was that if I could get 75 per cent I'd be happy and with nearly 80 I'd be ecstatic. We got the 75 with a couple of errors, so I was thrilled.

Then it was Valegro's turn. The first half of the test looked as if it was going to be a world record. It was brilliant. Then we got to the canter where lately Charlotte had been having a few problems with pirouettes and changes. In the pirouettes Valegro had been so sitting and slow it seemed to be taking him an age to get round it, and that's what he did in that test and he missed a beat. In the one-time changes her legs stopped moving. I think Charlotte thought the changes were going so well that he again would just do them. So what looked as if it would be an 85 to 86 per cent test ended up a little over 80. Still a brilliant score, and he won the class. The pace was beginning to pick up again.

We decided there that Charlotte would ride the special. Having done the music at Rotterdam she hadn't done one for a long time and, as I told her at the time, her special wasn't so special. Under the Hickstead format the freestyle was part of the team competition, which I didn't like, but it suited that as I was on the team we could again do different tests. Uti was hot, I had a great ride, we won with 81 per cent and it was a real boost for both of us.

We were also part way through filming again with Horse & Country

TV for our 'behind the scenes' on the way to the Europeans. It was becoming an annual documentary. We'd started filming before Hickstead, then planned for reporter Jenny Rudall and producer/director Kim Lomax to meet Michael Eilberg and Laura at Hickstead, as we were still presuming Laura would be on the team. Laura and Alf took part in a training display there with Dr B, and although Alf looked slightly more aged he still seemed his usual self. So nothing untoward had occurred at that moment.

I think Charlotte was then finding it quite stressful being in the middle of all this filming because after her special, where she'd made mistakes again in the changes with a couple of mistakes in the piaffe, she realised there was still a lot of polishing up to do and there were only a couple of weeks left to do it in. With Uthopia it was a question of getting to grips with it as we went on. I hadn't been riding at my best but the pieces of the jigsaw were coming together; Uthopia was back on the team, we had Michael and Half Moon Delphi as backup, with Valegro we knew where to tidy things, and hopefully Alf was ready to go again.

A week later I got the phone call from Laura. She wanted to be the first to tell me that she had decided to withdraw Alf. She felt he still wasn't quite right and she didn't want to take him to a championship if he wasn't going to be at his best. It was a blow for the team and sad for Laura, but a decision we all respected.

So then I knew that reserve Gareth Hughes, with three days' preparation, would be getting the call. I had said to him at Hickstead not to give up but to ride Nadonna right up until the last minute as if they were going, that you never know. And that's what he did. So on three days' notice to go to the Europeans, Gareth was as prepared as anyone can be.

I'd been teaching Gareth on and off for ages. He comes to us irregularly; it can be every three weeks or every three months as he's running a business as well. But Gareth is the easiest person to pick up and help, he's generally a very secure person in what he's doing and he just wants eyes on the ground when he needs them and of course confidence, which everybody does. So I thought that'll be great, if Gareth needs help I'll be there anyway, Ferdi will be there for Michael and then I'll look after Charlotte.

I knew, however, that Charlotte would now have to get the most unbelievable score to keep us in the hunt. If I could start to get back up towards eighty, and she managed to get high eighties, we knew Michael could get into the seventies and Gareth too, but we needed to up those scores. The action plan began with a phone call to Philip Cheetham at Hartpury. I do a lot of work there with Philip and they're always so accommodating, brilliant actually. When I told Philip I needed an arena set up, outside, as we had to run through tests, his response was simply, 'When do you want it?'

After Hickstead I'd impressed upon Charlotte what would happen if her legs didn't work in the changes and what could happen in the piaffe. Horses change and after three years at grand prix a horse will not be as hot and keen as he was as an inexperienced fresher. Valegro was at the stage where he needed moulding a bit more. Although he never says no and is always keen to do his work, he now needed riding.

So we went to Hartpury the week after Hickstead and I can honestly say it was the first time I have really yelled my guts out at Charlotte. We were there to practise the music test. She'd done the grand prix often enough and I knew how to fix the test in the warm-up. The special was all about her having Valegro in front of her leg and the music, well, I didn't want to see those same mistakes again.

I gave her the full lecture, telling her, 'You know what you did in London, you made the same mistakes at Olympia, and you also did it in Rotterdam, so that's three imperfect music tests and I don't care if you won them, they were not good enough to win gold.' Don't forget Charlotte is ultra competitive so a clear rally was to highlight her chief rivals: 'You've seen what Helen Langehanenburg's doing, and if the rumours are true that Parzival's coming back then we need to get cracking!!' Admittedly it's hard if not impossible to say 'Langehanen-burg' correctly while in lecture-delivering mode, but Charlotte knew exactly whom I meant by Helen Beefburger, and while Parzival had been diagnosed with arrhythmia earlier in the year and missed Rotterdam, after the Dutch team training camp it was announced he was fit and ready to go again.

We drove a car down to Hartpury, opened all four doors and turned that music on. There were a lot of busy workers there but everybody stopped to watch. They must have thought I was some kind of tormentor from a prison or something! Again! No, go back to the beginning – can't you HEAR that change of music? Again, again, again. But if I sounded like a stuck record it was all in aid of creating records. And it was being videoed.

Sometimes things can't sink in all in one go, you have to go away and watch it. We went through that freestyle three times, and that's a lot. I did have it in the back of my mind to be careful. I didn't want to over-push the horse as he had to be fresh for the Europeans, but I needed to take Charlotte to the full maximum and get her head around how to ride this music test and how to get him more forward in these piaffe pirouettes so he didn't get stuck. The most important thing was that I wanted, needed even to be certain that Valegro knew what was being asked of him.

The first two tests were riddled with mistakes; she didn't collect him enough, didn't ride him forward in the piaffe, made her pirouettes too tight, blah, blah, blah. But the third test, well, it was spectacular. We stopped. I loosened Valegro's girth, gave him a sugar, gave Charlotte a pat on the leg and said to her, 'That is what you will do at the Europeans' before sending her away to watch the videos. I expected Charlotte to be grumpy and miserable because she'd got it wrong and I'd shouted at her, but she sent me a text later that day which read 'Thank you very much'. Anyone who knows Charlotte will tell you that 'thank you very much' doesn't come that easily. So, I thought, she has really taken this on board. I felt confident after that.

I had actually qualified three horses for the Europeans. I trusted Bruno and I would have liked to have ridden him as I felt he had stepped up to the plate for it, but Uthopia if he went at his best would get the highest score. It was a bonus to have David Trott back in the driving seat as International Teams Director, to have our old friend 'Adrian Mole', as I call him, back there. David has been brilliant over the years when we came nowhere, and he has always listened. He's let me make my own decisions and gone along with them. Equally I've always been straight with him; I told him I didn't think Golly was ready and that I'd love to take Fine Time because my real pleasure is bringing a new one up, but I did feel that Uti at his best would get the highest score. I made my own decision, but David was supportive of that. He's a brilliant listener and that he agrees with my way of thinking is even better!

So the team was set and off we went. With each championship there's always a feeling of trepidation, especially with one of the key members missing from the team, but at the same time I felt that with Michael and Gareth we had brilliant backup. I was also thrilled for them, that they had made a breakthrough to team level, as I could just about remember how exciting it was for me. I only hoped we could do something in Herning, because for them to come onto the team and win a medal would not only be an amazing feeling but would also make them better competition riders and fill them with confidence for the future.

We all got on really well. Michael is very focused, like his father Ferdi, and Ferdi is very encompassing when it comes to teams. Very good at the side of the arena, Ferdi always has something to give not take away. Dickie Waygood is a great chef d'equipe. He started alongside Richard Davison at Windsor then took over as chef at the World Games in Kentucky. Teams are close units and for anyone new coming in, well, let's just say Dickie managed to slip into that role as only a Major could – with immaculate precision. Dickie's become a bastion for the team and he has a brilliant sense of humour. We laugh at his army precision and while I don't want to work to it, I certainly need it. You can talk to Dickie about anything and you can tell him secrets – how the horse went, how you don't want to do it – in complete confidence, which is exactly what you want in a chef d'equipe. He's a proper part of the team. But Dickie has evented at top level, and having been Riding Master to the Household Cavalry and director of their musical ride I suspect keeping four piaffe passage merchants in order is a walk in the park to him!

So we were a really good team, having really good fun and we were really on form, I thought. The horses all trotted up brilliantly and in the stadium practice all the horses seemed relaxed. We did a couple of fun things as well, like a trip out to the Blue Hors Stud, and we were lucky that a hotel had been secured for us right by the venue as most people had horrendous journeys to get there. It wasn't a great hotel but with the Queen's suite on the top floor, occupied that week by her sister Princess Benedikte as patron of the European Championships, it was good enough for us.

It had been decided that Gareth would go first, Michael second and because I knew there would be enough of a gap to help Charlotte I would ride third and Charlotte fourth. Poor Gareth didn't have the best start. His mare Nadonna had been working well but in hindsight we could possibly have worked her harder. She's a sensitive horse and one of the best tests I've seen Gareth do on her was at Hickstead where he got his times muddled up, so he had worked her properly in the morning only to be told at one o'clock he was on at two o'clock so he had to get her back out and work her again. She was brilliant there. Sometimes you stumble across these equations that work for individual horses. Gareth had been steadily creeping up and he'd been on the winning team for the Rotterdam Nations Cup, where they'd done a good job and the mare had been very good. She was fifteen but had matured later on in her career and they'd made a good partnership.

In the warm-up arena, a short walk from the main arena, you could look down at the big screen and see what was going on. As Gareth was called to go and started to walk to the main arena, Nadonna saw the big screen. That was an awful moment. We'd all seen it but she saw the horse on the screen and it flipped her light switch. She stood rigid with her head up in the air staring at this screen and it just blew her brain. If we'd had another ten minutes Gareth could have got her back down to earth again and unwound her. But they had to go, so Nadonna went on her twinkle toes down to the arena, breathing fire. I gave Gareth a pat on the leg and said, 'She'll be fine, mate, off you go,' then I crossed my fingers. I could see by the way she was trotting she was airborne. Going round the edge she was so lit up. Watching that test was like nails being slowly drawn down a blackboard. Anything that could go wrong went wrong, but Gareth managed to bring her home.

Something like that puts a lot of pressure on the other three, we know that, but I thought, 'We can still do it, it'll be fine.' It might not put us in a gold situation, but Gareth and Michael were going to be around the same score on paper so we just had to hope and pray now that the three of us could do it, we'd lost our safety net, that was all. So that afternoon Mike came out and did a great job. There were moments of inexperience from Delphi, but Mike rode like a mature competitor. The horse had a good attitude in the ring and did some lovely things, it was a joy to watch actually, and they scored nearly 73 per cent. The one blip was that the judging was slightly erratic, with one judge only awarding 65 per cent, but we had a good solid platform to launch from.

That night was another where no sleep was had. Hotel rooms I find at best irritating, but to be in a hotel room waiting to ride for a major championship is grim. We'd gone into town to have something to eat, so at least there was the walk out and the walk back, but it's all about filling time. After tossing and turning, not knowing which way it was going to go, I woke up the next day feeling upbeat. Charlotte was positive, Valegro had been going like a star, Uti had been brilliant, both horses had been working with their tails in the air, enjoying themselves, and I could see that the other teams were getting the vibe that they had to look out. We thought – we knew – that gold could have gone to either Germany, Holland or Britain, and in case of a disaster we knew Denmark had been coming up that year. Akeem had been bought for Andreas Helgstrand, Anna Kasprzak and Donnperignon had been going great guns. Princess Nathalie, who is lovely, had been popping up on 75 per cent on gorgeous old Digby, and Mummy was in the Queen's suite so things were looking good for them too.

Uti felt fine in the warm-up. I went down to that tunnel with a good feeling and the first part of my test went well, then I got to my first piaffe and what can I say – little turd – he did a little courbette. That's a nice move for the Spanish Riding School but it's never been part of a dressage test. Uti likes to do it when he's behind my leg, but I took a deep breath and thought, I'm not going to be fazed by it. And he did some good things and lovely pirouettes, which aren't my strongest point, but I unfortunately missed a two-time change. It was a miscommunication, that's all. I quite enjoyed it out there, though. Uti was very genuine and considering I hadn't been able to ride much it was OK. I took my hat off and saluted, and I thought, 'I've just ridden for 75 per cent.' As we walked out the score went up and that's what it was. We knew we had Charlotte and Valegro to come and that we were going to be in there somewhere.

Judging has grown so far removed from what it used to be twenty-five years ago when every German was going to get a whopping score and every Dutch rider was going to get a huge score and the rest of us got pot luck. You are generally going to get what you deserve and when you make a mistake you know you are going down. You're going down because the judges now have to be so honest about what they see as marks are flashed around the stadium for the audience. You're not going to get away with it with a judging supervisory panel in place scrutinising every decision, hopefully. It's great for the sport that we as riders, and the audience, can see what's going on. I am sure the pressure on the judges is huge.

Most of us, maybe none of us even, had any idea that Helen Langehanenburg was as strong and steely as Charlotte. From her petite body emerges an incredible hulk of a competitor. None of us had seen Damon Hill do a grand prix like that and if she didn't attack every single mark I'll eat my words in every copy of this book! She rode unbelievably. I was so impressed with her and so impressed with Damon Hill, and she shot the Germans straight back into a gold medal position. Yes, there's rivalry, but we're all horse lovers and I felt emotional for Helen that she'd got work out of that horse that no one else could have, then I felt emotional for Adelinde that she'd got her Parzival back. You could see how delighted she was.

As Charlotte went in and did her test on Blueberry I stood like a ramrod with my arms folded. In my mind I was saying yes, yes, yes to every movement. She had a small blip in the passage to canter where she made a mistake but it was so smooth to watch, so slick, the horse was so full of presence and had so much self-carriage it was without a doubt the best grand prix I have ever seen in my life.

They scored a world record – just shy of 86 per cent. It was deserved and Charlotte kept the three medal nations within 1 per cent. It was phenomenal to have those three riders going last for their teams to create this huge atmosphere, this amazing team competition and this great suspense.

The grand prix decided the team competition and we ended up in bronze medal position. I could say unfortunately, but it wasn't unfortunately. There was 'point nothing' in it, it was just how it panned out in the end, and because of the excitement that had been building all day, as each of these girls had come out rocketing these scores it didn't matter. Nobody cared that we'd won the bronze, and most of all I didn't care. What I remember is being so proud of all of them.

Damon Hill has the ability to get behind Helen's leg. He did it in London where the weather was a bit hot. He didn't really piaffe and rather gave up on all those things that are his forte. Stallions like Uti and Damon Hill have some of these traits in common; they're clever, they're hormonal, they have different seasons to other competition horses because they're also breeding and they can take exception to things.

In London, Helen rode as hard as she could but he gave up, then in the following winter World Cup season he worked for her like he's never worked before. I don't think you can ever be 100 per cent sure what you're going to get with a stallion. That old adage from my years with Jannie and Christopher always resonates, and stallions don't always agree with one's point in the discussion. In this competition there was no special to count as it had in London, the European medals were decided purely on the grand prix, so job done we went out that night on a real high. Will had, as usual, generously organised a party through World Class in the restaurant opposite the hotel with all the owners and supporters.

Roly managed to arrive ten minutes after Valegro's grand prix – I love her dearly, but she does get her timings mixed up! She was there for the evening celebrations though, and for the individual tests. We had a great night. We'd never won a bronze – any of us – and for Gareth and Michael to come onto a team and go away with a medal was absolutely fantastic.

We went on to the special. By that stage I just wanted to enjoy it, which was absolutely hysterical from my point of view. I was hoping to up my score. That was my plan. I think the fact that I was so relaxed as I didn't expect with my preparation to be thinking of an individual medal, despite two years earlier having taken silver in the special. I knew it was in there that I was going to have a good ride, and I did have a great ride. There were a couple of iffy moments, but my score went up to 78 per cent and I moved up a place to finish sixth. It was very close to the top and lots of people had good rides.

Michael did a good job again. It was great he was going forward to the music as well in fourteenth as it is special when the whole team can go through. Gareth didn't go, but he was completely cool and accepted the situation. He would rather have gone out with everything going wrong than thinking the horse had gone well and getting a bad score, and he knew he had more shows to come.

Then I went to prepare Charlotte. After all the build-up and our fixing of things, it was as if we'd reached this peak and there was an air of calm now. One week earlier we knew we'd got it all sorted. I just reminded her of what we'd done the week before, of what she had to do, that she had to get Valegro in front of her and that she must move her legs. And she did remember to do all of it, but it was the battle of the blondes, or the dumb blondes in this situation.

It had started earlier that morning when Sweden's Patrik Kittel went wrong, then Charlotte went wrong when she set off to do her two tempis instead of her canter half-passes, then Helen went the wrong way across the diagonal at the end, then Adelinde did what Charlotte did. Never before in the history of dressage have the three medallists all gone wrong like that. However in between those three wrongs they did a lot of rights.

Again Helen was on flying form, Valegro was spectacular. Adelinde was into the eighties but a couple of per cent behind. Those two really did go for it. You could see Helen's teeth gritted and I could also see on Charlotte's face she had the words ringing in her ears that were, I think, on *Eurodressage* earlier in the year, something like 'Nobody will catch Helen this year'. I'd brought that silly little line up and said, 'Nobody thinks you're going to win. But you are.'

And she did. Charlotte and Valegro took the gold again. It was SO close and although it was historic that they all went wrong, it was also fair because their marks were what they were, and no one could say they lost it because they went wrong, so that was brilliant.

Not satisfied with winning the special, we had to then think about the music. But Charlotte and I had gone through the music three times a week earlier and I had absolute faith that this was going to work. Of course, I still had to ride as well. Luckily, having finished sixth of fifteen riders we were drawn in batches of five, so no one could have been more delighted at being sixth than me. I again knew that with five in each group I'd be in the second group and with a break between each group I knew I'd have time, whatever happened, to prepare Charlotte for her freestyle.

Uti was great, out of the first ten riders he went up another 2 per cent to head the first two groups and I got my 81 to finish sixth overall. My overall feeling was that this was brilliant for me, Uti had gone better and better and it was brilliant to ride my London music again, it was definitely the right decision to take him. It was such a good feeling to hop off not worrying about where I'd come, but seeing him in first place going into the final five was perfect.

That last five was a very strong group who all went well and finished in the same placings as in the special. Kristina Sprehe was fifth (she'd sneaked point 0.2 per cent higher than me), Edward Gal fourth, Adelinde third, Helen second and Charlotte first. Charlotte's was a phenomenal test, and as Richard Davison said, 'I don't think the judges can ever have given so many tens as they did in that test.' However he was slightly wrong because she didn't quite pip Totilas and Edward Gal's record for freestyle – that's the only record she hadn't quite caught. But she would.

It was the London test, yet it seemed to work better. Having heard the music in competition a few times, Charlotte nailed every single movement. There was one bit in a pirouette where Valegro popped out when she accidentally caught him with her spur – where Edwina decided to use her legs for a change – but it was a truly great test.

What Charlotte says when she comes out of a test is dictated by the look on my face. Charlotte will say what she feels when she knows how I feel. And my look to her said there was literally nothing else you could have done, and that horse has done three brilliant tests. At eleven years old he has pulled out three great performances and he has worked for you in every single test; he's been genuine, he looked magnificent and he makes people cry, he makes people give him a standing ovation because of his charisma. And when she came out I told her, 'You nailed it, you did it, it worked' and she was ecstatic. I said to her, 'It doesn't matter what Helen does' – Helen was coming after her – 'I don't think we could wish for any more.' And by that stage Damon Hill had headed down the hill a bit.

So it was a brilliant end to a brilliant championship. Afterwards it was the same situation as always: everyone's so tired. We had an early flight the next morning from Billund – there was no flight that evening, much as we all wished we could get out, so we spent a quiet night in the hotel and went to bed early. It was nice to get a good night's sleep. After winning team gold, showjumpers Ben Maher and Scott Brash had won silver and bronze in the showjumping, so it had been a good show all round for Team GB and World Class. We were all in the same hotel and we were all stabled together. While we're not close, we're supportive. They're the new generation and I'm in the middle (I'm not as old as Nick Skelton, although he wasn't on the team in Herning). They'd finished on the Saturday and shipped out on the Sunday, so again there was that end-of-show feeling where you want to get back and get on with your life.

14

It's Not All about Riding

I came back and shot off to Spain for four days with lovely Jill Hodges whom I used to ride for; Jill and Jackie Moreton-Deakin have always been my little bolt-hole providers. If I need a few days away I go down to one of their apartments in Spain – great friends they have one each in nearby blocks – which I love doing. It was so good to hop on a plane with Jill and go off for four days to snooze, eat and drink. Brilliant.

I was looking forward to the nationals. Katherine Bateson was over from the States and had done such great work kindly keeping Bruno going for me. While we're away at championships the clock doesn't stop at home and horses have to be kept ticking over. Golly was being wound down ready for his break and I wanted to get Bruno to those nationals that I always love going to. Those days away were enough to recharge my batteries and I came back ready for a week on Bruno.

As it often does in these situations something pops up to put a spanner in the works and sure enough it did here. Bruno was shod on the Sunday and he was due in the grand prix the following Saturday. Life is pretty busy the week before the nationals, let's call it hectic actually, with lots of panicking people needing polish-ups, prop-ups, psychology sessions, test riding practice, advice. It's a crazy time because this is the dream of so many British competitors, the nationals is their Europeans, their World Games, their Olympics.

Anyway, having been shod and in the midst of all this organised chaos, Bruno decided to hobble on Monday morning so I rang Gemma in a panic. The only delight in this situation was that Gemma's husband, Nathan, shoes Gemma's horses. An excellent farrier, poor Nathan was absolutely horrified when he came out to see Bruno. As a result of one nail too high in his front foot he was lame and feeling sorry for himself, he didn't want to move. Nathan skilfully took the shoe off and said, 'Right, we'll do it with glue, he'll be OK by Wednesday or Thursday.' 'I've got a grand prix on Saturday,' I exclaimed, horrified. Poor Nathan got hell from Gemma back at home. She'd organised for her mum, Jenny, to come over from Jersey to watch. Paul, her dad, was sadly too ill to travel.

By Thursday morning Bruno decided that his feet felt fine and he trotted up sound. Even so, all I could think was, 'Oh my God he's had four days off, he's been lame, does he feel right?' He'd only been walking in hand during that time. Bruno obviously did feel fine, however, because on that Thursday he tried to buck me off, which is one thing he never does. Even so, my thought was, 'I won't work you too hard just in case.' I upped the work on Friday, then on Saturday we were at the nationals.

Bruno was so excited warming up. It's wonderful how a horse's personality develops when they know they're good and Bruno, who is the most laid-back stallion in the world, well, I knew this was going to be his time – his 'Fine Time' – as he felt frisky. If horses could speak I'm sure he would have said I should have taken him to the Europeans. But anyway, he gave me a super grand prix. He was a bit hot in the test but I couldn't have asked him to go any better considering the week we'd had and that I'd been away at the Europeans. He got nearly 73 and the next day to Uti's silver-medal-winning music Bruno flew, earning nearly 77 per cent, my eighth national title and my sixty-sixth national championship. He bucked his way round the lap of honour and that gave me so much pleasure. By showing how pleased he was with himself Bruno was following in the tradition started by Donnersong, our 'Otto'. I love it when they know they're the best and let rip!

One reason why I love the nationals so much is that it's a family network and there's nothing I like better than seeing the people who've worked for me bagging championships; that year it was Jo Hamilton (née Barry) and Spencer on Supernova, who has the makings of a good one. Then we were entertained in fine style, as always, by the reclusive Lady Malvern, but that's another story.

There are things you get asked to do after winning medals and attaining a certain profile and after the nationals one of my first jobs was to judge the BHS Instructor of the Year competition with Di Lampard and Darrell Scaife. Since I have been teaching for years but stopped taking exams after the BHSAI I wasn't sure how this would go down. Finding a winner who taught from the gut, not only improving the combination he had to teach but leaving them with smiles on their faces after a touch of the Irish blarney was great. Conan Rowan, shamrock luck to you, you're a man after my own heart.

There are treats too and one of the best was Wimbledon on my birthday. Laura, Charlotte and I were invited to join a host of Olympians in the Royal Box on Centre Court. After a fantastic lunch we took our seats while Sue Barker did live introductions. That she said it was my birthday but refrained from mentioning my age was a huge relief and I thank Sue for that, although our Char-of-the-garden wasn't thrilled about being introduced as Charlotte Dujar*deen*. The atmosphere was amazing as was the crowd's welcome for all of us, but while Gasquet and Tomic played out their match in front of us we could hear the screams and shouts for Laura Robson next door on Court Two. We were sitting at the back (as usual) but there were screens in the front row where we could get a glimpse of Laura so if we appeared to be looking at our feet that was why. Andy Murray was there on the way to his momentous win and Sir Chris Hoy was guest of honour. It was fabulous but did make me realise why people find a whole day of dressage too much. Having sat through a whole day of tennis I can now totally understand. Wimbledon presented me with a birthday cake to take home and I managed to get it there, safely, without dropping so much as a *soupçon* of it on anyone else, which rounded off a very special day.

That July I had finally got my moment to meet the Queen when I received my MBE at Windsor Castle. Her Majesty is, as everyone knows, a huge fan of horses and it was lovely that she found the Olympic dressage exciting and expressed her happiness in our success. I told her I had just given Zara her final lesson before her temporary break from riding until the birth of Mia Grace. What I didn't mention was that it was not actually the first time I had met the Queen. Years before on Sark I was selected, along with a little girl, to present a posy to the Queen and Prince Philip on one of their visits to the island. The little girl went up first and curtseyed. Then I went up, and also curtseyed.

People may not realise that if you want a photograph you can only have official portraits. The newspapers are there too and *The Times'* photographer zoomed in on Laura and me, taking us outside for the shot. By the time I got back in I was at the back of the queue for the official portrait and had to wait for an hour and a half. The best picture was snapped by Claire on her mobile. It's of me doing a rather spectacular *Strictly Come Dancing* high kick in the drive. I may have ballet dancer's feet but how I accomplished that without doing myself a major injury I do not know. Nicky and Richard Barrett had come too, so we nipped into Windsor and had lunch at Browns, which was delicious. That evening we had a wonderful dinner at the Hampshire Four Seasons thanks to Richard's successful blagging on the phone which secured us an unheard of outside table. It was a gorgeous weekend, and rare for being so relaxing.

The thrill, the joy, the satisfaction and sometimes the frustration of this sport for me is in bringing horses up, and their journey from being promising untried youngsters to expressing their talents and personalities, hopefully at international grand prix. Looking back on their careers, and seeing how they have developed, you realise not only are they are all individuals but you learn so much from each of them if you listen. Take Don Archie.

Archie was born at Kate's out of a mare she'd bought from Suzanne and Darren in foal to DiMaggio. Kate had sold him as a foal to Nicola Cooper. Darren broke him in as a four-year-old. Archie proved to be a naughty boy. He managed to buck someone off one day then, having clearly decided this was a bit of sport, continued to do so for another two years. Nicola as a young mother understandably did not want to put herself in that situation so she decided to sell him. He was then naughty again and the buyer pulled out, so Nicola, who has trained with me for ages after having been a leading young rider, came to see me. She was at her wits' end; he was that naughty she didn't know what to do with him and she offered him to me for a nominal amount, provided I would sign a letter saying I wouldn't sue her if he did anything horrible. I understood, and at that point realised I was probably taking on a monster. But there aren't many monsters that can't be turned into cuties so I thought we'd get there in the end.

Well, Archie turned into one of the most challenging horses of our time. He had a lovely walk and canter and no trot. Greg Smith was here then, riding for me and for Sandra up the road. Greg's a typical Kiwi in that he loves a challenge, but it's all approached in that 'no bother', laid-back way.

So we got Archie on the lunge. He was ultra cold-backed so doing up the girth was always interesting and we didn't know from one day to the next when he was going to do his turn and let rip – he didn't do it every day. He'd be good for five days then he'd dump you.

We were making some progress, but it reached the point where things were getting out of hand. Archie had been going down the drive absolutely fine, going for an hour's hack absolutely fine, then one day on the way home he decided to dump Greg on the tarmac. Given that Greg was pretty difficult to dislodge I said to him that I

Making it Happen

didn't want to go on for much longer as Archie was liable to hurt him or someone else. Archie could drop his shoulder faster than any horse you've ever seen, then put in a colossal buck.

We had him in the indoor school a few days later, Greg aboard, and I could see that his back was up so I clipped the lunge line onto him. I went to set him off in trot around me in a circle and he turned his back on me and headed in the other direction, so I had no pull whatsoever. I was running as fast as Mo Farah, legging it round the school determined not to let go of him so Greg wouldn't hit the deck. Greg managed to face him into the boards in a corner so he couldn't turn left or right. Archie couldn't get rid of him, and Greg then gave him a jolly good smacked bottom. He'd never had that before as no one had ever dared. Then Greg galloped him round the school and every time he stopped he got another spanking. That cured Archie of his lethal bucking.

It didn't cure him of his sense of humour, however. The time came when Charlotte took over to teach him the moves. Greg was heading back to New Zealand and as I'd given him a half-share in Archie because the horse was such a bastard, it was only fair that I would buy Greg out if Charlotte was going to ride him, despite the fact he was probably worth about 10p!

Jannie would have loved Archie and all his tricks and I have looked deep into my old box of tricks inherited from her for solutions. Jannie would have said he's got a great big brain; she'd always say about a horse with what looks like a bump on his head that he had a 'Badminton head'. When I asked her what she meant, she said, 'It's got a lot of brains – it'll go round Badminton if it can jump big enough.' Those old horsemanship ideas she used to have, Romany many of them I think, are definitely quirky and I always took note. Still do.

Thanks to Charlotte's ability to teach a horse to trot, Archie began to move like a swan. He was six by this time and, for obvious reasons, he hadn't been competed. We were going to Spain that year – it was 2011 by this time, the year that Charlotte and Valegro launched at small tour – so I said, 'Let's take him. We'll see how he behaves for three weeks and if he does you can do the six-year-old class on him.'

The first week he was so naughty; every time she asked him to do something he stuck his head up in the air and effed off. He never gave me the feeling he was frightened, he was obstinate. The second week was hilarious because he had to do a test to qualify for the final. I can honestly say that in all the dressage tests I've watched I have never felt so nervous. I thought any minute Archie's going to stick his head up and bugger off wherever he wants to go, but Charlotte was riding as tactfully as she could possibly have ridden and he won the class. The beginning of the next week was horrific as Archie had decided since he'd been submissive for one day he wasn't going to do it again, and he literally stuck his head in the air and galloped across two arenas and into a hedge. I have this lasting memory of Charlotte's *trasero* and his sticking out of this hedge. Archie carefully pulled himself out, stuck his head up again and galloped back across those two arenas. Jan Bemelmans – who is a lovely man, vastly experienced and intuitive – was there training the Spanish team. Jan suggested I put Archie in a double bridle.

That's what we did, there and then, and when Archie went to disappear and Charlotte said no, stay here, he said, 'OK, hands up, I give in.' It was absolutely brilliant. Archie competed that final weekend, he looked absolutely gorgeous and he won the six-year-old championship. Archie's fine when he has learnt something, but while he's learning he's like the naughtiest of naughty kids and throws his toys out of the pram like missiles.

He has always been on the back burner. He's been that classic situation that no one else would want him – until they know *we* want him. He lives in the field with his mate Barney (Nip Tuck) and only comes in to work. Barney the bolter was also started by Greg. Barney's more of an event type, which was Greg's passion, and he only used to want to go all the time. Greg loved those two naughty kids and he did turn them round.

Archie won the advanced medium winter championship in 2013. He was great on that day, then he went out did his first prix st georges to score 77 per cent, and in his second he scored 10 per cent lower as he couldn't be bothered. He's only nine; I ride him now, and I've always thought it's a case of just sweet-talking him along until he is ready for grand prix. He has an amazing piaffe but does four steps and says I'm not doing it any more. He is incredibly clever, so I'm building up a step a month at the moment. That's all he needs to learn. I know he's going to be great. He has a fantastic hind leg, amazing piaffe and passage, a great trot and a lovely canter. He does everything, but he's still disobedient and I know we have to wait for his obedience as he isn't ready to give himself over yet. Archie is a very, very strong-willed horse – and he has that bump between his eyes.

Ann Cory, the proud owner of 'Donald', Dolendo, has always been involved. She has been a big supporter of British Eventing too and goes on every European and world tour. Dolendo was her dream machine, so when he retired I knew she would love another involvement. On Ann's seventieth birthday, a lovely sunny day, I gave her a card. Inside it said that her birthday present was a share in Archie. It's only a nail in his hoof, though. In the tiniest print I could muster, I wrote: *There is no financial gain if he is to be sold.* Dear Ann couldn't see to read it, which was the funniest thing, but we have plans for Archie so she need not worry.

Every sportsman needs a great support network and with horses it's even more crucial. We couldn't do it without the help of the vet, the farrier, the physio, etc. The support we get from the World Class Performance programme, which is run by UK Sport and administers the lottery funding, makes all the difference. We can now go out and concentrate purely on the competition in hand, instead of worrying about how to pay for it when we get home. And then we have the support blanket of the 'British Army' looking after all the logistics and details – we never used to get into the nearest and best hotel to the show in the old days!

After Kentucky, when Catherine moved on, Fiona Lawrence stepped up to the plate to take over the running of the yard, and she's made a fantastic job of it. Fiona had been introduced by Catherine and had covered while Catherine was away, so it was a natural transition. She's also brilliant at showing people round the yard and introduces the horses with all their personal stories.

I had realised I also needed someone who could be away from the yard and travel with us. I'd known Alan Davies since for ever. He'd come to me for lessons at Stow – he was into showing and produced Trumpcard to win the 1996 ladies hunter champion at the Horse of the Year Show for Tanya Nicol – and he'd groomed for Emile in Sydney. In fact, as only two dressage grooms were allowed to fly with the horses, he'd looked after Gullit while Jo flew on ahead. I bumped into Alan at a dinner party and asked what he was doing. He was freelancing, so I put it to him that I had two horses that would probably go to the Europeans the following year, how would he fancy it? He came to Vidauban with us and ended up staying. He's now a vital member of our team.

Alan is the crème de la crème of travelling head lads, as the job's known in racing circles. We call him the supergroom. The lorry is his home from home, and at the shows – his passion in life – he is in his element and he knows everyone. To have someone that can take away the stress of competing, who is so in tune with the horses that he knows their legs, their bodies, their minds, their feed patterns, is a huge boon. It means all I have to think about is my test. I still take an interest in the horses' welfare, but that is Alan's top priority.

I've only had two supergrooms in my life, Catherine being the other. She was of the same ilk as Alan; she did the Europeans in 2009 and WEG a year later. They are HGV truckers, fully competent at travelling the world. With a supergroom it's as simple as saying, 'I'm competing in Austria, see you there.' Given my history and those early trucking experiences, I was never going to be cut out for dealing with everything involved!

Alan has been the mainstay for Uthopia and Valegro; the horses love him and he loves them, and he's been with us the whole way through. He's more emotional than Charlotte and I. It works, because Alan doesn't tell me how to do my job and I don't tell him how to do his. I would never question his professionalism, he doesn't question mine, and we're both aiming for the same thing. He's also been a good influence on Charlotte. Let's face it, she's been very spoilt in that all this infrastructure has been in place for her, but it has released her from a lot of unnecessary pressure. It is the cog in the wheel that is probably the most crucial, bar the performance itself.

Charlotte doesn't know the other side of it, and I'm happy for her that she doesn't. It's a hard life. Still, people do it. I'll never forget one night when I was coming back from a show in the car and we stopped in Oxford for fuel. And there was William Fox-Pitt in the petrol station; he had been competing all that weekend but he was sitting in a petrol station waiting for a lorry that was coming up to meet him so he could do a swap and drive a new batch of horses straight to another event while the four horses he'd just competed would be taken home. I take my hat off to the eventers and don't ever complain, because that really was an eye-opener. It absolutely amazes me how they keep it up.

Alan and I are of the same vintage and he knows that for as long as I keep going so must he. If he were to retire, that would mean I would have to. And since Roly and I have made the decision that Valegro will never be sold, I have no choice but to carry on! Meanwhile Alan's also competing. After the Olympics he won the champion miniature Shetland title at the Wessex show with Halstock Casandra. Needless to say, Alan's turnout is impeccable.

I did a talk for the BHS about what the Olympics did for us and what the future holds, and despite not having a crystal ball I do know we've got a future. The continuing success of British Dressage means capitalising on a lot of shining examples such as Charlotte's ascent to stardom and the fact it wasn't about coming from a moneyed background. I didn't either. Inspiration is the key to the London 2012 legacy.

Sport is demanding, we all know that. A horse doesn't get to the top by feeding it apples and asking would it mind doing a grand prix or jumping a six-foot fence. We know that we are so lucky to be able to have horses to help us in our competition quest and that we also have to have fair training methods, so Richard Davison and I came up with the idea of the Dressage Convention to encourage people of course to use horse-friendly methods but also to try and get the message over that we are all wanting the same end. It was subtitled 'where training methods meet' and we invited a diverse panel with the aim of showing that it was all about inclusivity. And we had new methods of including people in the discussions via that new generation communications tool, Twitter. It was ground-breaking, yet it wasn't rocket-science, just getting across the basic philosophy of horsemanship, irrespective of whether people are gold medal winners or not.

Riding is one aspect of it, but in training horses need methods to follow that are understandable. We have to keep them, physically and mentally, in good environments, put them in the right spaces. They are all different – that's what makes my life with horses so joyous to wake up to every morning – but it means that you have to develop a relationship of trust and mutual respect with each individual horse. The horse world needs positive images, positive people and positive training methods that are kind. It was great to be able to do the Convention with Richard, who is still bringing me up today.

Richard had orchestrated so much in his years as team manager and in London, and before, Richard had my back. It was at a dinner, after 'those' Europeans I think, that Richard stood up and congratulated all the hard-working members of the team – the farrier, vet and grooms – then turned to the hierarchy and told them what he really thought and what should be done so no other rider had to be put through what I had. It meant a lot to me that Richard spoke up and stuck his neck out for me, which was why I was so glad to be able to do the same for him after London.

Athens was pretty pivotal for both of us. We were hacking around the racetrack and chatting about Richard's response to a fellow Olympic rider who had bent his ear over something very tiresome and trivial. He couldn't be doing with it, so graphically told them where to go. He asked me whether I had ever done that, and thinking about it, I hadn't really, not even at school, but maybe it was about time I did.

Richard reminded me much later that over the following months we'd be chatting and he had noticed I'd casually wrap up the story by saying something like, 'Oh I just got tired of their bickering so I told them where to go,' and he was worried that he'd started something he shouldn't have. But, to be serious, I had realised that life is too short to waste time listening to negative people bickering on about unimportant crap and far better to spend time listening to people who are positive and deserve to be listened to. It was an important lesson.

What a long way we have come since then, and how many miles travelled in the course of winning medals and setting records. Valegro and Charlotte nailed that freestyle world record at Olympia, which was a phenomenal Christmas present. And when you've been doing it for a while you get to see how things come round in circles. For example, who should be coming home with Valegro from his triumphant World Cup qualifier in Amsterdam but dear Lenny, to retire with us. The minute she heard, Fiona was getting the bananas in and an extra sack of carrots, and of course making his favourite cucumber sandwiches.

The first summer I was at Jannie's I told her about Mitch, Rossford de Carteret's son of L'Arret and one of the lady carriage horses. He was a fantastic jumper and I had shown Jannie pictures of me jumping him. She had said he looked pretty special and that we'd better bring him over as he was wasted on Sark. I thought he'd appeal to Jannie's sense of humour. I called him the Dachshund because he had his mother's short cobby legs and a long body, but he had his father's beautiful Arab head. At 14.2, technically a pony, he was too small to pull the tourist carriages, so Rossford agreed I could take him to the mainland and sell him. When I went home for a holiday that first summer, I took Kate with me and we brought Mitch back to the mainland with us.

On the docks he was put in a crate. I loved him so much and thought he was so cool that I went in with him, holding him pressed up against the side of the open crate. There was no breast bar or anything. It was a sunny, lovely day and one moment I could hear the clank of the chains tightening, then the next we were swung out over the edge of the pier, way up in the air looking down at the cargo boat. Thank God Mitch didn't panic or I would have been squashed! Instead that horse just gazed out of the front of the crate as it was lowered onto the front of the boat – the *Ile de Sercq*, I think it was. When we got to Guernsey the crate had to come off the same way. Well, Guernsey harbour in the middle of the day in the middle of summer is crammed with roll-on roll-off ferries and boats coming in from Jersey, France and the mainland. One of the guys from the riding school had brought a horsebox and we had to get Mitch on that to get the big boat to England. Even in the middle of all this, Mitch calmly walked up the ramp, no fuss, onto this lorry.

We sailed that night to Portsmouth. The driver was taking antique furniture to sell, so furniture had gone in first, then Mitch, then more furniture. It was around ten at night when we got to Portsmouth and Customs decided they wanted to check the horsebox. There were cars coming off the boat, it was dark and I tried to explain that this horse had come from Sark so had never seen a car. I only had him in a head collar and I didn't want to take him off the lorry as I might never get him back on. But Customs insisted and Mitch had to get off that lorry on Portsmouth docks late at night. He stood coolly next to me while all the cars drove past. To be honest, I think he was in shock. Everything was fine, Customs gave us the go-ahead, and amazingly

Mitch went straight back on that lorry. We arrived at Kate's in the early hours.

I moved him up to Jannie's the next day and Jannie just loved him. I remember I'd got up on the garden wall and pulled him towards me so I could get on, at which point he suddenly jumped straight over the wall. Jannie thought that was the funniest thing she'd ever seen. She could not stop laughing.

We took him up to the Faerie Glen that day and Jannie put these jumps up. Mitch was like a mini-Milton (John Whitaker's famous white stallion), and having watched him jump a few Jannie said, 'That's a freak!' She rang David Tatlow that night and told him he wouldn't believe what we had here. He came and bought Mitch the next day. The worst thing was that beloved Mitch was gone within a week, and then he came down with a virus, a really bad one. Having lived on Sark, he had no immunity and had had no injections. It was a whole year before he was well again. But he went to a well-known showjumping family and was a prolific winner.

Why do I tell that story now? Because it's about a beloved horse being discovered and having the chance to realise his talent and lead a happy life. That's what I want for my horses, and what I try to make happen for every last one of them. But most of all it's a story of a long, eventful, but exciting journey from Sark. Just like my story.

Career Highlights

Key: GPS – Grand Prix Special; GPF – Grand Prix Freestyle

Olympic Games

2012	London GB	Uthopia	Team Gold, GPS 3rd, GPF 5th
2004	Athens GRE	Escapado	Team 7th, GPS 9th, GPF 13th
2000	Sydney AUS	Argentile Gullit	Team 8th
1992	Barcelona ESP	Giorgione	Team 7th, GPS 16th

World Championships

| 2010 | Kentucky USA | Liebling II | Team Silver, GPS 17th |
| 1990 | Stockholm SWE | Rubelit von Unkenruf | Team 5th, GPS 18th |

European Championships

2013	Herning DEN	Uthopia	Team Bronze, GPS 6th, GPF 6th
2011	Rotterdam NED	Uthopia	Team Gold, GPS Silver, GPF Silver
2009	Windsor GB	Liebling II	Team Silver, GPS 10th GPF 10th
2005	Hagen GER	Escapado	Team 5th, GPS 5th, GPF 11th

1999	Arnhem NED	Legal Democrat	Team 5th, GPS 15th
1997	Verden GER	Legal Democrat	Team 8th
1991	Donaueschingen, GER	Rubelit von Unkenruf	Team 10th

National Champion

2013	Fine Time
2012	Uthopia
2009	Liebling II
2004	Escapado
1999	Legal Democrat
1998	Legal Democrat
1997	Legal Democrat
1992	Giorgione

Carl has amassed an incredible sixty-six national titles over his career at medium, advanced medium and small tour including level. And of course eight at the ultimate grand prix level, which earns the title 'National Champion'.

Index

For competitions, author interviews,
pre-publication extracts, news and events,
sign up to the monthly

Orion Books Newsletter

at

www.orionbooks.co.uk

Prefer your updates daily?
Follow us 🐦 @orionbooks